THE ELEMENTS OF
DRAWING

THE ELEMENTS OF
DRAWING

John Ruskin

WITH

A NEW INTRODUCTION BY

LAWRENCE CAMPBELL

ASSOCIATE PROFESSOR OF ART, BROOKLYN COLLEGE,
UNIVERSITY OF THE CITY OF NEW YORK

DOVER PUBLICATIONS, INC.
NEW YORK

This Dover edition, first published in 1971, is an unabridged republication of the text of *The Elements of Drawing. In three letters to beginners* as edited by E. T. Cook and Alexander Wedderburn in Volume XV (1904) of the Library Edition of *The Works of John Ruskin* (published by George Allen, London), which also contains *The Elements of Perspective* and *The Laws of Fésole. The Elements of Drawing* was originally published by Smith, Elder, & Co., London, in 1857.

A new Introduction has been written for the present edition by Lawrence Campbell.

The publisher is grateful to the Brooklyn College Library for making a copy of the book available for reproduction.

International Standard Book Number: 0-486-22730-8
Library of Congress Catalog Card Number: 79-132553

Manufactured in the United States of America
Dover Publications, Inc., 31 East 2nd Street, Mineola, N.Y. 11501

INTRODUCTION TO THE DOVER EDITION

JOHN RUSKIN wrote *The Elements of Drawing* during the winter of 1856–1857. The book, published by Smith, Elder, & Co. of London, appeared for sale on June 22, 1857, and promptly sold out. It was necessary to bring out a second edition by October. A third, issued in three separate thousands, came out in 1859, 1860 and 1861. When the third edition was exhausted, the book remained out of print until Ruskin's permission was obtained for a fourth edition in 1892. This was followed by a fifth in 1895, then by a sixth in February 1898, and impressions of this edition were dated 1900, 1901 and May 1904, making a total sale of 16,000—a considerable sale for a book of its kind. In 1904, a new pocket edition appeared on the market, in which the reverse of the title page stated that the total printing had then reached 19,000. This figure does not include the 2062 copies in the Library Edition of all of Ruskin's writings in 39 volumes, edited magnificently and thoroughly by E. T. Cook and Alexander Wedderburn, and published by George Allen of London; nor could it include the Everyman Library edition published by J. M. Dent, London, associated with E. P. Dutton, New York, in 1907, reprinted in 1911. And it does not include the portions of the text which were published in *Our Sketching Club: Letters and Studies on Landscape Art* by the Rev. R. St. John Tyrwhitt of Oxford, published by Macmillan of London in 1874, and subsequently published in Boston, in 1875, by Roberts Brothers. There were also several unauthorized editions in the United States, the first being published by Wiley & Halstead of New York, in 1857, the same year the first English edition came out.

 The Elements of Drawing was one of a triad of books on drawing written by Ruskin. The second book, *The Elements of Perspective*, came out in 1859. The third, *The Laws of Fésole*, a volume of revised lessons on drawing, belongs to a later period in Ruskin's life, 1877–1878. It appeared in 1879, published by George Allen of Orpington, Kent, and London. Ruskin planned *The Laws of Fésole* as a two-volume work, the first devoted to drawing, the second, to painting and color. The subtitle of Volume I was "A familiar treatise on the elementary principles and practice of drawing and painting as determined by the Tuscan masters. Arranged for the use of schools." The condition of Ruskin's health, mental as well as physical, discouraged him from writing, or even beginning, Volume II.

Ruskin undertook *The Elements of Drawing* as a way of answering the many requests he received after the publication of Volume I of *Modern Painters* in 1843 for advice and assistance in the practice of drawing. These requests came to him from people in all walks of life: from ladies in high society, from old and close friends, from art students and from workmen like Thomas Dixon, the cork-cutter at Sunderland, to whom Ruskin was later to address the letters which form the volume of his writings entitled *Time and Tide*.

Ruskin had been in the habit of giving drawing lessons by letter from a much earlier date. In a letter to his friend, Sir Henry Wentworth Acland, he observes: "I know of no book which is a sufficient guide to this study. Most artists learn their rules mechanically and never trouble themselves about the reason of them."

Two years before writing *The Elements of Drawing*, in 1854, he began teaching at the newly opened Working Men's College in London (where one of his colleagues was Dante Gabriel Rossetti) and soon people began to talk about his classes. By this time Ruskin was chief among contemporary English writers on art and certainly the only critic with both the will and the ability to translate principles into practice. For Ruskin had been drawing since early youth. Even when totally absorbed in the writing of *The Stones of Venice*, or at work on the different volumes of his great work, *Modern Painters*, there was hardly a day when Ruskin did not draw or paint for several hours.

Cook and Wedderburn, the editors of the Library Edition of Ruskin's writings, state that an examination of the proofsheets from the paragraph numbered 99 onwards shows that one set was corrected by Ruskin himself, the other by his friend W. H. Harrison. From the condition of these galley proofs, one learns that Ruskin attained simplicity and clarity of writing only by the most careful of revisions—and these by the costliest of indulgences, rewriting in proof.

Ruskin, not always a modest man, was yet modest about his methods of instruction, according to one of his students. He did not attach supreme importance to a particular method, believing that in teaching, the personality of the teacher is of more importance than the method. His object was not to instruct professional artists, but to show how the elements of drawing might best become a factor in general education. For his system he claimed only that it was calculated to encourage refinement of individual perception, to train the eye in close observation of natural beauties and the hand in delicacy and precision of manipulation—thus, to help his students understand what masterly work meant and be able to recognize it when they saw it.

But although he believed that people who wanted to enter into art as professionals should study it in academies or art schools, there is nothing in *The Elements of Drawing* unworthy of the attention of the professional artist or art student. Indeed, the book is a gem of information and clarity. Not a footnote could be removed from it without harming the book as a whole.

The form in which Ruskin cast the work and the method he adopted in his teaching were conditioned in large measure by the times he lived in. First, he wished in a practical way to protest against certain tendencies in the current teaching of art. Second, he wished to encourage closeness of observation rather than manual dexterity and neatness of execution. And third, he wished to fix the attention on natural objects rather than upon plaster casts of sculpture, or upon "nonsense lines" as they were to be found in the manuals of drawing which were then the only books available to students.

Of his system, Ruskin made the claim that although it was at variance with the practices of all recent European academy schools, yet it was founded on that of Leonardo da Vinci.

What of the book's influence? Though it was directed to the

student and amateur, artists read it also. At least parts of it were known to some of those whom we consider today as the giants of French painting of the later nineteenth century.

In an article in the March 1911 *Contemporary Review* on "What is Impressionism?" Wynford Dewhurst quotes Monet as having told a British journalist in 1900 that "ninety per cent of the theory of Impressionist painting is in . . . Ruskin's *Elements of Drawing*." This opinion by one of the greatest masters of direct perceptual painting outdoors is remarkable in view of the fact that it is doubtful if Monet could have read English with any real fluency, and that *The Elements of Drawing* was never translated into French. (It was, however, translated into German and Italian.) And yet he may have struggled through it, just as Marcel Proust, known to have had a poor knowledge of English, nonetheless read deeply in Ruskin and was the translator into French of *The Bible of Amiens* and *Sesame and Lilies*.

More probably Monet's acquaintance with Ruskin's ideas came from reading the two long passages from *The Elements of Drawing* which Ogden Rood, the New York physicist and professor at Columbia, quoted in his book *Modern Chromatics*, a review of everything then known on the perception of color. This book, published in New York in 1879 by D. Appleton & Co., was subsequently reissued by the same publisher as *The Students' Text-Book of Color, or Modern Chromatics with Application to Art and Industry*, in 1881. A translation of *The Students' Textbook* appeared in Paris in the same year, entitled *Théorie Scientifique des Couleurs*. A review of the book by Philippe Gille drew the attention of the young Georges Seurat, who obtained the book and read it carefully. The parts quoted by Rood from Ruskin were paragraph 172, part C, headed "Breaking one colour in small points through or over another," in Letter III *On Colour and Composition*, and the even more striking passages from paragraphs 169 (4) and 168 (3)—in Rood's order of selection, not Ruskin's order of writing. In the last section one literally *sees* Seurat's Neo-Impressionist technique.

Near the end of Rood's book, he again refers to Ruskin, to his method of isolating the different colors in a landscape with the aid of a small aperture in a piece of white cardboard, by which the student is able to convince himself of the true nature of the colors composing a scene. For when these are seen isolated from the colors next to them, they are not heightened or altered by contrast; also, with such patches of color, the judgment is not affected by the memory of the colors which the objects exhibit at short distances, or by what artists call "local color."

It is instructive to compare this with the piece of advice attributed to Monet quoted by Charles Biederman in *Art as the Evolution of Visual Knowledge*, published by the author privately in Redwing, Minnesota, in 1948. Says Monet: "When you go out to paint, try to forget what object you have before you, a tree, a house, a field, or whatever. Merely think, here is a little square of blue, here an oblong of pink, here a streak of yellow, and paint it just as it looks to you, the exact color and shape, until it gives you your own naïve impression of the scene before you."

Apropos this passage, it seems timely to mention Ruskin's own theory about unclarity, or "mystery," in nature. It is impossible for the human intelligence to perceive all of nature. Thus he who represents what he sees before him, but is able to see either not at all or only in part, produces an abstraction which will be a projection of his own being or soul, providing he can rid himself—as much as is humanly possible—of the pictorial conventions through which he, and to a great extent, all of us who have been exposed to paintings, illustrations or photographs, have learnt, since infancy, to grasp nature conceptually. The following lines are from *Modern Painters*, Volume IV, Chapter 4. "Take the commonest, closest, most familiar thing, and strive to draw it verily as you see it. Be sure of this last fact, for otherwise you will find yourself continually drawing, not what you *see*, but what you *know*. The best practice to begin with is, sitting about three yards from a bookcase (not your own, so that you may *know* none of the titles of the books), to try to draw the books accurately, with the titles of the backs and patterns on the bindings as you see them. You are not to stir from your place to seek what they are, but to draw them simply as they appear, giving the perfect look of neat lettering; which, nevertheless, must be (as you will find it on most of the books) absolutely illegible. Next, try to draw a piece of patterned muslin or lace (of which you do not know the pattern), a little way off, and rather in the shade; and be sure you get all the grace and look of the pattern without going a step nearer to see what it is. Then try to draw a bank of grass, with all its blades; or a bush, with all its leaves; and you will soon begin to understand under what a universal law of obscurity we live, and perceive that all *distinct* drawing must be *bad* drawing, and that nothing can be right, till it is unintelligible."

One of the popular misconceptions about Ruskin, repeated without end by those who have not read him, but only books about him, or have seen quotations out of context, is that what he meant by visual truth meant only a literal, factual recording of visual information with each fact recorded quite separately from the facts next to it—the remorseless technique of the Pre-Raphaelite Holman Hunt. To such misconceptions, *Elements of Drawing* is an antidote. It is true, however, that Ruskin in his own drawings had difficulty in quenching his enthusiasm for individual detail. And so we find many of his drawings with brilliantly drawn "facts" isolated in surroundings of generalized unfinished effects (which may remind the viewer of some of the most recent developments in modern art). But Ruskin made these drawings for himself and sometimes for his friends. He gave them away freely. He did not think of them as drawings for sale. There are examples of an unflagging attention throughout the length and breadth of a single drawing, but for the most part it is as though his interest gave out at a certain point, or was exhausted by the intensity of his concentration upon one particular aspect of a building or a scene.

As a writer, Ruskin is sometimes silly, but always brilliant. Yet for us today, he is often a difficult writer. The reason is his inability to concentrate. As Kenneth Clark states in his introduction to his admirable anthology of Ruskin's writings entitled *Ruskin Today*, published by Penguin Books: "This inability was part of his genius. In his mind, as in the eye of an impressionist painter, everything was more or less reflected in everything else; and when he tries too hard to keep his mind in a single track, as in the second volume of *Modern Painters*, some of its beautiful

colour is lost. Still, it must be admitted that after the age of
about thirty, his inability to stick to the point becomes rather
frustrating, and in his later writings, where literally every sentence starts a new train of thought, he reduces his reader to a
kind of hysterical despair."

But the modern reader should have no difficulty reading
The Elements of Drawing. Only perhaps where Ruskin refers to
painters well known to mid-nineteenth-century readers but
hardly known today except to specialists, will the reader come
up against any hurdles. Also, when he speaks of "cakes" of
watercolor, the best substitute today will be the small pan containing watercolor rather than the watercolor in the tube. There
will be other passages about art supplies where the modern
reader may have to use his own judgment in making modern
substitutions. One exception is the Gillott lithograph crowquill
pen, which, if the present writer is not mistaken, is still to be
had on the market.

The essence of Ruskin's art credo may be understood by
assembling three widely quoted passages from different books:
"The greatest thing a human soul ever does in this world is to
see something, and tell what it *saw* in a plain way. Hundreds
of people can talk for one who can think, but thousands think
for one who can see. To see clearly is poetry, prophecy and
religion, all in one" (*Modern Painters*, Vol. III, Part IV, Chapter
16, Section 28; published in 1856). "In order that people may
be happy in their work, these three things are needed. They
must be for it; they must not do too much of it; and they must
have a sense of success in it" (*Pre-Raphaelitism*, published in
1851). "There is no Wealth but Life" (*Unto this Last, four essays
on the principles of political economy*, published in 1860).

In his introduction to *The Art Criticism of John Ruskin*, a
useful as well as delightful selection of Ruskin's writings on art
made in 1964 (published by Doubleday in its Anchor Books
series, but unhappily now out of print) Robert L. Herbert sums
up Ruskin's principles in a statement based on Ruskin's own
summary in *The Eagle's Nest*, 1872. "First, to represent visual
appearances only, never memory knowledge. This is what placed
him in opposition to conventional art circles and allied him,

unknowingly, with progressive French art. Second, to test these appearances only by the aspect of knowledge that pertains to visual appearances so that, for example, one would avoid the error of drawing each lash of an eye because one can't really see them as individual hairs. Third, having learned to represent actual appearances faithfully, if you have any human faculty of your own, visionary appearances will take place to you which will be nobler and more true than any actual or material appearances; and the realization of these is the function of every fine art, which is founded absolutely, therefore, in truth, and consists absolutely in imagination."

One should not, Ruskin says over and again, leave the truth of visual appearance by one iota, unless directed by the play of imagination. For it is the imagination, unrestrained by scientific knowledge or preconceived ideas, which enables the artist to travel beyond appearance. The works of art which result from the state of exaltation resulting from knowing the truth of nature's appearances—which means the artist's own subjective experience—and contemplating these appearances to the point of ecstasy, will not resemble what we think nature looks like because we shall be seeing it through another mind, that of the artist.

Says Ruskin: "We do not want his mind to be like a badly-blown glass, that distorts what we see through it, but like a glass of sweet and strange colour, that gives new tones to what we see through it; and a glass of rare strength and clearness too, to let us see more than we could see ourselves."

Concludes Herbert, a perfect modern Ruskinite: "We therefore return again to that central precept; the artistic imagination as the source of great art."

It is on this note of heroic optimism that this introduction may conveniently close.

1970   LAWRENCE CAMPBELL

CONTENTS

LETTER I

LETTER II

LETTER III

APPENDIX I

APPENDIX II

LIST OF ILLUSTRATIONS

PLATES

WOODCUTS AND DIAGRAMS

(Drawn and Cut on the Wood by Miss Byfield from Drawings by the Author)

LIST OF ILLUSTRATIONS

In the original Library Edition volume, page 1 was the part title page of 'The Elements of Drawing,' page 2 was blank, page 3 the title page, page 4 blank; pages 5 to 8 contained a Bibliographical Note (as of 1904) which is summarized in the Introduction to the present edition. The text thus opens with page 9.

PREFACE

[1857]

1. It may perhaps be thought, that in prefacing a manual of drawing, I ought to expatiate on the reasons why drawing should be learned; but those reasons appear to me so many and so weighty, that I cannot quickly state or enforce them.[1] With the reader's permission, as this volume is too large already, I will waive all discussion respecting the importance of the subject, and touch only on those points which may appear questionable in the method of its treatment.

2. In the first place, the book is not calculated for the use of children under the age of twelve or fourteen. I do not think it advisable to engage a child in any but the most voluntary practice of art. If it has talent for drawing, it will be continually scrawling on what paper it can get; and should be allowed to scrawl at its own free will, due praise being given for every appearance of care, or truth, in its efforts. It should be allowed to amuse itself with cheap colours almost as soon as it has sense enough to wish for them. If it merely daubs the paper with shapeless stains, the colour-box may be taken away till it knows better: but as soon as it begins painting red coats on soldiers, striped flags to ships, etc., it should have colours at command; and, without restraining its choice of subject in that imaginative and historical art, of a military tendency, which children delight in, (generally quite as valuable, by the way, as any historical art delighted in

---

[1] ["The Value of Drawing" was taken by Ruskin as the subject of an Address in 1857 to the St. Martin's School of Art (see Vol. XVI., App. iii.); and see in the same volume the paper on "Education in Art" (pp. 143–151).]

by their elders,[1]) it should be gently led by the parents to try to draw, in such childish fashion as may be, the things it can see and likes,—birds, or butterflies, or flowers, or fruit.

3. In later years, the indulgence of using the colour should only be granted as a reward, after it has shown care and progress in its drawings with pencil. A limited number of good and amusing prints should always be within a boy's reach: in these days of cheap illustration he can hardly possess a volume of nursery tales without good woodcuts in it, and should be encouraged to copy what he likes best of this kind; but should be firmly restricted to a *few* prints and to a few books. If a child has many toys, it will get tired of them and break them; if a boy has many prints he will merely dawdle and scrawl over them; it is by the limitation of the number of his possessions that his pleasure in them is perfected, and his attention concentrated.[2] The parents need give themselves no trouble in instructing him, as far as drawing is concerned, beyond insisting upon economical and neat habits with his colours and paper, showing him the best way of holding pencil and rule, and, so far as they take notice of his work, pointing out where a line is too short or too long, or too crooked, when compared with the copy; *accuracy* being the first and last thing they look for. If the child shows talent for inventing or grouping figures, the parents should neither check, nor praise it. They may laugh with it frankly, or show pleasure in what it has done, just as they show pleasure in seeing it well, or cheerful; but they must not praise it for being clever, any more than they would praise it for being stout. They should praise it only for what costs it self-denial, namely, attention and hard work; otherwise they will make it work

[1] [For Ruskin's views on "historical" art, wrongly and rightly so called, see *Modern Painters*, vol. iii. (Vol. V. p. 64); *Lectures on Architecture and Painting*, Vol. XII. pp. 151–153; Vol. XIV. p. 84; *Cestus of Aglaia*, § 2.]

[2] [Ruskin is here speaking from the personal experience of his own childhood: see *Præterita*, i. ch. i. § 14.]

for vanity's sake, and always badly. The best books to
put into its hands are those illustrated by George Cruikshank or by Richter. (See Appendix.[1]) At about the age
of twelve or fourteen, it is quite time enough to set youth
or girl to serious work; and then this book will, I think,
be useful to them; and I have good hope it may be so,
likewise, to persons of more advanced age wishing to know
something of the first principles of art.

4. Yet observe, that the method of study recommended
is not brought forward as absolutely the best, but only as
the best which I can at present devise for an isolated
student. It is very likely that farther experience in teaching may enable me to modify it with advantage in several
important respects; but I am sure the main principles of
it are sound, and most of the exercises as useful as they
can be rendered without a master's superintendence. The
method differs, however, so materially from that generally
adopted by drawing-masters, that a word or two of explanation may be needed to justify what might otherwise be
thought wilful eccentricity.

5. The manuals at present published on the subject of
drawing are all directed, as far as I know, to one or other
of two objects. Either they propose to give the student a
power of dexterous sketching with pencil or water-colour,
so as to emulate (at considerable distance) the slighter
work of our second-rate artists; or they propose to give
him such accurate command of mathematical forms [2] as may
afterwards enable him to design rapidly and cheaply for
manufactures. When drawing is taught as an accomplishment, the first is the aim usually proposed; while the
second is the object kept chiefly in view at Marlborough
House,[3] and in the branch Government Schools of Design.

6. Of the fitness of the modes of study adopted in those

---

[1] [Below, pp. 222, 224.]
[2] [So also in architecture: see *Two Paths*, § 28.]
[3] [Then the seat of the Science and Art Department, afterwards transferred to
South Kensington. On the general subject of the Department's methods, see the
Introduction to Vol. XVI.]

schools, to the end specially intended, judgment is hardly yet possible; only, it seems to me, that we are all too much in the habit of confusing art as *applied* to manufacture, with manufacture itself.[1] For instance, the skill by which an inventive workman designs and moulds a beautiful cup, is skill of true art; but the skill by which that cup is copied and afterwards multiplied a thousandfold, is skill of manufacture: and the faculties which enable one workman to design and elaborate his original piece, are not to be developed by the same system of instruction as those which enable another to produce a maximum number of approximate copies of it in a given time. Farther: it is surely inexpedient that any reference to purposes of manufacture should interfere with the education of the artist himself. Try first to manufacture a Raphael; then let Raphael direct your manufacture. He will design you a plate, or cup, or a house, or a palace, whenever you want it, and design them in the most convenient and rational way; but do not let your anxiety to reach the platter and the cup interfere with your education of the Raphael. Obtain first the best work you can, and the ablest hands, irrespective of any consideration of economy or facility of production. Then leave your trained artist to determine how far art can be popularised, or manufacture ennobled.

7. Now, I believe that (irrespective of differences in individual temper and character) the excellence of an artist, as such, depends wholly on refinement of perception, and that it is this, mainly, which a master or a school can teach; so that while powers of invention distinguish man from man, powers of perception distinguish school from school. All great schools enforce delicacy of drawing and subtlety of sight: and the only rule which I have, as yet, found to be without exception respecting art, is that all great art is delicate.[2]

[1] [On this subject, compare *Laws of Fésole*, Preface, § 6 (p. 344, below), and *Two Paths*, §§ 51 *seq.*]

[2] [See below, § 16; and compare *Modern Painters*, vol. iii. (Vol. V. p. 63).]

8. Therefore, the chief aim and bent of the following system is to obtain, first, a perfectly patient, and, to the utmost of the pupil's power, a delicate method of work, such as may ensure his seeing truly. For I am nearly convinced that, when once we see keenly enough, there is very little difficulty in drawing what we see; but, even supposing that this difficulty be still great, I believe that the sight is a more important thing than the drawing; and I would rather teach drawing that my pupils may learn to love Nature, than teach the looking at Nature that they may learn to draw. It is surely also a more important thing, for young people and unprofessional students, to know how to appreciate the art of others, than to gain much power in art themselves. Now the modes of sketching ordinarily taught are inconsistent with this power of judgment. No person trained to the superficial execution of modern water-colour painting, can understand the work of Titian or Leonardo; they must for ever remain blind to the refinement of such men's pencilling, and the precision of their thinking. But, however slight a degree of manipulative power the student may reach by pursuing the mode recommended to him in these letters, I will answer for it that he cannot go once through the advised exercises without beginning to understand what masterly work means; and, by the time he has gained some proficiency in them, he will have a pleasure in looking at the painting of the great schools, and a new perception of the exquisiteness of natural scenery, such as would repay him for much more labour than I have asked him to undergo.

9. That labour is, nevertheless, sufficiently irksome, nor is it possible that it should be otherwise, so long as the pupil works unassisted by a master. For the smooth and straight road which admits unembarrassed progress must, I fear, be dull as well as smooth; and the hedges need to be close and trim when there is no guide to warn or bring back the erring traveller. The system followed in this work will, therefore, at first, surprise somewhat sorrowfully

those who are familiar with the practice of our class at the Working Men's College ;[1] for there, the pupil, having the master at his side to extricate him from such embarrassments as his first efforts may lead into, is *at once* set to draw from a solid object, and soon finds entertainment in his efforts and interest in his difficulties. Of course the simplest object which it is possible to set before the eye is a sphere ; and, practically, I find a child's toy, a white leather ball, better than anything else ; as the gradations on balls of plaster of Paris, which I use sometimes to try the strength of pupils who have had previous practice, are a little too delicate for a beginner to perceive. It has been objected that a circle, or the outline of a sphere, is one of the most difficult of all lines to draw. It is so ;* but I do not want it to be drawn. All that his study of the ball is to teach the pupil, is the way in which shade gives the appearance of projection. This he learns most satisfactorily from a sphere ; because any solid form, terminated by straight lines or flat surfaces, owes some of its appearance of projection to its perspective ; but in the sphere, what, without shade, was a flat circle, becomes, merely by the added shade, the image of a solid ball ; and this fact is just as striking to the learner, whether his circular outline be true or false. He is, therefore, never allowed to trouble himself about it ; if he makes the ball look as oval as an egg, the degree of error is simply pointed out to him, and he does better next time, and better still the next. But his mind is always fixed on the gradation of shade, and the outline left to take, in due time, care of itself. I call it outline, for the sake of immediate intelligibility,—strictly speaking, it is merely the edge of the shade ; no pupil in my class being ever allowed to draw an outline, in the ordinary sense. It is pointed out to him, from the

---

* Or, more accurately, appears to be so, because any one can see an error in a circle.

[1] [See above, Introduction, pp. xix.–xxii. ; and compare Vol. V. pp. xxxvi.–xli.]

first, that Nature relieves one mass, or one tint, against another; but outlines none.[1] The outline exercise, the second suggested in this letter, is recommended, not to enable the pupil to draw outlines, but as the only means by which, unassisted, he can test his accuracy of eye, and discipline his hand. When the master is by, errors in the form and extent of shadows can be pointed out as easily as in outline, and the handling can be gradually corrected in details of the work. But the solitary student can only find out his own mistakes by help of the traced limit, and can only test the firmness of his hand by an exercise in which nothing but firmness is required; and during which all other considerations (as of softness, complexity, etc.) are entirely excluded.

10. Both the system adopted at the Working Men's College, and that recommended here, agree, however, in one principle, which I consider the most important and special of all that are involved in my teaching: namely, the attaching its full importance, from the first, to local colour.[2] I believe that the endeavour to separate, in the course of instruction, the observation of light and shade from that of local colour, has always been, and must always be, destructive of the student's power of accurate sight, and that it corrupts his taste as much as it retards his progress. I will not occupy the reader's time by any discussion of the principle here, but I wish him to note it as the only distinctive one in my system, so far as it *is* a system. For the recommendation to the pupil to copy faithfully, and without alteration, whatever natural object he chooses to study, is serviceable, among other reasons, just because it gets rid of systematic rules altogether, and teaches people to draw,

---

[1] [Compare "Addresses on Decorative Colour," § 10, Vol. XII. p. 482.]

[2] [Compare Leonardo's *Treatise on Painting*, § 175 : "The student who is desirous of making great proficiency in the art of imitating the works of Nature, should not only learn the shape of figures or other objects, and be able to delineate them with truth and precision, but he must also accompany them with their proper lights and shadows, *according to the situation in which those objects appear.*" The references in this volume to Leonardo's *Treatise* are to the English version by J. F. Rigaud ("Bohn's Library").]

as country lads learn to ride, without saddle or stirrups; my main object being, at first, not to get my pupils to hold their reins prettily, but to "sit like a jackanapes, never off."[1]

11. In these written instructions, therefore, it has always been with regret that I have seen myself forced to advise anything like monotonous or formal discipline. But, to the unassisted student, such formalities are indispensable, and I am not without hope that the sense of secure advancement, and the pleasure of independent effort, may render the following out of even the more tedious exercises here proposed, possible to the solitary learner, without weariness. But if it should be otherwise, and he finds the first steps painfully irksome, I can only desire him to consider whether the acquirement of so great a power as that of pictorial expression of thought be not worth some toil; or whether it is likely, in the natural order of matters in this working world, that so great a gift should be attainable by those who will give no price for it.

12. One task, however, of some difficulty, the student will find I have not imposed upon him: namely, learning the laws of perspective. It would be worth while to learn them, if he could do so easily; but without a master's help, and in the way perspective is at present explained in treatises, the difficulty is greater than the gain. For perspective is not of the slightest use, except in rudimentary work. You can draw the rounding line of a table in perspective, but you cannot draw the sweep of a sea bay; you can foreshorten a log of wood by it, but you cannot foreshorten an arm. Its laws are too gross and few to be applied to any subtle form; therefore, as you must learn to draw the subtle forms by the eye, certainly you may draw the simple ones. No great painters ever trouble themselves about perspective, and very few of them know its laws; they draw everything by the eye, and, naturally enough, disdain in the easy parts of their work rules which cannot help them in difficult ones.

[1] [*Henry V.*, v. 2.]

It would take about a month's labour to draw imperfectly, by laws of perspective, what any great Venetian will draw perfectly in five minutes, when he is throwing a wreath of leaves round a head, or bending the curves of a pattern in and out among the folds of drapery. It is true that when perspective was first discovered, everybody amused themselves with it; and all the great painters put fine saloons and arcades behind their Madonnas, merely to show that they could draw in perspective: but even this was generally done by them only to catch the public eye, and they disdained the perspective so much, that though they took the greatest pains with the circlet of a crown, or the rim of a crystal cup, in the heart of their picture, they would twist their capitals of columns and towers of churches about in the background in the most wanton way, wherever they liked the lines to go, provided only they left just perspective enough to please the public.

13. In modern days, I doubt if any artist among us, except David Roberts, knows so much perspective as would enable him to draw a Gothic arch to scale at a given angle and distance.[1] Turner, though he was professor of perspective to the Royal Academy, did not know what he professed,[2] and never, as far as I remember, drew a single building in true perspective in his life; he drew them only with as much perspective as suited him. Prout also knew nothing of perspective, and twisted his buildings, as Turner did, into whatever shapes he liked.[3] I do not justify this; and would recommend the student at least to treat perspective with common civility, but to pay no court to it. The best way he can learn it, by himself, is by taking a pane of glass, fixed in a frame, so that it can be

[1] [For a similar statement, see *Pre-Raphaelitism*, § 19 (Vol. XII. p. 356); and for Roberts as an architectural draughtsman, see also *Modern Painters*, vol. i. (Vol. III. p. 223).]

[2] [But see *Modern Painters*, vol. i. (Vol. III. p. 607), and for his diagrams prepared for his Academy lectures—"of the most difficult perspective subjects"—*ibid.*, vol. v. pt. ix. ch. xii. § 4 *n.*, and Vol. XIII. p. 307.]

[3] [For a full discussion of Prout's characteristic virtues and limitations, see Vol. XIV. pp. 384–404.]

set upright before the eye, at the distance at which the proposed sketch is intended to be seen.[1] Let the eye be placed at some fixed point, opposite the middle of the pane of glass, but as high or as low as the student likes; then with a brush at the end of a stick, and a little body-colour that will adhere to the glass, the lines of the landscape may be traced on the glass, as you see them through it. When so traced they are all in true perspective. If the glass be sloped in any direction, the lines are still in true perspective, only it is perspective calculated for a sloping plane, while common perspective always supposes the plane of the picture to be vertical. It is good, in early practice, to accustom yourself to enclose your subject, before sketching it, with a light frame of wood held upright before you; it will show you what you may legitimately take into your picture, and what choice there is between a narrow foreground near you, and a wide one farther off; also, what height of tree or building you can properly take in, etc.*

14. Of figure drawing, nothing is said in the following pages, because I do not think figures, as chief subjects, can be drawn to any good purpose by an amateur. As accessaries in landscape, they are just to be drawn on the same principles as anything else.

15. Lastly: If any of the directions given subsequently to the student should be found obscure by him, or if at any stage of the recommended practice he find himself in difficulties which I have not enough provided against, he may apply by letter to Mr. Ward,[2] who is my under drawing-master at the Working Men's College (45 Great Ormond

* If the student is fond of architecture, and wishes to know more of perspective than he can learn in this rough way, Mr. Runciman (of 49 Acacia Road, St. John's Wood), who was my first drawing-master, and to whom I owe many happy hours, can teach it him quickly, easily, and rightly.[3]

1 [See the opening of Ruskin's own *Elements of Perspective*, below, p. 241.]
2 [Mr. William Ward's present address (1904) is 2 Church Terrace, Richmond, Surrey; but he is no longer engaged in teaching.]
3 [For some account of Mr. Runciman, see *Præterita*, i. ch. iv. § 84.]

Street[1]), and who will give any required assistance, on the lowest terms that can remunerate him for the occupation of his time. I have not leisure myself in general to answer letters of inquiry, however much I may desire to do so; but Mr. Ward has always the power of referring any question to me when he thinks it necessary. I have good hope, however, that enough guidance is given in this work to prevent the occurrence of any serious embarrassment; and I believe that the student who obeys its directions will find, on the whole, that the best answerer of questions is perseverance; and the best drawing-masters are the woods and hills.

[1] [Now (1904) about to be removed to new buildings on a site facing Oakley Square, a little north of St. Pancras Station.]

ADVERTISEMENT TO THE SECOND EDITION

[1857]

As one or two questions, asked of me since the publication of this work, have indicated points requiring elucidation, I have added a few short notes in the first Appendix. It is not, I think, desirable otherwise to modify the form or add to the matter of a book as it passes through successive editions; I have, therefore, only mended the wording of some obscure sentences;[1] with which exception the text remains, and will remain, in its original form, which I had carefully considered. Should the public find the book useful, and call for further editions of it, such additional notes as may be necessary will be always placed in the first Appendix, where they can be at once referred to, in any library, by the possessors of the earlier editions; and I will take care they shall not be numerous.[2]

August 3, 1857.

[1] [See the list of "Variæ Lectiones" above, pp. 7, 8.]
[2] [No such notes were, however, added.]

THE ELEMENTS OF
DRAWING

THE
ELEMENTS OF DRAWING

LETTER I

ON FIRST PRACTICE

1. MY DEAR READER,—Whether this book is to be of use to you or not, depends wholly on your reason for wishing to learn to draw. If you desire only to possess a graceful accomplishment, to be able to converse in a fluent manner about drawing, or to amuse yourself listlessly in listless hours, I cannot help you: but if you wish to learn drawing that you may be able to set down clearly, and usefully, records of such things as cannot be described in words, either to assist your own memory of them, or to convey distinct ideas of them to other people;[1] if you wish to obtain quicker perceptions of the beauty of the natural world, and to preserve something like a true image of beautiful things that pass away, or which you must yourself leave; if, also, you wish to understand the minds of great painters, and to be able to appreciate their work sincerely, seeing it for yourself, and loving it, not merely taking up the thoughts of other people about it; then I *can* help you, or, which is better, show you how to help yourself.

2. Only you must understand, first of all, that these powers, which indeed are noble and desirable, cannot be got without work. It is much easier to learn to draw well, than it is to learn to play well on any musical instrument; but you know that it takes three or four years of practice, giving

---

[1] [Compare the paper on "Education in Art" in *A Joy for Ever*, § 153 (Vol. XVI. p. 143).]

three or four hours a day, to acquire even ordinary command over the keys of a piano; and you must not think that a masterly command of your pencil, and the knowledge of what may be done with it, can be acquired without pains-taking, or in a *very* short time. The kind of drawing which is taught, or supposed to be taught, in our schools, in a term or two, perhaps at the rate of an hour's practice a week, is not drawing at all. It is only the performance of a few dexterous (not always even that) evolutions on paper with a black-lead pencil; profitless alike to performer and beholder, unless as a matter of vanity, and that the smallest possible vanity. If any young person, after being taught what is, in polite circles, called "drawing," will try to copy the commonest piece of real work—suppose a lithograph on the title-page of a new opera air, or a woodcut in the cheapest illustrated newspaper of the day,—they will find themselves entirely beaten. And yet that common litho-graph was drawn with coarse chalk, much more difficult to manage than the pencil of which an accomplished young lady is supposed to have command; and that woodcut was drawn in urgent haste, and half spoiled in the cutting after-wards; and both were done by people whom nobody thinks of as artists, or praises for their power; both were done for daily bread, with no more artist's pride than any simple handicraftsmen feel in the work they live by.

3. Do not, therefore, think that you can learn drawing, any more than a new language, without some hard and disagreeable labour. But do not, on the other hand, if you are ready and willing to pay this price, fear that you may be unable to get on for want of special talent. It is in-deed true that the persons who have peculiar talent for art, draw instinctively, and get on almost without teaching; though never without toil. It is true, also, that of inferior talent for drawing there are many degrees: it will take one person a much longer time than another to attain the same results, and the results thus painfully attained are never quite so satisfactory as those got with greater ease

when the faculties are naturally adapted to the study. But I have never yet, in the experiments I have made, met with a person who could not learn to draw at all; and, in general, there is a satisfactory and available power in every one to learn drawing if he wishes, just as nearly all persons have the power of learning French, Latin, or arithmetic, in a decent and useful degree, if their lot in life requires them to possess such knowledge.

4. Supposing then that you are ready to take a certain amount of pains, and to bear a little irksomeness and a few disappointments bravely, I can promise you that an hour's practice a day for six months, or an hour's practice every other day for twelve months, or, disposed in whatever way you find convenient, some hundred and fifty hours' practice, will give you sufficient power of drawing faithfully whatever you want to draw, and a good judgment, up to a certain point, of other people's work: of which hours if you have one to spare at present, we may as well begin at once.

EXERCISE I.

5. Everything that you can see in the world around you, presents itself to your eyes only as an arrangement of patches of different colours variously shaded.* Some of

* (*N.B.*—This note is only for the satisfaction of incredulous or curious readers. You may miss it if you are in a hurry, or are willing to take the statement in the text on trust.)

The perception of solid Form is entirely a matter of experience. We *see* nothing but flat colours; and it is only by a series of experiments that we find out that a stain of black or grey indicates the dark side of a solid substance, or that a faint hue indicates that the object in which it appears is far away. The whole technical power of painting depends on our recovery of what may be called the *innocence of the eye;* that is to say, of a sort of childish perception of these flat stains of colour, merely as such, without consciousness of what they signify,—as a blind man would see them if suddenly gifted with sight.

For instance: when grass is lighted strongly by the sun in certain directions, it is turned from green into a peculiar and somewhat dusty-looking yellow. If we had been born blind, and were suddenly endowed with sight on a piece of grass thus lighted in some parts by the sun, it

these patches of colour have an appearance of lines or texture within them, as a piece of cloth or silk has of threads, or an animal's skin shows texture of hairs: but whether this be the case or not, the first broad aspect of the thing is that of a patch of some definite colour; and the first thing to be learned is, how to produce extents of smooth colour, without texture.

6. This can only be done properly with a brush; but a brush, being soft at the point, causes so much uncertainty in the touch of an unpractised hand, that it is hardly possible to learn to draw first with it, and it is better to take, in early practice, some instrument with a hard and fine point, both that we may give some support to the hand, and that by working over the subject with so delicate a point, the attention may be properly directed to all the most minute

would appear to us that part of the grass was green, and part a dusty yellow (very nearly of the colour of primroses); and, if there were primroses near, we should think that the sunlighted grass was another mass of plants of the same sulphur-yellow colour. We should try to gather some of them, and then find that the colour went away from the grass when we stood between it and the sun, but not from the primroses; and by a series of experiments we should find out that the sun was really the cause of the colour in the one,—not in the other. We go through such processes of experiment unconsciously in childhood; and having once come to conclusions touching the signification of certain colours, we always suppose that we *see* what we only know, and have hardly any consciousness of the real aspect of the signs we have learned to interpret. Very few people have any idea that sunlighted grass is yellow.

Now, a highly accomplished artist has always reduced himself as nearly as possible to this condition of infantine sight. He sees the colours of nature exactly as they are, and therefore perceives at once in the sunlighted grass the precise relation between the two colours that form its shade and light. To him it does not seem shade and light, but bluish green barred with gold.

Strive, therefore, first of all, to convince yourself of this great fact about sight. This, in your hand, which you know by experience and touch to be a book, is to your eye nothing but a patch of white, variously gradated and spotted; this other thing near you, which by experience you know to be a table, is to your eye only a patch of brown, variously darkened and veined; and so on: and the whole art of Painting consists merely in perceiving the shape and depth of these patches of colour, and putting patches of the same size, depth, and shape on canvas. The only obstacle to the success of painting is, that many of the real colours are brighter and paler than it is possible to put on canvas: we must put darker ones to represent them.

parts of it. Even the best artists need occasionally to study subjects with a pointed instrument, in order thus to discipline their attention: and a beginner must be content to do so for a considerable period.

7. Also, observe that before we trouble ourselves about differences of colour, we must be able to lay on *one* colour properly, in whatever gradations of depth and whatever shapes we want. We will try, therefore, first to lay on tints or patches of grey, of whatever depth we want, with a pointed instrument. Take any finely pointed steel pen (one of Gillott's lithographic crowquills is best), and a piece of quite smooth, but not shining, note-paper, cream laid, and get some ink that has stood already some time in the inkstand, so as to be quite black, and as thick as it can be without clogging the pen. Take a rule, and draw four straight lines, so as to enclose a square, or nearly a square, about as large as *a*, Fig. 1. I say nearly a square, because it does not in

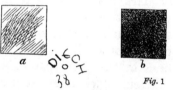

the least matter whether it is quite square or not, the object being merely to get a space enclosed by straight lines.

8. Now, try to fill in that square space with crossed lines, so completely and evenly that it shall look like a square patch of grey silk or cloth, cut out and laid on the white paper, as at *b*. Cover it quickly, first with straightish lines, in any direction you like, not troubling yourself to draw them much closer or neater than those in the square *a*. Let them quite dry before retouching them. (If you draw three or four squares side by side, you may always be going on with one while the others are drying.) Then cover these lines with others in a different direction, and let those dry; then in another direction still, and let those dry. Always wait long enough to run no risk of blotting, and then draw the lines as quickly as you can. Each ought to be laid on as swiftly as the dash of the pen of a good writer; but if you try to reach this great speed at

first, you will go over the edge of the square, which is a
fault in this exercise. Yet it is better to do so now and
then than to draw the lines very slowly; for if you do, the
pen leaves a little dot of ink at the end of each line, and
these dots spoil your work. So draw each line quickly,
stopping always as nearly as you can at the edge of the
square. The ends of lines which go over the edge are afterwards to be removed with the penknife, but not till you
have done the whole work, otherwise you roughen the paper,
and the next line that goes over the edge makes a blot.

9. When you have gone over the whole three or four
times, you will find some parts of the square look darker
than other parts. Now try to make the lighter parts as
dark as the rest, so that the whole may be of equal depth
or darkness. You will find, on examining the work, that
where it looks darkest the lines are closest, or there are
some much darker lines than elsewhere; therefore you must
put in other lines, or little scratches and dots, *between* the
lines in the paler parts ; and where there are any very conspicuous dark lines, scratch them out lightly with the penknife, for the eye must not be attracted by any line in
particular. The more carefully and delicately you fill in
the little gaps and holes, the better ; you will get on faster
by doing two or three squares perfectly than a great many
badly. As the tint gets closer and begins to look even,
work with very little ink in your pen, so as hardly to make
any mark on the paper; and at last, where it is too dark,
use the edge of your penknife very lightly, and for some
time, to wear it softly into an even tone. You will find
that the greatest difficulty consists in getting evenness : one
bit will always look darker than another bit of your square ;
or there will be a granulated and sandy look over the whole.
When you find your paper quite rough and in a mess, give
it up and begin another square, but do not rest satisfied
till you have done your best with every square. The tint
at last ought at least to be as close and even as that in *b*,
Fig. 1. You will find, however, that it is very difficult to

get a pale tint; because, naturally, the ink lines necessary to produce a close tint at all, blacken the paper more than you want. You must get over this difficulty not so much by leaving the lines wide apart as by trying to draw them excessively fine, lightly and swiftly; being very cautious in filling in; and, at last, passing the penknife over the whole. By keeping several squares in progress at one time, and reserving your pen for the light one just when the ink is nearly exhausted, you may get on better. The paper ought, at last, to look lightly and evenly toned all over, with no lines distinctly visible.

EXERCISE II.

10. As this exercise in shading is very tiresome, it will be well to vary it by proceeding with another at the same time. The power of shading rightly depends mainly on lightness of hand and keenness of sight; but there are other qualities required in drawing, dependent not merely on lightness, but steadiness of hand; and the eye, to be perfect in its power, must be made accurate as well as keen, and not only see shrewdly, but measure justly.

11. Possess yourself therefore of any cheap work on botany containing *outline* plates of leaves and flowers, it does not matter whether bad or good: Baxter's *British Flowering Plants*[1] is quite good enough. Copy any of the simplest outlines, first with a soft pencil, following it, by the eye, as nearly as you can; if it does not look right in proportions, rub out and correct it, always by the eye, till you think it is right: when you have got it to your mind, lay tracing-paper on the book; on this paper trace the outline you have been copying, and apply it to your own; and having thus ascertained the faults, correct them all patiently, till you have got it as nearly accurate as may be. Work with

---

[1] [William Baxter (Curator of the Oxford Botanic Gardens): *British Phænogamous Botany; or, Figures and Descriptions of the genera of British Flowering Plants*, Oxford, 1834–1843, 6 vols.]

a very soft pencil, and do not rub out so hard * as to spoil
the surface of your paper; never mind how dirty the paper
gets, but do not roughen it; and let the false outlines alone
where they do not really interfere with the true one. It is
a good thing to accustom yourself to hew and shape your
drawing out of a dirty piece of paper. When you have got
it as right as you can, take a quill pen, not very fine at the
point; rest your hand on a book about an inch and a half
thick, so as to hold the pen long; and go over your pencil
outline with ink, raising your pen point as seldom as possible, and never leaning more heavily on one part of the line
than on another. In most outline drawings of the present
day, parts of the curves are thickened to give an effect of
shade; all such outlines are bad, but they will serve well
enough for your exercises, provided you do not imitate this
character: it is better, however, if you can, to choose a book
of pure outlines. It does not in the least matter whether
your pen outline be thin or thick; but it matters greatly
that it should be *equal*, not heavier in one place than in
another. The power to be obtained is that of drawing an
even line slowly and in any direction; all dashing lines, or
approximations to penmanship, are bad. The pen should, as
it were, walk slowly over the ground, and you should be
able at any moment to stop it, or to turn it in any other
direction, like a well-managed horse.

12. As soon as you can copy every curve *slowly* and
accurately, you have made satisfactory progress; but you
will find the difficulty is in the slowness. It is easy to draw
what appears to be a good line with a sweep of the hand, or

---

* Stale crumb of bread is better, if you are making a delicate drawing,
than India-rubber, for it disturbs the surface of the paper less: but it
crumbles about the room and makes a mess; and, besides, you waste the
good bread, which is wrong; and your drawing will not for a long while
be worth the crumbs. So use India-rubber very lightly; or, if heavily,
pressing it only, not passing it over the paper, and leave what pencil marks
will not come away so, without minding them. In a finished drawing the
uneffaced pencilling is often serviceable, helping the general tone, and en-
abling you to take out little bright lights.

with what is called freedom; * the real difficulty and master-liness is in never letting the hand *be* free, but keeping it under entire control at every part of the line.

EXERCISE III.

13. Meantime, you are always to be going on with your shaded squares, and chiefly with these, the outline exercises being taken up only for rest.

As soon as you find you have some command of the

Fig. 2

pen as a shading instrument, and can lay a pale or dark tint as you choose, try to produce gradated spaces like Fig. 2, the dark tint passing gradually into the lighter ones. Nearly

---

* What is usually so much sought after under the term "freedom" is the character of the drawing of a great master in a hurry, whose hand is so thoroughly disciplined, that when pressed for time he can let it fly as it will, and it will not go far wrong. But the hand of a great master at real *work* is *never* free: its swiftest dash is under perfect government. Paul Veronese or Tintoret could pause within a hair's-breadth of any appointed mark, in their fastest touches; and follow, within a hair's-breadth, the previously intended curve. You must never, therefore, aim at freedom. It is not required of your drawing that it should be free, but that it should be right; in time you will be able to do right easily, and then your work will be free in the best sense; but there is no merit in doing wrong easily.

These remarks, however, do not apply to the lines used in shading, which, it will be remembered, are to be made as quickly as possible. The reason of this is, that the quicker a line is drawn, the lighter it is at the ends, and therefore the more easily joined with other lines, and concealed by them; the object in perfect shading being to conceal the lines as much as possible.

And observe, in this exercise, the object is more to get firmness of hand than accuracy of eye for outline; for there are no outlines in Nature, and the ordinary student is sure to draw them falsely if he draws them at all. Do not, therefore, be discouraged if you find mistakes continue to occur in your outlines; be content at present if you find your hand gaining command over the curves.

all expression of form, in drawing, depends on your power of gradating delicately; and the gradation is always most skilful which passes from one tint into another very little paler.   Draw, therefore, two parallel lines for limits to your work, as in Fig. 2, and try to gradate the shade evenly from white to black, passing over the greatest possible distance, yet so that every part of the band may have visible change in it.   The perception of gradation is very deficient in all beginners (not to say, in many artists), and you will probably, for some time, think your gradation skilful enough, when it is quite patchy and imperfect.   By getting a piece of grey shaded riband, and comparing it with your drawing, you may arrive, in early stages of your work, at a wholesome dissatisfaction with it.   Widen your band little by little as you get more skilful, so as to give the gradation more lateral space, and accustom yourself at the same time to look for gradated spaces in Nature.   The sky is the largest and the most beautiful; watch it at twilight, after the sun is down, and try to consider each pane of glass in the window you look through as a piece of paper coloured blue, or grey, or purple, as it happens to be, and observe how quietly and continuously the gradation extends over the space in the window, of one or two feet square.   Observe the shades on the outside and inside of a common white cup or bowl, which make it look round and hollow;* and then on folds of white drapery; and thus gradually you will be led to observe the more subtle transitions of the light as it increases or declines on flat surfaces.   At last, when your eye gets keen and true, you will see gradation on everything in Nature.

14. But it will not be in your power yet awhile to draw from any objects in which the gradations are varied and complicated; nor will it be a bad omen for your future progress, and for the use that art is to be made of by you,

---

* If you can get any pieces of dead white porcelain, not glazed, they will be useful models.

if the first thing at which you aim should be a little bit of sky. So take any narrow space of evening sky, that you can usually see, between the boughs of a tree, or between two chimneys, or through the corner of a pane in the window you like best to sit at, and try to gradate a little space of white paper as evenly as that is gradated—as *tenderly*, you cannot gradate it without colour, no, nor with colour either; but you may do it as evenly; or, if you get impatient with your spots and lines of ink, when you look at the beauty of the sky, the sense you will have gained of that beauty is something to be thankful for. But you ought not to be impatient with your pen and ink; for all great painters, however delicate their perception of colour, are fond of the peculiar effect of light which may be got in a pen-and-ink sketch, and in a woodcut, by the gleaming of the white paper between the black lines; and if you cannot gradate well with pure black lines, you will never gradate well with pale ones. By looking at any common woodcuts, in the cheap publications of the day, you may see how gradation is given to the sky by leaving the lines farther and farther apart; but you must make your lines as fine as you can, as well as far apart, towards the light; and do not try to make them long or straight, but let them cross irregularly in any direction easy to your hand, depending on nothing but their gradation for your effect. On this point of direction of lines, however, I shall have to tell you more, presently; in the meantime, do not trouble yourself about it.

EXERCISE IV.

15. As soon as you find you can gradate tolerably with the pen, take an H. or HH. pencil, using its point to produce shade, from the darkest possible to the palest, in exactly the same manner as the pen, lightening, however, now with India-rubber instead of the penknife. You will

find that all *pale* tints of shade are thus easily producible with great precision and tenderness, but that you cannot get the same dark power as with the pen and ink, and that the surface of the shade is apt to become glossy and metallic, or dirty-looking, or sandy. Persevere, however, in trying to bring it to evenness with the fine point, removing any single speck or line that may be too black, with the *point* of the knife: you must not scratch the whole with the knife as you do the ink. If you find the texture very speckled-looking, lighten it all over with India-rubber, and recover it again with sharp, and excessively fine touches of the pencil point, bringing the parts that are too pale to perfect evenness with the darker spots.

You cannot use the point too delicately or cunningly in doing this; work with it as if you were drawing the down on a butterfly's wing.

16. At this stage of your progress, if not before, you may be assured that some clever friend will come in, and hold up his hands in mocking amazement, and ask you who could set you to that "niggling"; and if you persevere in it, you will have to sustain considerable persecution from your artistical acquaintances generally, who will tell you that all good drawing depends on "boldness." But never mind them. You do not hear them tell a child, beginning music, to lay its little hand with a crash among the keys, in imitation of the great masters: yet they might, as reasonably as they may tell you to be bold in the present state of your knowledge.[1] Bold, in the sense of being undaunted, yes; but bold in the sense of being careless, confident, or exhibitory,—no,—no, and a thousand times no; for, even if you were not a beginner, it would be bad advice that made you bold. Mischief may easily be done quickly, but good and beautiful work is generally done slowly; you will find no boldness in the way a flower or a

---

[1] [So Leonardo in his *Treatise*, § 167, which is headed "Accuracy ought to be learnt before despatch in the execution."]

bird's wing is painted; and if Nature is not bold at her work, do you think you ought to be at yours? So never mind what people say, but work with your pencil point very patiently; and if you can trust me in anything, trust me when I tell you, that though there are all kinds and ways of art,—large work for large places, small work for narrow places, slow work for people who can wait, and quick work for people who cannot,—there is one quality, and, I think, only one, in which all great and good art agrees;— it is all delicate art. Coarse art is always bad art.[1] You cannot understand this at present, because you do not know yet how much tender thought, and subtle care, the great painters put into touches that at first look coarse; but, believe me, it is true, and you will find it is so in due time.

17. You will be perhaps also troubled, in these first essays at pencil drawing, by noticing that more delicate gradations are got in an instant by a chance touch of the India-rubber, than by an hour's labour with the point; and you may wonder why I tell you to produce tints so painfully, which might, it appears, be obtained with ease. But there are two reasons: the first, that when you come to draw forms, you must be able to gradate with absolute precision, in whatever place and direction you wish; not in any wise vaguely, as the India-rubber does it: and, secondly, that all natural shadows are more or less mingled with gleams of light. In the darkness of ground there is the light of the little pebbles or dust; in the darkness of foliage, the glitter of the leaves; in the darkness of flesh, transparency; in that of a stone, granulation: in every case there is some mingling of light, which cannot be represented by the leaden tone which you get by rubbing, or by an instrument known to artists as the "stump." When you can manage the point properly, you will indeed be able to do much also with this instrument, or with your fingers;

---

[1] [See above, Preface, § 7, p. 14.]

but then you will have to retouch the flat tints afterwards, so as to put life and light into them, and that can only be done with the point. Labour on, therefore, courageously, with that only.

18. When you can manage to tint and gradate tenderly with the pencil point, get a good large alphabet, and try to *tint* the letters into shape with the pencil point. Do not outline them first, but measure their height and ex-

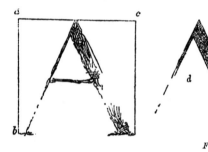

treme breadth with the compasses,[1] as *a b, a c,* Fig. 3, and then scratch in their shapes gradually; the letter A, enclosed within the lines, being in what Turner would have called a "state of for-wardness." Then, when you are satisfied with the

Fig. 3

shape of the letter, draw pen-and-ink lines firmly round the tint, as at *d,* and remove any touches outside the limit, first with the India-rubber, and then with the penknife, so that all may look clear and right. If you rub out any of the pencil inside the outline of the letter, retouch it, closing it up to the inked line. The straight lines of the outline are all to be ruled,* but the curved lines are to be drawn by

---

* Artists who glance at this book may be surprised at this permission. My chief reason is, that I think it more necessary that the pupil's eye should be trained to accurate perception of the relations of curve and right lines, by having the latter absolutely true, than that he should practise drawing straight lines. But also, I believe, though I am not quite sure of this, that he never *ought* to be able to draw a straight line. I do not believe a perfectly trained hand ever can draw a line without some curvature in it, or some variety of direction. Prout could draw a straight line, but I do not believe Raphael could, nor Tintoret. A great draughtsman can, as far as I have observed, draw every line *but* a straight one.

---

[1] [So in §§ 30 and 47, below, pp. 44, 51, the use of compasses is recommended; compare the Preface to *The Laws of Fésole,* below, p. 342.]

the eye and hand; and you will soon find what good practice there is in getting the curved letters, such as Bs, Cs, etc., to stand quite straight, and come into accurate form.

19. All these exercises are very irksome, and they are not to be persisted in alone; neither is it necessary to acquire perfect power in any of them. An entire master of the pencil or brush ought, indeed, to be able to draw any form at once, as Giotto his circle;[1] but such skill as this is only to be expected of the consummate master, having pencil in hand all his life, and all day long,—hence the force of Giotto's proof of his skill; and it is quite possible to draw very beautifully, without attaining even an approximation to such a power; the main point being, not that every line should be precisely what we intend or wish, but that the line which we intended or wished to draw should be right. If we always see rightly and mean rightly, we shall get on, though the hand may stagger a little; but if we mean wrongly, or mean nothing, it does not matter how firm the hand is. Do not therefore torment yourself because you cannot do as well as you would like; but work patiently, sure that every square and letter will give you a certain increase of power; and as soon as you can draw your letters pretty well, here is a more amusing exercise for you.

EXERCISE VI.

20. Choose any tree that you think pretty, which is nearly bare of leaves, and which you can see against the sky, or against a pale wall, or other light ground: it must not be against strong light, or you will find the looking at it hurt your eyes; nor must it be in sunshine, or you will be puzzled by the lights on the boughs. But the tree must be in shade; and the sky blue, or grey, or dull

---

[1] [The reference is to Vasari's story of the round O of Giotto, quoted in full by Ruskin in *Giotto and his Works in Padua*, § 5; referred to also at p. 372 below, and n *Queen of the Air*, § 144, and *Lectures on Art*, § 74.]

white. A wholly grey or rainy day is the best for this practice.

21. You will see that all the boughs of the tree are dark against the sky. Consider them as so many dark rivers, to be laid down in a map with absolute accuracy; and, without the least thought about the roundness of the stems, map them all out in flat shade, scrawling them in with pencil, just as you did the limbs of your letters; then correct and alter them, rubbing out and out again, never minding how much your paper is dirtied (only not destroying its surface), until every bough is exactly, or as near as your utmost power can bring it, right in curvature and in thickness. Look at the white interstices between them with as much scrupulousness as if they were little estates which you had to survey, and draw maps of, for some important lawsuit, involving heavy penalties if you cut the least bit of a corner off any of them, or give the hedge anywhere too deep a curve; and try continually to fancy the whole tree nothing but a flat ramification on a white ground. Do not take any trouble about the little twigs, which look like a confused network or mist; leave them all out,* drawing only the main branches as far as you can see them distinctly, your object at present being not to draw a tree, but to learn how to do so. When you have got the thing as nearly right as you can,—and it is better to make one good study, than twenty left unnecessarily inaccurate,—take your pen, and put a fine outline to all the boughs, as you did to your letter, taking care, as far as possible, to put the outline within the edge of the shade, so as not to make the boughs thicker: the main use of the outline is to affirm the whole more clearly; to do away with little accidental roughnesses and excrescences, and especially to mark where boughs cross, or come in front of each other, as at such points their

---

* Or, if you feel able to do so, scratch them in with confused quick touches, indicating the general shape of the cloud or mist of twigs round the main branches; but do not take much trouble about them.

arrangement in this kind of sketch is unintelligible without the outline. It may perfectly well happen that in Nature it should be less distinct than your outline will make it; but it is better in this kind of sketch to mark the facts clearly. The temptation is always to be slovenly and careless, and the outline is like a bridle,[1] and forces our indolence into attention and precision. The outline should be about the thickness of that in Fig. 4, which represents the ramification of a small stone pine, only I have not endeavoured to represent the pencil shading within the outline, as I could not easily express it in a woodcut; and you have nothing to do at present with the indication of foliage above, of which in another place. You may also draw your trees as much larger than this figure as you like; only, however large they

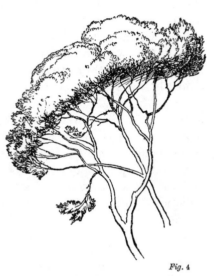

Fig. 4

may be, keep the outline as delicate, and draw the branches far enough into their outer sprays to give quite as slender ramification as you have in this figure, otherwise you do not get good enough practice out of them.

22. You cannot do too many studies of this kind: every one will give you some new notion about trees. But when you are tired of tree boughs, take any forms whatever which are drawn in flat colour, one upon another; as patterns on any kind of cloth, or flat china (tiles, for instance), executed in two colours only; and practise drawing

[1] [So Leonardo (§ 113): " Perspective is to painting what the bridle is to a horse."]

them of the right shape and size by the eye, and filling them in with shade of the depth required.

In doing this, you will first have to meet the difficulty of representing depth of colour by depth of shade. Thus a pattern of ultramarine blue will have to be represented by a darker tint of grey than a pattern of yellow.

23. And now it is both time for you to begin to learn the mechanical use of the brush; and necessary for you to do so in order to provide yourself with the gradated scale of colour which you will want. If you can, by any means, get acquainted with any ordinary skilful water-colour painter, and prevail on him to show you how to lay on tints with a brush, by all means do so; not that you are yet, nor for a long while yet, to begin to colour, but because the brush is often more convenient than the pencil for laying on masses or tints of shade, and the sooner you know how to manage it as an instrument the better. If, however, you have no opportunity of seeing how water-colour is laid on by a workman of any kind, the following directions will help you :—

EXERCISE VII.

24. Get a shilling cake of Prussian blue.[1] Dip the end of it in water so as to take up a drop, and rub it in a white saucer till you cannot rub much more, and the colour gets dark, thick, and oily-looking. Put two teaspoonfuls of water to the colour you have rubbed down, and mix it well up with a camel's-hair brush about three-quarters of an inch long.

25. Then take a piece of smooth, but not glossy, Bristol board or pasteboard; divide it, with your pencil and rule, into squares as large as those of the very largest chess-board: they need not be perfect squares, only as nearly so

---

[1] [So in §§ 121, 156, 163, colour in cakes is recommended. That was in 1857. Now that moist water-colours are sold in tubes, so that they can be set on the palette, clean every morning, the tubes are recommended (see *The Laws of Fésole*, x. 13, below, p. 469).—*Editor's note in index, ed. 1892 and later.*]

as you can quickly guess. Rest the pasteboard on something sloping as much as an ordinary desk; then, dipping your brush into the colour you have mixed, and taking up as much of the liquid as it will carry, begin at the top of one of the squares, and lay a pond or runlet of colour along the top edge. Lead this pond of colour gradually downwards, not faster at one place than another, but as if you were adding a row of bricks to a building, all along (only building down instead of up), dipping the brush frequently so as to keep the colour as full in that, and in as great quantity on the paper, as you can, so only that it does not run down anywhere in a little stream. But if it should, never mind; go on quietly with your square till you have covered it all in. When you get to the bottom, the colour will lodge there in a great wave. Have ready a piece of blotting-paper; dry your brush on it, and with the dry brush take up the superfluous colour as you would with a sponge, till it all looks even.

26. In leading the colour down, you will find your brush continually go over the edge of the square, or leave little gaps within it. Do not endeavour to retouch these, nor take much care about them; the great thing is to get the colour to lie smoothly where it reaches, not in alternate blots and pale patches; try, therefore, to lead it over the square as fast as possible, with such attention to your limit as you are able to give. The use of the exercise is, indeed, to enable you finally to strike the colour up to the limit with perfect accuracy; but the first thing is to get it even,—the power of rightly striking the edge comes only by time and practice: even the greatest artists rarely can do this quite perfectly.

27. When you have done one square, proceed to do another which does not communicate with it. When you have thus done all the alternate squares, as on a chessboard, turn the pasteboard upside down, begin again with the first, and put another coat over it, and so on over all the others. The use of turning the paper upside down

is to neutralise the increase of darkness towards the bottom of the squares, which would otherwise take place from the ponding of the colour.

28. Be resolved to use blotting-paper, or a piece of rag, instead of your lips, to dry the brush. The habit of doing so, once acquired, will save you from much partial poisoning. Take care, however, always to draw the brush from root to point, otherwise you will spoil it. You may even wipe it as you would a pen when you want it very dry, without doing harm, provided you do not crush it upwards. Get a good brush at first, and cherish it; it will serve you longer and better than many bad ones.

29. When you have done the squares all over again, do them a third time, always trying to keep your edges as neat as possible. When your colour is exhausted, mix more in the same proportions, two teaspoonfuls to as much as you can grind with a drop; and when you have done the alternate squares three times over, as the paper will be getting very damp, and dry more slowly, begin on the white squares, and bring them up to the same tint in the same way. The amount of jagged dark line which then will mark the limits of the squares will be the exact measure of your unskilfulness.

30. As soon as you tire of squares draw circles (with compasses); and then draw straight lines irregularly across circles, and fill up the spaces so produced between the straight line and the circumference ; and then draw any simple shapes of leaves, according to the exercise No. II., and fill up those, until you can lay on colour quite evenly in any shape you want.

31. You will find in the course of this practice, as you cannot always put exactly the same quantity of water to the colour, that the darker the colour is, the more difficult it becomes to lay it on evenly. Therefore, when you have gained some definite degree of power, try to fill in the forms required with a full brush, and a dark tint, at once, instead of laying several coats one over another; always

taking care that the tint, however dark, be quite liquid; and that, after being laid on, so much of it is absorbed as to prevent its forming a black line at the edge as it dries. A little experience will teach you how apt the colour is to do this, and how to prevent it; not that it needs always to be prevented, for a great master in water-colours will sometimes draw a firm outline, when he *wants* one, simply by letting the colour dry in this way at the edge.

32. When, however, you begin to cover complicated forms with the darker colour, no rapidity will prevent the tint from drying irregularly as it is led on from part to part. You will then find the following method useful. Lay in the colour very pale and liquid; so pale, indeed, that you can only just see where it is on the paper. Lead it up to all the outlines, and make it precise in form, keeping it thoroughly wet everywhere. Then, when it is all in shape, take the darker colour, and lay some of it *into* the middle of the liquid colour. It will spread gradually in a branchy kind of way, and you may now lead it up to the outlines already determined, and play it with the brush till it fills its place well; then let it dry, and it will be as flat and pure as a single dash, yet defining all the complicated forms accurately.

33. Having thus obtained the power of laying on a tolerably flat tint, you must try to lay on a gradated one. Prepare the colour with three or four teaspoonfuls of water; then, when it is mixed, pour away about two thirds of it, keeping a teaspoonful of pale colour. Sloping your paper as before, draw two pencil lines all the way down, leaving a space between them of the width of a square on your chess-board. Begin at the top of your paper, between the lines; and having struck on the first brushful of colour, and led it down a little, dip your brush deep in water, and mix up the colour on the plate quickly with as much more water as the brush takes up at that one dip: then, with this paler colour, lead the tint farther down. Dip in water again, mix the colour again, and thus

lead down the tint, always dipping in water once between each replenishing of the brush, and stirring the colour on the plate well, but as quickly as you can. Go on until the colour has become so pale that you cannot see it ; then wash your brush thoroughly in water, and carry the wave down a little farther with that, and then absorb it with the dry brush, and leave it to dry.

34. If you get to the bottom of your paper before your colour gets pale, you may either take longer paper, or begin, with the tint as it was when you left off, on another sheet ; but be sure to exhaust it to pure whiteness at last. When all is quite dry, recommence at the top with another similar mixture of colour, and go down in the same way. Then again, and then again, and so continually until the colour at the top of the paper is as dark as your cake of Prussian blue, and passes down into pure white paper at the end of your column, with a perfectly smooth gradation from one into the other.

35. You will find at first that the paper gets mottled or wavy, instead of evenly gradated ; this is because at some places you have taken up more water in your brush than at others, or not mixed it thoroughly on the plate, or led one tint too far before replenishing with the next. Practice only will enable you to do it well ; the best artists cannot always get gradations of this kind quite to their minds ; nor do they ever leave them on their pictures without after-touching.

36. As you get more power, and can strike the colour more quickly down, you will be able to gradate in less compass ;* beginning with a small quantity of colour, and adding a drop of water, instead of a brushful ; with finer brushes, also, you may gradate to a less scale. But slight skill will enable you to test the relations of colour to shade

---

* It is more difficult, at first, to get, in colour, a narrow gradation than an extended one ; but the ultimate difficulty is, as with the pen, to make the gradation go *far*.

as far as is necessary for your immediate progress, which is to be done thus:—

37. Take cakes of lake, of gamboge, of sepia, of blue-black, of cobalt, and vermilion; and prepare gradated columns (exactly as you have done with the Prussian blue) of the lake and blue-black.* Cut a narrow slip, all the way down, of each gradated colour, and set the three slips side by side; fasten them down, and rule lines at equal distances across all the three, so as to divide them into fifty degrees, and number the degrees of each, from light to dark, 1, 2, 3, etc. If you have gradated them rightly, the darkest part either of the red or blue will be nearly equal in power to the darkest part of the blue-black, and any degree of the black slip will also, accurately enough for our purpose, balance in weight the degree similarly numbered in the red or the blue slip. Then, when you are drawing from objects of a crimson or blue colour, if you can match their colour by any compartment of the crimson or blue in your scales, the grey in the compartment of the grey scale marked with the same number is the grey which must represent that crimson or blue in your light and shade drawing.

38. Next, prepare scales with gamboge, cobalt, and vermilion. You will find that you cannot darken these beyond a certain point;† for yellow and scarlet, so long as they remain yellow and scarlet, cannot approach to black; we cannot have, properly speaking, a dark yellow or dark scarlet. Make your scales of full yellow, blue, and scarlet, half-way down; passing *then* gradually to white. Afterwards use lake to darken the upper half of the vermilion and gamboge; and Prussian blue to darken the cobalt. You will thus have three more scales, passing from white nearly to black, through yellow and orange, through

---

* Of course, all the columns of colour are to be of equal length.

† The degree of darkness you can reach with the given colour is always indicated by the colour of the solid cake in the box.

sky-blue, and through scarlet. By mixing the gamboge and
Prussian blue you may make another with green; mixing
the cobalt and lake, another with violet; the sepia alone
will make a forcible brown one; and so on, until you have
as many scales as you like, passing from black to white
through different colours.   Then, supposing your scales
properly gradated and equally divided, the compartment or
degree No. 1 of the grey will represent in chiaroscuro the
No. 1 of all the other colours; No. 2 of grey the No. 2
of the other colours, and so on.

39. It is only necessary, however, in this matter that
you should understand the principle; for it would never
be possible for you to gradate your scales so truly as to
make them practically accurate and serviceable; and even
if you could, unless you had about ten thousand scales,
and were able to change them faster than ever juggler
changed cards, you could not in a day measure the tints
on so much as one side of a frost-bitten apple. But when
once you fully understand the principle, and see how all
colours contain as it were a certain quantity of darkness,
or power of dark relief from white—some more, some less;
and how this pitch or power of each may be represented
by equivalent values of grey, you will soon be able to
arrive shrewdly at an approximation by a glance of the
eye, without any measuring scale at all.

40. You must now go on, again with the pen, drawing
patterns, and any shapes of shade that you think pretty,
as veinings in marble or tortoiseshell, spots in surfaces of
shells, etc., as tenderly as you can, in the darknesses that
correspond to their colours; and when you find you can
do this successfully, it is time to begin rounding.

EXERCISE VIII.

41. Go out into your garden, or into the road, and pick
up the first round or oval stone you can find, not very
white, nor very dark; and the smoother it is the better,

only it must not *shine*. Draw your table near the window, and put the stone, which I will suppose is about the size of *a* in Fig. 5 (it had better not be much larger), on a piece of not very white paper, on the table in front of you. Sit so that the light may come from your left, else the shadow of the pencil point interferes with your sight of your work. You must not let the *sun* fall on the stone, but only ordinary light: therefore choose a window which the sun does not come in at.[1] If you can shut the shutters

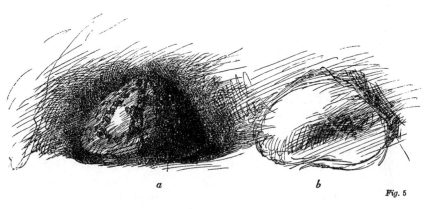

a   *b*

Fig. 5

of the other windows in the room it will be all the better; but this is not of much consequence.

42. Now if you can draw that stone, you can draw anything;[2] I mean, anything that is drawable. Many things (sea foam, for instance) cannot be drawn at all, only the idea of them more or less suggested; but if you can draw the stone *rightly*, everything within reach of art is also within yours.[3]

---

[1] [Compare Leonardo, § 186: "To paint well from nature, your window should be to the north, that the lights may not vary. If it be to the south, you must have paper blinds, that the sun, in going round, may not alter the shadows. The situation of the light should be such as to produce upon the ground a shadow from your model as long as that is high."]

[2] [So in *Modern Painters,* vol. v. pt. vi. ch. v. § 2: "If you can paint *one* leaf, you can paint the world."]

[3] [For a discussion of stone-drawing, illustrated by various examples, see *Modern Painters,* vol. iv. ch. xviii. §§ 10 *seq.* (Vol. VI. pp. 370 *seq.*).]

For all drawing depends, primarily, on your power of representing *Roundness*. If you can once do that, all the rest is easy and straightforward; if you cannot do that, nothing else that you may be able to do will be of any use. For Nature is all made up of roundnesses; not the roundness of perfect globes, but of variously curved surfaces. Boughs are rounded, leaves are rounded, stones are rounded, clouds are rounded, cheeks are rounded, and curls are rounded: there is no more flatness in the natural world than there is vacancy. The world itself is round, and so is all that is in it, more or less, except human work, which is often very flat indeed.

Therefore, set yourself steadily to conquer that round stone, and you have won the battle.

43. Look your stone antagonist boldly in the face. You will see that the side of it next the window is lighter than most of the paper; that the side of it farthest from the window is darker than the paper; and that the light passes into the dark gradually, while a shadow is thrown to the right on the paper itself by the stone: the general appearance of things being more or less as in *a*, Fig. 5, the spots on the stone excepted, of which more presently.

44. Now, remember always what was stated in the outset, that everything you can see in Nature is seen only so far as it is lighter or darker than the things about it, or of a different colour from them. It is either seen as a patch of one colour on a ground of another; or as a pale thing relieved from a dark thing, or a dark thing from a pale thing. And if you can put on patches of colour or shade of exactly the same size, shape, and gradations as those on the object and its ground, you will produce the appearance of the object and its ground. The best draughtsmen— Titian and Paul Veronese themselves—could do no more than this; and you will soon be able to get some power of doing it in an inferior way, if you once understand the exceeding simplicity of what is to be done. Suppose you have a brown book on a white sheet of paper, on a red

tablecloth. You have nothing to do but to put on spaces of red, white, and brown, in the same shape, and gradated from dark to light in the same degrees, and your drawing is done. If you will not look at what you see, if you try to put on brighter or duller colours than are there, if you try to put them on with a dash or a blot, or to cover your paper with "vigorous" lines, or to produce anything, in fact, but the plain, unaffected, and finished tranquillity of the thing before you, you need not hope to get on. Nature will show you nothing if you set yourself up for her master. But forget yourself, and try to obey her, and you will find obedience easier and happier than you think.

45. The real difficulties are to get the refinement of the forms and the evenness of the gradations. You may depend upon it, when you are dissatisfied with your work, it is always too coarse or too uneven. It may not be wrong—in all probability is not wrong, in any (so-called) great point. But its edges are not true enough in outline; and its shades are in blotches, or scratches, or full of white holes. Get it more tender and more true, and you will find it is more powerful.[1]

46. Do not, therefore, think your drawing must be weak because you have a finely pointed pen in your hand. Till you can draw with that, you can draw with nothing; when you can draw with that, you can draw with a log of wood charred at the end. True boldness and power are only to be gained by care. Even in fencing and dancing, all ultimate ease depends on early precision in the commencement; much more in singing or drawing.

47. Now I do not want you to copy my sketch in Fig. 5, but to copy the stone before you in the way that my sketch is done. To which end, first measure the extreme length of the stone with compasses, and mark that

---

[1] [So Leonardo (§ 181): "Take care that the shadows and lights be united, or lost in each other; without any hard strokes or lines; as smoke loses itself in the air, so are your lights and shadows to pass from the one to the other, without any apparent separation."]

length on your paper; then, between the points marked,
leave something like the form of the stone in light, scrawling the paper all over, round it; *b*, in Fig. 5, is a beginning
of this kind.[1] Rather leave too much room for the high
light, than too little; and then more cautiously fill in the
shade, shutting the light gradually up, and putting in the
dark slowly on the dark side. You need not plague yourself about accuracy of shape, because, till you have practised a great deal, it is impossible for you to draw the
shape of the stone quite truly, and you must gradually
gain correctness by means of these various exercises : what
you have mainly to do at present is, to get the stone to
look solid and round, not much minding what its exact
contour is—only draw it as nearly right as you can without
vexation; and you will get it more right by thus feeling
your way to it in shade, than if you tried to draw the outline at first. For you can *see* no outline; what you see is
only a certain space of gradated shade, with other such
spaces about it; and those pieces of shade you are to imitate as nearly as you can, by scrawling the paper over till
you get them to the right shape, with the same gradations
which they have in Nature. And this is really more likely
to be done well, if you have to fight your way through a
little confusion in the sketch, than if you have an accurately
traced outline. For instance, having sketched the fossil
sea-urchin at *a*, in Fig. 5, whose form, though irregular,
required more care in following than that of a common
stone, I was going to draw it also under another effect;[2]
reflected light bringing its dark side out from the background: but when I had laid on the first few touches I
thought it would be better to stop, and let you see how I
had begun it, at *b*. In which beginning it will be observed

---

[1] [Ed. 1 adds :—
   "You cannot rightly see what the form of the stone really is till you
   begin finishing, so sketch it in quite rudely; only rather leave too *much*
   room for the high light . . ."]
[2] [Here ed. 1 reads simply :—
   "For instance, I was going to draw, beside *a*, another effect on the stone;
   reflected light . . ."]

that nothing is so determined but that I can more or less modify, and add to or diminish the contour as I work on, the lines which suggest the outline being blended with the others if I do not want them; and the having to fill up the vacancies and conquer the irregularities of such a sketch will probably secure a higher completion at last, than if half an hour had been spent in getting a true outline before beginning.

48. In doing this, however, take care not to get the drawing too dark. In order to ascertain what the shades of it really are, cut a round hole, about half the size of a pea, in a piece of white paper the colour of that you use to draw on. Hold this bit of paper with the hole in it, between you and your stone; and pass the paper backwards and forwards, so as to see the different portions of the stone (or other subject) through the hole. You will find that, thus, the circular hole looks like one of the patches of colour you have been accustomed to match, only changing in depth as it lets different pieces of the stone be seen through it. You will be able thus actually to *match* the colour of the stone at any part of it, by tinting the paper beside the circular opening. And you will find that this opening never looks quite *black*, but that all the roundings of the stone are given by subdued greys.*

49. You will probably find, also, that some parts of the stone, or of the paper it lies on, look luminous through the opening; so that the little circle then tells as a light spot instead of a dark spot. When this is so, you cannot imitate it, for you have no means of getting light brighter than white paper: but by holding the paper more sloped towards the light, you will find that many parts of the stone, which before looked light through the hole, then look dark through it; and if you can place the paper in such a position that every part of the stone looks slightly dark, the little hole will tell always as a spot of shade, and

* The figure *a*, Fig. 5, is very dark, but this is to give an example of all kinds of depths of tint, without repeated figures.

if your drawing is put in the same light, you can imitate or match every gradation.   You will be amazed to find, under these circumstances, how slight the differences of tint are, by which, through infinite delicacy of gradation, Nature can express form.

If any part of your subject will obstinately show itself as a light through the hole, that part you need not hope to imitate.   Leave it white; you can do no more.

50. When you have done the best you can to get the general form, proceed to finish, by imitating the texture and all the cracks and stains of the stone as closely as you can; and note, in doing this, that cracks or fissures of any kind, whether between stones in walls, or in the grain of timber or rocks, or in any of the thousand other conditions they present, are never expressible by single black lines, or lines of simple shadow.   A crack must always have its complete system of light and shade, however small its scale. It is in reality a little ravine, with a dark or shady side, and light or sunny side, and, usually, shadow in the bottom. This is one of the instances in which it may be as well to understand the reason of the appearance; it is not often so in drawing, for the aspects of things are so subtle and confused that they cannot in general be explained; and in the endeavour to explain some, we are sure to lose sight of others, while the natural over-estimate of the importance of those on which the attention is fixed causes us to exaggerate them, so that merely scientific draughtsmen caricature a third part of Nature, and miss two thirds.   The best scholar is he whose eye is so keen as to see at once how the thing looks, and who need not therefore trouble himself with any reasons why it looks so: but few people have this acuteness of perception; and to those who are destitute of it, a little pointing out of rule and reason will be a help, especially when a master is not near them.   I never allow my own pupils to ask the reason of anything, because, as I watch their work, I can always show them how the thing is, and what appearance they are missing in it; but when

a master is not by to direct the sight, science may, here and there, be allowed to do so in his stead.

51. Generally, then, every solid illumined object—for instance, the stone you are drawing—has a light side turned towards the light, a dark side turned away from the light, and a shadow, which is cast on something else (as by the stone on the paper it is set upon). You may sometimes be placed so as to see only the light side and shadow, sometimes only the dark side and shadow, and sometimes both or either without the shadow; but in most positions solid objects will show all the three, as the stone does here.

52. Hold up your hand with the edge of it towards you, as you sit now with your side to the window, so that the flat of your hand is turned to the window. You will see one side of your hand distinctly lighted, the other distinctly in shade. Here are light side and dark side, with no seen shadow; the shadow being detached, perhaps on the table, perhaps on the other side of the room; you need not look for it at present.

53. Take a sheet of note-paper, and holding it edgewise, as you hold your hand, wave it up and down past the side of your hand which is turned from the light, the paper being of course farther from the window. You will see, as it passes, a strong gleam of light strike on your hand, and light it considerably on its dark side. This light is *reflected* light. It is thrown back from the paper (on which it strikes first in coming from the window) to the surface of your hand, just as a ball would be if somebody threw it through the window at the wall and you caught it at the rebound.[1]

Next, instead of the note-paper, take a red book, or a piece of scarlet cloth. You will see that the gleam of light falling on your hand, as you wave the book, is now reddened. Take a blue book, and you will find the gleam

[1] [So Leonardo (§ 213): "Reverberations are produced by all bodies of a bright nature, that have a smooth and tolerably hard surface, which, repelling the light it receives, makes it rebound like a football (*balzo della palla*) against the first object opposed to it."]

is blue. Thus every object will cast some of its own colour back in the light that it reflects.

54. Now it is not only these books or papers that reflect light to your hand: every object in the room on that side of it reflects some, but more feebly, and the colours mixing all together form a neutral* light, which lets the colour of your hand itself be more distinctly seen than that of any object which reflects light to it; but if there were no reflected light, that side of your hand would look as black as a coal.

55. Objects are seen therefore, in general, partly by direct light, and partly by light reflected from the objects around them, or from the atmosphere and clouds. The colour of their light sides depends much on that of the direct light, and that of the dark sides on the colours of the objects near them. It is therefore impossible to say beforehand what colour an object will have at any point of its surface, that colour depending partly on its own tint, and partly on infinite combinations of rays reflected from other things. The only certain fact about dark sides is, that their colour will be changeful, and that a picture which gives them merely darker shades of the colour of the light sides must assuredly be bad.[1]

56. Now, lay your hand flat on the white paper you are drawing on. You will see one side of each finger lighted, one side dark, and the shadow of your hand on the paper. Here, therefore, are the three divisions of shade seen at once. And although the paper is white, and your hand of a rosy colour somewhat darker than white, yet you will see that the shadow all along, just under the finger

---

* Nearly neutral in ordinary circumstances, but yet with quite different tones in its neutrality, according to the colours of the various reflected rays that compose it.

---

[1] [Ultimately Ruskin found it advisable to direct beginners in his Oxford Drawing School to "shade simply with a deeper and (if you already know what the word means) a warmer tone of the colour you are using" (*Laws of Fésole*, viii. 9, below, p. 434), this being an approach to the practice of the Venetians, as opposed to that of the Bolognese and Roman schools (*Lectures on Art*, § 134).—*Editor's note in index, ed. 1892 and later.*]

which casts it, is darker than the flesh, and is of a very deep grey. The reason of this is, that much light is reflected from the paper to the dark side of your finger, but very little is reflected from other things to the paper itself in that chink under your finger.

57. In general, for this reason, a shadow, or, at any rate, the part of the shadow nearest the object, is darker than the dark side of the object. I say in general, because a thousand accidents may interfere to prevent its being so. Take a little bit of glass, as a wine-glass, or the ink-bottle, and play it about a little on the side of your hand farthest from the window; you will presently find you are throwing gleams of light all over the dark side of your hand, and in some positions of the glass the reflection from it will annihilate the shadow altogether, and you will see your hand dark on the white paper. Now a stupid painter would represent, for instance, a drinking-glass beside the hand of one of his figures, and because he had been taught by rule that "shadow was darker than the dark side," he would never think of the reflection from the glass, but paint a dark grey under the hand, just as if no glass were there. But a great painter would be sure to think of the true effect, and paint it; and then comes the stupid critic, and wonders why the hand is so light on its dark side.

58. Thus it is always dangerous to assert anything as a *rule* in matters of art; yet it is useful for you to remember that, in a general way, a shadow is darker than the dark side of the thing that casts it, supposing the colours otherwise the same; that is to say, when a white object casts a shadow on a white surface, or a dark object on a dark surface: the rule will not hold if the colours are different, the shadow of a black object on a white surface being, of course, not so dark, usually, as the black thing casting it. The only way to ascertain the ultimate truth in such matters is to *look* for it; but, in the meantime, you will be helped by noticing that the cracks in the stone are little ravines, on one side of which the light strikes

sharply, while the other is in shade. This dark side usually casts a little darker shadow at the bottom of the crack; and the general tone of the stone surface is not so bright as the light bank of the ravine. And, therefore, if you get the surface of the object of a uniform tint, more or less indicative of shade, and then scratch out a white spot or streak in it of any shape; by putting a dark touch beside this white one, you may turn it, as you choose, into either a ridge or an incision, into either a boss or a cavity. If you put the dark touch on the side of it nearest the sun, or rather, nearest the place that the light comes from, you will make it a cut or cavity; if you put it on the opposite side, you will make it a ridge or mound; and the complete success of the effect depends less on depth of shade than on the rightness of the drawing; that is to say, on the evident correspondence of the form of the shadow with the form that casts it. In drawing rocks, or wood, or anything irregularly shaped, you will gain far more by a little patience in following the forms carefully, though with slight touches, than by laboured finishing of texture of surface and transparencies of shadow.

59. When you have got the whole well into shape, proceed to lay on the stains and spots with great care, quite as much as you gave to the forms. Very often, spots or bars of local colour do more to express form than even the light and shade, and they are always interesting as the means by which Nature carries light into her shadows, and shade into her lights; an art of which we shall have more to say hereafter, in speaking of composition. *a*, in Fig. 5, is a rough sketch of a fossil sea-urchin, in which the projections of the shell are of black flint, coming through a chalky surface. These projections form dark spots in the light; and their sides, rising out of the shadow, form smaller whiter spots in the dark. You may take such scattered lights as these out with the penknife, provided you are just as careful to place them rightly as if you got them by a more laborious process.

60. When you have once got the feeling of the way in which gradation expresses roundness and projection, you may try your strength on anything natural or artificial that happens to take your fancy, provided it be not too complicated in form. I have asked you to draw a stone first, because any irregularities and failures in your shading will be less offensive to you, as being partly characteristic of the rough stone surface, than they would be in a more delicate subject; and you may as well go on drawing rounded stones of different shapes for a little while, till you find you can really shade delicately. You may then take up folds of thick white drapery, a napkin or towel thrown carelessly on the table is as good as anything, and try to express them in the same way; only now you will find that your shades must be wrought with perfect unity and tenderness, or you will lose the flow of the folds. Always remember that a little bit perfected is worth more than many scrawls; whenever you feel yourself inclined to scrawl, give up work resolutely, and do not go back to it till next day. Of course your towel or napkin must be put on something that may be locked up, so that its folds shall not be disturbed till you have finished. If you find that the folds will not look right, get a photograph of a piece of drapery (there are plenty now to be bought, taken from the sculpture of the cathedrals of Rheims, Amiens, and Chartres, which will at once educate your hand and your taste), and copy some piece of that; you will then ascertain what it is that is wanting in your studies from Nature, whether more gradation, or greater watchfulness of the disposition of the folds. Probably for some time you will find yourself failing painfully in both, for drapery is very difficult to follow in its sweeps; but do not lose courage, for the greater the difficulty, the greater the gain in the effort. If your eye is more just in measurement of form than delicate in perception of tint, a pattern on the folded surface will help you. Try whether it does or not: and if the patterned drapery confuses you, keep for a time to the simple white one; but if

it helps you, continue to choose patterned stuffs (tartans and simple chequered designs are better at first than flowered ones), and even though it should confuse you, begin pretty soon to use a pattern occasionally, copying all the distortions and perspective modifications of it among the folds with scrupulous care.

61. Neither must you suppose yourself condescending in doing this. The greatest masters are always fond of drawing patterns; and the greater they are, the more pains they take to do it truly.* Nor can there be better practice at any time, as introductory to the nobler complication of natural detail. For when you can draw the spots which follow the folds of a printed stuff, you will have some chance of following the spots which fall into the folds of the skin of a leopard as he leaps; but if you cannot draw the manufacture, assuredly you will never be able to draw the creature. So the cloudings on a piece of wood, carefully drawn, will be the best introduction to the drawing of the clouds of the sky, or the waves of the sea; and the dead leaf-patterns on a damask drapery, well rendered, will enable you to disentangle masterfully the living leaf-patterns of a thorn thicket or a violet bank.

62. Observe, however, in drawing any stuffs, or bindings of books, or other finely textured substances, do not trouble yourself, as yet, much about the woolliness or gauziness of the thing; but get it right in shade and fold, and true in pattern. We shall see, in the course of after-practice, how the penned lines may be made indicative of texture; but at present attend only to the light and shade and pattern.

---

* If we had any business with the reasons of this, I might perhaps be able to show you some metaphysical ones for the enjoyment, by truly artistical minds, of the changes wrought by light and shade and perspective in patterned surfaces; but this is at present not to the point; and all that you need to know is that the drawing of such things is good exercise, and moreover a kind of exercise which Titian, Veronese, Tintoret, Giorgione, and Turner, all enjoyed, and strove to excel in.[1]

---

[1] [Compare *Inaugural Address at Cambridge*, § 10 (Vol. XVI.).]

You will be puzzled at first by *lustrous* surfaces, but a little attention will show you that the expression of these depends merely on the right drawing of their light and shade, and reflections. Put a small black japanned tray on the table in front of some books; and you will see it reflects the objects beyond it as in a little black rippled pond; its own colour mingling always with that of the reflected objects. Draw these reflections of the books properly, making them dark and distorted, as you will see that they are, and you will find that this gives the lustre to your tray. It is not well, however, to draw polished objects in general practice; only you should do one or two in order to understand the aspect of any lustrous portion of other things, such as you cannot avoid; the gold, for instance, on the edges of books, or the shining of silk and damask, in which lies a great part of the expression of their folds. Observe also that there are very few things which are totally without lustre; you will frequently find a light which puzzles you, on some apparently dull surface, to be the dim image of another object.

63. And now, as soon as you can conscientiously assure me that with the point of the pen or pencil you can lay on any form and shade you like, I give you leave to use the brush with one colour,—sepia, or blue black, or mixed cobalt and blue black, or neutral tint; and this will much facilitate your study, and refresh you. But, preliminarily, you must do one or two more exercises in tinting.

EXERCISE IX.

64. Prepare your colour as directed for Exercise vii. Take a brush full of it, and strike it on the paper in any irregular shape; as the brush gets dry, sweep the surface of the paper with it as if you were dusting the paper very lightly; every such sweep of the brush will leave a number of more or less minute interstices in the colour. The lighter and faster every dash the better. Then leave the

whole to dry; and, as soon as it is dry, with little colour in your brush, so that you can bring it to a fine point, fill up all the little interstices one by one, so as to make the whole as even as you can, and fill in the larger gaps with more colour, always trying to let the edges of the first and of the newly applied colour exactly meet, and not lap over each other. When your new colour dries, you will find it in places a little paler than the first. Retouch it therefore, trying to get the whole to look quite one piece. A very small bit of colour thus filled up with your very best care, and brought to look as if it had been quite even from the first, will give you better practice and more skill than a great deal filled in carelessly; so do it with your best patience, not leaving the most minute spot of white; and do not fill in the large pieces first and then go to the small, but quietly and steadily cover in the whole up to a marked limit; then advance a little farther, and so on; thus always seeing distinctly what is done and what undone.

EXERCISE X.

65. Lay a coat of the blue, prepared as usual, over a whole square of paper. Let it dry. Then another coat over four fifths of the square, or thereabouts, leaving the edge rather irregular than straight, and let it dry. Then another coat over three fifths; another over two fifths; and the last over one fifth; so that the square may present the appearance of gradual increase in darkness in five bands, each darker than the one beyond it. Then, with the brush rather dry, (as in the former exercise, when filling up the interstices), try, with small touches, like those used in the pen etching, only a little broader, to add shade delicately beyond each edge, so as to lead the darker tints into the paler ones imperceptibly. By touching the paper very lightly, and putting a multitude of little touches, crossing and recrossing in every direction, you will gradually be

able to work up to the darker tints, outside of each, so as quite to efface their edges, and unite them tenderly with the next tint. The whole square, when done, should look evenly shaded from dark to pale, with no bars, only a crossing texture of touches, something like chopped straw, over the whole.*

66. Next, take your rounded pebble; arrange it in any light and shade you like; outline it very loosely with the pencil. Put on a wash of colour, prepared *very* pale, quite flat over all of it, except the highest light, leaving the edge of your colour quite sharp. Then another wash, extending only over the darker parts, leaving the edge of that sharp also, as in tinting the square. Then another wash over the still darker parts, and another over the darkest, leaving each edge to dry sharp. Then, with the small touches, efface the edges, reinforce the darks, and work the whole delicately together as you would with the pen, till you have got it to the likeness of the true light and shade. You will find that the tint underneath is a great help, and that you can now get effects much more subtle and complete than with the pen merely.

67. The use of leaving the edges always sharp is that you may not trouble or vex the colour, but let it lie as it falls suddenly on the paper: colour looks much more lovely when it has been laid on with a dash of the brush, and left to dry in its own way, than when it has been dragged about and disturbed; so that it is always better to let the edges and forms be a little wrong, even if one cannot correct them afterwards, than to lose this fresh quality of the tint. Very great masters in water colour can lay on the true forms at once with a dash, and bad masters in water colour lay on grossly false forms with a dash, and leave them false; for people in general, not knowing false from true, are as much pleased with the appearance of power in

---

* The use of acquiring this habit of execution is that you may be able, when you begin to colour, to let one hue be seen in minute portions, gleaming between the touches of another.

the irregular blot as with the presence of power in the determined one; but *we*, in our beginnings, must do as much
as we can with the broad dash, and then correct with the
point, till we are quite right. We must take care to be
right, at whatever cost of pains; and then gradually we
shall find we can be right with freedom.

68. I have hitherto limited you to colour mixed with
two or three teaspoonfuls of water; but, in finishing your
light and shade from the stone, you may, as you efface
the edge of the palest coat towards the light, use the
colour for the small touches with more and more water,
till it is so pale as not to be perceptible. Thus you may
obtain a perfect gradation to the light. And in reinforcing
the darks, when they are very dark, you may use less and
less water. If you take the colour tolerably dark on your
brush, only always liquid (not pasty), and dash away the
superfluous colour on blotting paper, you will find that,
touching the paper very lightly with the dry brush, you
can, by repeated touches, produce a dusty kind of bloom,
very valuable in giving depth to shadow; but it requires
great patience and delicacy of hand to do this properly.
You will find much of this kind of work in the grounds
and shadows of William Hunt's drawings.*

69. As you get used to the brush and colour, you will
gradually find out their ways for yourself, and get the
management of them. And you will often save[1] yourself
much discouragement by remembering what I have so often
asserted,[2]—that if anything goes wrong, it is nearly sure to
be refinement that is wanting, not force; and connexion,
not alteration. If you dislike the state your drawing is in,
do not lose patience with it, nor dash at it, nor alter its

---

* William Hunt, of the Old Water-Colour Society.[3]

[1] [Ed. 1 reads :—
        " . . . management of them. Nothing but practice will do this perfectly ;
   but you will often save . . ."]
[2] [See above, Preface, § 7, and §§ 16, 45.]
[3] [For whose technique, see Vol. XIV. pp. 376, 383, 437 ; *Two Paths*, § 69
(Vol. XVI.). See also § 175, below, p. 152.]

plan, nor rub it desperately out, at the place you think wrong; but look if there are no shadows you can gradate more perfectly; no little gaps and rents you can fill; no forms you can more delicately define: and do not *rush* at any of the errors or incompletions thus discerned, but efface or supply slowly, and you will soon find your drawing take another look. A very useful expedient in producing some effects, is to wet the paper, and then lay the colour on it, more or less wet, according to the effect you want. You will soon see how prettily it gradates itself as it dries; when dry, you can reinforce it with delicate stippling when you want it darker. Also, while the colour is still damp on the paper, by drying your brush thoroughly, and touching the colour with the brush so dried, you may take out soft lights with great tenderness and precision. Try all sorts of experiments of this kind, noticing how the colour behaves; but remembering always that your final results must be obtained, and can only be obtained, by pure work with the point, as much as in the pen drawing.

70. You will find also, as you deal with more and more complicated subjects, that Nature's resources in light and shade are so much richer than yours, that you cannot possibly get all, or anything like all, the gradations of shadow in any given group. When this is the case, determine first to keep the broad masses of things distinct: if, for instance, there is a green book, and a white piece of paper, and a black inkstand in the group, be sure to keep the white paper as a light mass, the green book as a middle tint mass, the black inkstand as a dark mass; and do not shade the folds in the paper, or corners of the book, so as to equal in depth the darkness of the inkstand. The great difference between the masters of light and shade, and imperfect artists, is the power of the former to draw so delicately as to express form in a dark-coloured object with little light, and in a light-coloured object with little darkness; and it is better even to leave the forms here and there unsatisfactorily rendered than to lose the general

relations of the great masses. And this, observe, not because masses are grand or desirable things in your composition (for with composition at present you have nothing whatever to do), but because it is a fact that things do so present themselves to the eyes of men, and that we see paper, book, and inkstand as three separate things, before we see the wrinkles, or chinks, or corners of any of the three. Understand, therefore, at once, that no detail can be as strongly expressed in drawing as it is in reality; and strive to keep all your shadows and marks and minor markings on the masses, lighter than they appear to be in Nature; you are sure otherwise to get them too dark. You will in doing this find that you cannot get the projection of things sufficiently shown; but never mind that; there is no need that they should appear to project, but great need that their relations of shade to each other should be preserved. All deceptive projection is obtained by partial exaggeration of shadow; and whenever you see it, you may be sure the drawing is more or less bad: a thoroughly fine drawing or painting will always show a slight tendency towards flatness.

71. Observe, on the other hand, that, however white an object may be, there is always some small point of it whiter than the rest. You must therefore have a slight tone of grey over everything in your picture except on the extreme high lights; even the piece of white paper, in your subject, must be toned slightly down, unless (and there are thousand chances against its being so) it should all be turned so as fully to front the light. By examining the treatment of the white objects in any pictures accessible to you by Paul Veronese or Titian, you will soon understand this.*

---

* At Marlborough House, among the four principal examples of Turner's later water-colour drawing, perhaps the most neglected was that of fishing-boats and fish at sunset.[1] It is one of his most wonderful works, though

---

[1] [The reference is to the first exhibition of Turner's water-colour sketches; see Vol. XIII. p. xxxiii. The drawing referred to is No. 372 in the National Gallery; *ibid.*, p. 97.]

72. As soon as you feel yourself capable of expressing with the brush the undulations of surfaces and the relations of masses, you may proceed to draw more complicated and beautiful things.* And first, the boughs of trees, now not in mere dark relief, but in full rounding. Take the first bit of branch or stump that comes to hand, with a fork in it; cut off the ends of the forking branches, so as to leave the whole only about a foot in length; get a piece of paper the same size, fix your bit of branch in some place where its position will not be altered, and draw it thoroughly, in all its light and shade, full size; striving, above all things, to get an accurate expression of its structure at the fork of the branch. When once you have mastered the tree at its *arm-pits*, you will have little more trouble with it.

73. Always draw whatever the background happens to be, exactly as you see it. Wherever you have fastened the bough, you must draw whatever is behind it, ugly or not, else you will never know whether the light and shade are right;[1] they may appear quite wrong to you, only for want of the background. And this general law is to be observed in all your studies: whatever you draw, draw completely and unalteringly, else you never know if what you have done is right, or whether you *could* have done it rightly had you tried. There is nothing *visible* out of which you may not get useful practice.

unfinished. If you examine the larger white fishing-boat sail, you will find it has a little spark of pure white in its right-hand upper corner, about as large as a minute pin's head, and that all the surface of the sail is gradated to that focus. Try to copy this sail once or twice, and you will begin to understand Turner's work. Similarly, the wing of the Cupid in Correggio's large picture in the National Gallery is focussed to two little grains of white at the top of it. The points of light on the white flower in the wreath round the head of the dancing child-faun, in Titian's Bacchus and Ariadne, exemplify the same thing.[2]

* I shall not henceforward number the exercises recommended; as they are distinguished only by increasing difficulty of subject, not by difference of method.

---

[1] [Compare Leonardo's *Treatise*, § 262.]
[2] [The Correggio is No. 10; the Titian, No. 35.]

74. Next, to put the leaves on your boughs. Gather a small twig with four or five leaves on it, put it into water, put a sheet of light-coloured or white paper behind it, so that all the leaves may be relieved in dark from the white field; then sketch in their dark shape carefully with pencil as you did the complicated boughs, in order to be sure that all their masses and interstices are right in shape before you begin shading, and complete as far as you can with pen and ink, in the manner of Fig. 6, which is a young shoot of lilac.

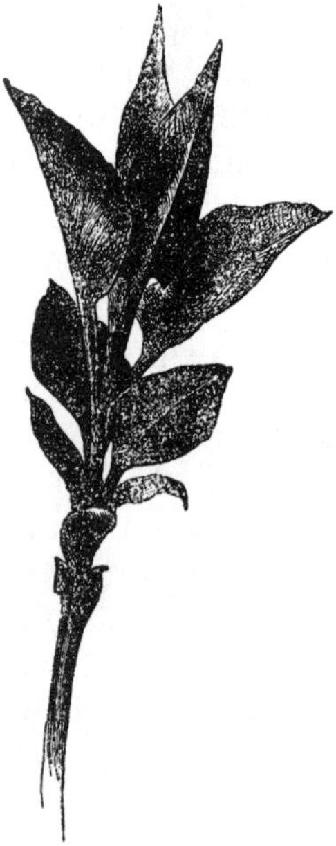

75. You will probably, in spite of all your pattern drawings, be at first puzzled by leaf foreshortening; especially because the look of retirement or projection depends not so much on the perspective of the leaves themselves as on the double sight of the two eyes. Now there are certain artifices by which good painters can partly conquer this difficulty; as slight exaggerations of force or colour in the nearer parts, and of obscurity in the more distant ones; but you must not attempt anything of this kind. When you are first sketching the leaves, shut one of your eyes, fix a point in the background, to bring the point of one of the leaves against; and so sketch the whole bough as you see it in a fixed position, looking with one eye only. Your drawing never can be made to look like the object itself, as you see that object with *both* eyes,* but it can be made perfectly like the object seen with one, and you must be content when you have got a resemblance on these terms.

Fig. 6

* If you understand the principle of the stereoscope you will know why; if not, it does not matter; trust me for the truth of the statement,

76. In order to get clearly at the notion of the thing
to be done, take a single long leaf, hold it with its point
towards you, and as flat as you can, so as to see nothing
of it but its thinness, as if you wanted to know how
thin it was; outline it so. Then slope it down gradually
towards you, and watch it as it lengthens out to its full
length, held perpendicularly down before you. Draw it in
three or four different positions between these extremes,
with its ribs as they appear in each position, and you will
soon find out how it must be.

77. Draw first only two or three of the leaves; then
larger clusters; and practise, in this way, more and more
complicated pieces of bough and leafage, till you find you
can master the most difficult arrangements, not consisting
of more than ten or twelve leaves. You will find as you
do this, if you have an opportunity of visiting any gallery
of pictures, that you take a much more lively interest
than before in the work of the great masters; you will
see that very often their best backgrounds are composed
of little more than a few sprays of leafage, carefully studied,
brought against the distant sky; and that another wreath
or two form the chief interest of their foregrounds. If
you live in London you may test your progress *accurately*
by the degree of admiration you feel for the leaves of
vine round the head of the Bacchus, in Titian's Bacchus
and Ariadne.[1] All this, however, will not enable you to
draw a mass of foliage. You will find, on looking at any
rich piece of vegetation, that it is only one or two of
the nearer clusters that you can by any possibility draw

as I cannot explain the principle without diagrams and much loss of time.[2]
See, however, Note 1, in Appendix I. [p. 215].

---

[1] [No. 35 in the National Gallery: see § 71 *n.*, above, and compare *Academy Notes*, 1855 (Vol. XIV. p. 21).]
[2] [See the diagram in Leonardo's *Treatise* (§ 124), where he says. " Painters often despair of being able to imitate Nature, from observing, that their pictures have not the same relief, nor the same life, as natural objects have in a looking-glass. . . . It is impossible that objects in painting should appear with the same relief as those in the looking-glass, unless we look at them with only one eye."]

in this complete manner. The mass is too vast, and too
intricate, to be thus dealt with.

78. You must now therefore have recourse to some
confused mode of execution, capable of expressing the confusion of Nature. And, first, you must understand what
the character of that confusion is. If you look carefully
at the outer sprays of any tree at twenty or thirty yards'
distance, you will see them defined against the sky in
masses, which, at first, look quite definite; but if you
examine them, you will see, mingled with the real shapes
of leaves, many indistinct lines, which are, some of them,

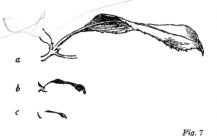

stalks of leaves, and some,
leaves seen with the edge
turned towards you, and
coming into sight in a
broken way; for, supposing
the real leaf shape to be
as at *a*, Fig. 7, this, when
removed some yards from
the eye, will appear dark
against the sky, as at *b;*

Fig. 7

then, when removed some yards farther still, the stalk and
point disappear altogether, the middle of the leaf becomes
little more than a line; and the result is the condition at
c, only with this farther subtlety in the look of it, inexpressible in the woodcut, that the stalk and point of the
leaf, though they have disappeared to the eye, have yet
some influence in *checking the light* at the places where
they exist, and cause a slight dimness about the part of
the leaf which remains visible, so that its perfect effect could
only be rendered by two layers of colour, one subduing the
sky tone a little, the next drawing the broken portions of
the leaf, as at *c*, and carefully indicating the greater darkness of the spot in the middle, where the under side of
the leaf is.

This is the perfect theory of the matter. In practice
we cannot reach such accuracy; but we shall be able to

render the general look of the foliage satisfactorily by the following mode of practice.

79. Gather a spray of any tree, about a foot or eighteen inches long. Fix it firmly by the stem in anything that will support it steadily; put it about eight feet away from you, or ten if you are far-sighted. Put a sheet of not very white paper behind it, as usual. Then draw very carefully, first placing them with pencil, and then filling them up with ink, every leaf-mass and stalk of it in simple black profile, as you see them against the paper: Fig. 8 is a bough of Phillyrea so drawn. Do not be afraid of running the leaves into a black mass when they come together; this exercise is only to teach you what the actual shapes of such masses are when seen against the sky.

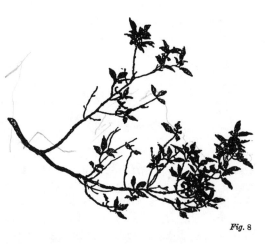

Fig. 8

80. Make two careful studies of this kind of one bough of every common tree,—oak, ash, elm, birch, beech, etc.; in fact, if you are good, and industrious, you will make one such study carefully at least three times a week, until you have examples of every sort of tree and shrub you can get branches of. You are to make two studies of each bough, for this reason,—all masses of foliage have an upper and under surface, and the side view of them, or profile, shows a wholly different organisation of branches from that seen in the view from above. They are generally seen more or less in profile, as you look at the whole tree, and Nature puts her best composition into the profile arrangement. But the view from above or below occurs not unfrequently,

also, and it is quite necessary you should draw it if you wish to understand the anatomy of the tree. The difference between the two views is often far greater than you could easily conceive. For instance, in Fig. 9, *a* is the upper view and *b* the profile, of a single spray of Phillyrea. Fig. 8 is an intermediate view of a larger bough; seen from beneath, but at some lateral distance also.

81. When you have done a few branches in this manner, take one of the drawings you have made, and put it first a yard away from you, then a yard and a half, then two yards; observe how the thinner stalks and leaves gradually disappear, leaving only a vague and slight darkness where they were; and make another study of

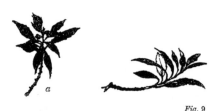

Fig. 9

the effect at each distance, taking care to draw nothing more than you really see, for in this consists all the difference between what would be merely a miniature drawing of the leaves seen near, and a full-size drawing of the same leaves at a distance. By full size, I mean the size which they would really appear of if their outline were traced through a pane of glass held at the same distance from the eye at which you mean to hold your drawing.[1] You can always ascertain this full size of any object by holding your paper upright before you, at the distance from your eye at which you wish your drawing to be seen. Bring its edge across the object you have to draw, and mark upon this edge the points where the outline of the object crosses, or goes behind, the edge of the paper. You will always find it, thus measured, smaller than you supposed.

82. When you have made a few careful experiments of this kind on your own drawings, (which are better for

---

[1] [Compare Leonardo's advice (§ 126): "Take a glass as large as your paper, fasten it well between your eye and the object you mean to draw," etc.]

practice, at first, than the real trees, because the black profile in the drawing is quite stable, and does not shake, and
is not confused by sparkles of lustre on the leaves,) you
may try the extremities of the real trees, only not doing
much at a time, for the brightness of the sky will dazzle
and perplex your sight. And this brightness causes, I believe, some loss of the outline itself; at least the chemical
action of the light in a photograph extends much within
the edges of the leaves, and, as it were, eats them away,
so that no tree extremity, stand it ever so still, nor any
other form coming against bright sky, is truly drawn by
a photograph; and if you once succeed in drawing a few
sprays rightly, you will find the result much more lovely
and interesting than any photograph can be.

83. All this difficulty, however, attaches to the rendering
merely the dark form of the sprays as they come against
the sky. Within those sprays, and in the heart of the tree,
there is a complexity of a much more embarrassing kind;
for nearly all leaves have some lustre, and all are more or
less translucent (letting light through them); therefore, in
any given leaf, besides the intricacies of its own proper
shadows and foreshortenings, there are three series of circumstances which alter or hide its forms. First, shadows
cast on it by other leaves,—often very forcibly. Secondly,
light reflected from its lustrous surface, sometimes the blue
of the sky, sometimes the white of clouds, or the sun itself
flashing like a star. Thirdly, forms and shadows of other
leaves, seen as darknesses through the translucent parts of
the leaf; a most important element of foliage effect, but
wholly neglected by landscape artists in general.

84. The consequence of all this is, that except now and
then by chance, the form of a complete leaf is never seen;
but a marvellous and quaint confusion, very definite, indeed, in its evidence of direction of growth, and unity of
action, but wholly indefinable and inextricable, part by part,
by any amount of patience. You cannot possibly work it
out in facsimile, though you took a twelvemonth's time to

a tree; and you must therefore try to discover some mode of execution which will more or less imitate, by its own variety and mystery, the variety and mystery of Nature, without absolute delineation of detail.

85. Now I have led you to this conclusion by observation of tree form only, because in that the thing to be proved is clearest. But no natural object exists which does not involve in some part or parts of it this inimitableness, this mystery of quantity, which needs peculiarity of handling and trick of touch to express it completely. If leaves are intricate, so is moss, so is foam, so is rock cleavage, so are fur and hair, and texture of drapery, and of clouds. And although methods and dexterities of handling are wholly useless if you have not gained first the thorough knowledge of the form of the thing; so that if you cannot draw a branch perfectly, then much less a tree; and if not a wreath of mist perfectly, much less a flock of clouds; and if not a single grass blade perfectly, much less a grass bank; yet having once got this power over decisive form, you may safely — and must, in order to perfection of work — carry out your knowledge by every aid of method and dexterity of hand.

86. But, in order to find out what method can do, you must now look at Art as well as at Nature, and see what means painters and engravers have actually employed for the expression of these subtleties. Whereupon arises the question, what opportunity you have to obtain engravings? You ought, if it is at all in your power, to possess yourself of a certain number of good examples of Turner's engraved works: if this be not in your power, you must just make the best use you can of the shop windows, or of any plates of which you can obtain a loan. Very possibly, the difficulty of getting sight of them may stimulate you to put them to better use. But, supposing your means admit of your doing so, possess yourself, first, of the illustrated edition either of Rogers's *Italy* or Rogers's *Poems*, and then of about a dozen of the plates named in the annexed lists.

The prefixed letters indicate the particular points deserving your study in each engraving.* Be sure, therefore, that your selection includes, at all events, one plate marked with each letter.[1] Do not get more than twelve of these plates,

* The plates marked with a star are peculiarly desirable. See note at the end of Appendix I. [p. 217].[2] The letters mean as follows:—

a stands for architecture, including distant grouping of towns, cottages, etc.
c clouds, including mist and aerial effects.
f foliage.
g ground, including low hills, when not rocky.
l effects of light.
m mountains, or bold rocky ground.
p power of general arrangement and effect.
q quiet water.
r running or rough water; or rivers, even if calm, when their line of flow is beautifully marked.

From the " England Series."

a c f r. Arundel.
  a f l. Ashby de la Zouche.
a l q r. Barnard Castle.*
 f m r. Bolton Abbey.
  f g r. Buckfastleigh.*
  a l p. Caernarvon.
  c l q. Castle Upnor.
  a f l. Colchester.
    l q. Cowes.
  c f p. Dartmouth Cove.*
  c l q. Flint Castle.*
a f g l. Knaresborough.*
  a f p. Lancaster.
c l m r. Lancaster Sands.*

  a g f. Launceston.*
c f l r. Leicester Abbey.
    f r. Ludlow.
  a f l. Margate.
  a l q. Orford.
    c p. Plymouth.
     f. Powis Castle.
  l m q. Prudhoe Castle.
f l m r. Chain Bridge over Tees.*
    m r. High Force of Tees.*
  a f q. Trematon.
    m q. Ulleswater.
    f m. Valle Crucis.

From the " Keepsake."

m p q. Arona.
    l m. Drachenfels.*
     f l. Marly.*

     p. St. Germain en Laye.
  l p q. Florence.
    l m. Ballyburgh Ness.*

---

[1] [Ed. 1 adds here:—
  "... each letter—of course the plates marked with two or three letters are, for the most part, the best. Do not ..."]
[2] [For other references—in some cases very numerous—to these engraved drawings, see General Index. The years of the *Keepsake* containing the plates mentioned are 1829 (Arona, *i.e.*, Lago Maggiore"), 1832 (Marly and St. Germain en Laye), and 1828 (Florence). "Drachenfels" was engraved, not in the *Keepsake*, but in vol. 2 of Finden's *Landscape and Portrait Illustrations to the Life and Works of Byron* (1833); and "Ballyburgh Ness" in *The Prose Works of Scott*, 1834 (*The Antiquary*).]

nor even all the twelve at first; for the more engravings you have, the less attention you will pay to them. It is a general truth, that the enjoyment derivable from art cannot be increased in quantity, beyond a certain point, by quantity of possession; it is only spread, as it were, over a larger surface, and very often dulled by finding ideas repeated in different works.[1] Now, for a beginner, it is always better that his attention should be concentrated on one or two good things, and all his enjoyment founded on them, than that he should look at many, with divided thoughts. He has much to discover; and his best way of discovering it is to think long over few things, and watch them earnestly. It is one of the worst errors of this age to try to know and to see too much: the men who seem to know everything, never in reality know anything rightly. Beware of *hand-book* knowledge.

87. These engravings are, in general, more for you to look at than to copy; and they will be of more use to you

From the " Bible Series." [2]

f m.	Mount Lebanon.	*c l p q.*	Solomon's Pools.*
m.	Rock of Moses at Sinai.	*a l.*	Santa Saba.
a l m.	Jericho.	*a l.*	Pool of Bethesda.
a c g.	Joppa.		

From " Scott's Works."

p r.	Melrose.*	*c m.*	Glencoe.
f r.	Dryburgh.*	*c m.*	Loch Coriskin.*
	a l.	Caerlaverock.	

From the " Rivers of France."

a q.	Château of Amboise, with large bridge on right.	*a p.*	Rouen Cathedral.
l p r.	Rouen, looking down the river, poplars on right.*	*f p.*	Pont de l'Arche.
		f l p.	View on the Seine, with avenue.
a l p.	Rouen, with cathedral and rainbow, avenue on left.	*a c p.*	Bridge of Meulan.
		c g p r.	Caudebec.*

---

[1] [A fact constantly insisted upon by Ruskin : see, for example, Vol. XIII. p. 501, and Vol. XVI., Appendix i. § 4.]
[2] [See below, Appendix i. § 254, p. 217.]

when we come to talk of composition, than they are at present; still, it will do you a great deal of good, sometimes to try how far you can get their delicate texture, or gradations of tone: as your pen-and-ink drawing will be apt to incline too much to a scratchy and broken kind of shade. For instance, the texture of the white convent wall, and the drawing of its tiled roof, in the vignette at p. 227 of Rogers's *Poems*, is as exquisite as work can possibly be; and it will be a great and profitable achievement if you can at all approach it. In like manner, if you can at all imitate the dark distant country at p. 7, or the sky at p. 80, of the same volume, or the foliage at pp. 12 and 144, it will be good gain; and if you can once draw the rolling clouds and running river at p. 9 of the *Italy*, or the city in the vignette of Aosta at p. 25, or the moonlight at p. 223, you will find that even Nature herself cannot afterwards very terribly puzzle you with her torrents, or towers, or moonlight.[1]

88. You need not copy touch for touch, but try to get the same effect. And if you feel discouraged by the delicacy required, and begin to think that engraving is not drawing, and that copying it cannot help you to draw, remember that it differs from common drawing only by the difficulties it has to encounter. You perhaps have got into a careless habit of thinking that engraving is a mere business, easy enough when one has got into the knack of it. On the contrary, it is a form of drawing more difficult than common drawing, by exactly so much as it is more difficult to cut steel than to move the pencil over paper. It is true that there are certain mechanical aids and methods which reduce it at certain stages either to pure machine work, or to more or less a habit of hand and arm; but this is not so in the foliage you are trying to copy, of which the best

---

[1] [The drawings for all these vignettes are in the National Gallery. They are, in the order named, 246 ("Columbus at La Rabida"); 226 ("Twilight"); 230 ("Tornaro"); 231 ("Gipsies"); 243 ("The Falls at Vallombré"); 205 ("St. Maurice"); 203 ("Aosta"); and 223 ("Padua: moonlight").]

and prettiest parts are always etched—that is, drawn with a fine steel point and free hand: only the line made is white instead of black, which renders it much more difficult to judge of what you are about. And the trying to copy these plates will be good for you, because it will awaken you to the real labour and skill of the engraver, and make you understand a little how people must work, in this world, who have really to *do* anything in it.

89. Do not, however, suppose that I give you the engraving as a model—far from it; but it is necessary you should be able to do as well* before you think of doing better, and you will find many little helps and hints in the various work of it. Only remember that *all* engravers' foregrounds are bad; whenever you see the peculiar wriggling parallel lines of modern engravings become distinct, you must not copy; nor admire: it is only the softer masses, and distances, and portions of the foliage in the plates marked *f*, which you may copy. The best for this purpose, if you can get it, is the "Chain bridge over the Tees," of the England series; the thicket on the right is very beautiful and instructive, and very like Turner. The foliage in the "Ludlow" and "Powis" is also remarkably good.

90. Besides these line engravings, and to protect you from what harm there is in their influence, you are to provide yourself, if possible, with a Rembrandt etching, or a photograph of one (of figures, not landscape). It does not matter of what subject, or whether a sketchy or finished one, but the sketchy ones are generally cheapest, and will teach you most. Copy it as well as you can, noticing especially that Rembrandt's most rapid lines have steady purpose; and that they are laid with almost inconceivable precision when the object becomes at all interesting. The "Prodigal Son," "Death of the Virgin," "Abraham and

---

* As *well*;—not as minutely: the diamond cuts finer lines on the steel than you can draw on paper with your pen; but you must be able to get tones as even, and touches as firm.

Isaac,"[1] and such others, containing incident and character rather than chiaroscuro, will be the most instructive. You can buy one; copy it well; then exchange it, at little loss, for another; and so, gradually, obtain a good knowledge of his system. Whenever you have an opportunity of examining his work at museums, etc., do so with the greatest care, not looking at *many* things, but a long time at each. You must also provide yourself, if possible, with an engraving of Albert Dürer's. This you will not be able to copy; but you must keep it beside you, and refer to it as a standard of precision in line. If you can get one with a *wing* in it, it will be best.[2] The crest with the cock, that with the skull and satyr, and the " Melancholy," are the best you could have, but any will do. Perfection in chiaroscuro drawing lies between these two masters, Rembrandt and Dürer. Rembrandt is often too loose and vague; and Dürer has little or no effect of mist or uncertainty. If you can see anywhere a drawing by Leonardo, you will find it balanced between the two characters; but there are no engravings which present this perfection, and your style will be best formed, therefore, by alternate study of Rembrandt and Dürer. Lean rather to Dürer; it is better, for amateurs, to err on the side of precision than on that of vagueness: and though, as I have just said, you cannot copy a Dürer, yet try every now and then a quarter of an inch square or so, and see how much nearer you can come; you cannot possibly try to draw the leafy crown of the " Melancholia " too often.

91. If you cannot get either a Rembrandt or a Dürer, you may still learn much by carefully studying any of George Cruikshank's etchings, or Leech's woodcuts in *Punch*,

---

[1] [Fine states of these etchings may be seen in the Print Room of the British Museum. The " Death of the Virgin " is dated 1639; " Abraham caressing Isaac," 1636; and the " Prodigal Son," 1636.]

[2] [See Fig. 49 in *Modern Painters*, vol. iv. (Vol. VI. p. 247). Fine states of the engravings by Dürer here mentioned may also be seen in the British Museum. A reproduction of the " Coat of Arms, with a Cock " is given at p. 55 of Lionel Cust's *Albert Dürer's Engravings*, 1894; for another reference to it, see *A Joy for Ever*, § 164 (Vol. XVI. p. 151). For other references to the " Melancholia," see Vol. VI. p. 64 *n*.]

on the free side; with Alfred Rethel's and Richter's * on the severe side. But in so doing you will need to notice the following points:

92. When either the material (as the copper or wood) or the time of an artist does not permit him to make a perfect drawing,—that is to say, one in which no lines shall be prominently visible,—and he is reduced to show the black lines, either drawn by the pen, or on the wood, it is better to make these lines help, as far as may be, the expression of texture and form. You will thus find many textures, as of cloth or grass or flesh, and many subtle effects of light, expressed by Leech with zigzag or crossed or curiously broken lines; and you will see that Alfred Rethel and Richter constantly express the direction and rounding of surfaces by the direction of the lines which shade them. All these various means of expression will be useful to you, as far as you can learn them, provided you remember that they are merely a kind of shorthand; telling certain facts not in quite the right way, but in the only possible way under the conditions: and provided in any after use of such means, you never try to show your own dexterity; but only to get as much record of the object as you can in a given time; and that you continually make efforts to go beyond such shorthand, and draw portions of the objects rightly.

93. And touching this question of direction of lines as indicating that of surface, observe these few points:

If lines are to be distinctly shown, it is better that, so far as they *can* indicate anything by their direction, they should explain rather than oppose the general character of the object. Thus, in the piece of woodcut from Titian, Fig. 10, the lines are serviceable by expressing, not only the shade of the trunk, but partly also its roundness, and the flow of its grain. And Albert Dürer, whose work

* See, for account of these plates, the Appendix on "Works to be studied." [1]

---

[1] [Below, pp. 222–224; but the Appendix is headed "Things to be Studied."]

was chiefly engraving, sets himself always thus to make
his lines as *valuable* as possible; telling much by them,
both of shade and direction of surface: and if you were
always to be limited to engraving on copper (and did not
want to express effects of mist or darkness, as well as
delicate forms), Albert Dürer's way of work would be the
best example for you. But, inasmuch as the perfect way
of drawing is by shade without lines, and the great painters
always conceive their subject as complete, even when they
are sketching it most rapidly, you will find that, when they
are not limited in means, they do not much trust to direc-

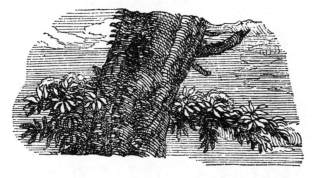

Fig. 10

tion of line, but will often scratch in the shade of a rounded
surface with nearly straight lines, that is to say, with the
easiest and quickest lines possible to themselves. When the
hand is free, the easiest line for it to draw is one inclining
from the left upwards to the right, or *vice versâ*, from the
right downwards to the left; and when done very quickly,
the line is hooked a little at the end by the effort at return
to the next. Hence, you will always find the pencil, chalk,
or pen sketch of a *very* great master full of these kind of
lines; and even if he draws carefully, you will find him using
simple straight lines from left to right, when an inferior
master would have used curved ones. Fig. 11 is a fair facsimile of part of a sketch of Raphael's, which exhibits these
characters very distinctly. Even the careful drawings of

Leonardo da Vinci are shaded most commonly with straight lines; and you may always assume it as a point increasing the probability of a drawing being by a great master if you find rounded surfaces, such as those of cheeks or lips, shaded with straight lines.

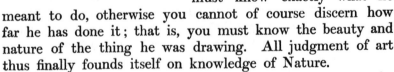

94. But you will also now understand how easy it must be for dishonest dealers to forge or imitate scrawled sketches like Fig. 11, and pass them for the work of great masters; and how the power of determining the genuineness of a drawing depends entirely on your knowing the facts of the objects drawn, and perceiving whether the hasty handling is *all* conducive to the expression of those truths. In a great man's work, at its fastest, no line is thrown away, and it is not by the rapidity, but the *economy* of the execution that you know him to be great. Now to judge of this economy, you must know exactly what he

Fig. 11

meant to do, otherwise you cannot of course discern how far he has done it; that is, you must know the beauty and nature of the thing he was drawing. All judgment of art thus finally founds itself on knowledge of Nature.

95. But farther observe, that this scrawled, or economic, or impetuous execution is never affectedly impetuous. If a great man is not in a hurry, he never pretends to be; if he has no eagerness in his heart, he puts none into his hand; if he thinks his effect would be better got with *two* lines, he never, to show his dexterity, tries to do it with one.

Be assured, therefore (and this is a matter of great importance), that you will never produce a great drawing by imitating the execution of a great master. Acquire his knowledge
and share his feelings, and the easy execution will fall from
your hand as it did from his: but if you merely scrawl
because he scrawled, or blot because he blotted, you will
not only never advance in power, but every able draughtsman, and every judge whose opinion is worth having, will
know you for a cheat, and despise you accordingly.

96. Again, observe respecting the use of outline:

All merely outlined drawings are bad, for the simple
reason, that an artist of any power can always do more,
and tell more, by quitting his outlines occasionally, and
scratching in a few lines for shade, than he can by restricting himself to outline only. Hence the fact of his
so restricting himself, whatever may be the occasion, shows
him to be a bad draughtsman, and not to know how to
apply his power economically. This hard law, however,
bears only on drawings meant to remain in the state in
which you see them; not on those which were meant to
be proceeded with, or for some mechanical use. It is
sometimes necessary to draw pure outlines, as an incipient
arrangement of a composition, to be filled up afterwards
with colour, or to be pricked through and used as patterns
or tracings; but if, with no such ultimate object, making
the drawing wholly for its own sake, and meaning it to
remain in the state he leaves it, an artist restricts himself
to outline, he is a bad draughtsman, and his work is bad.
There is no exception to this law. A good artist habitu-
ally sees masses, not edges, and can in every case make
his drawing more expressive (with any given quantity of
work) by rapid shade than by contours; so that all good
work whatever is more or less touched with shade, and
more or less interrupted as outline.

97. Hence, the published works of Retzsch,[1] and all the

---

[1] [For whom, see Vol. IV. pp. 259, 371; Vol. XIII. p. 275; and *Art of England*, § 101.]

English imitations of them, and all outline engravings from pictures, are bad work, and only serve to corrupt the public taste. And of such outlines, the worst are those which are darkened in some part of their course by way of expressing the dark side, as Flaxman's from Dante,[1] and such others; because an outline can only be true so long as it accurately represents the form of the given object with *one* of its edges. Thus, the outline *a* and the outline *b*, Fig. 12, are both *true* outlines of a ball; because, how-ever thick the line may be, whether we take the interior or exterior edge of it, that edge of it always draws a true circle. But *c* is a false out-line of a ball, because either the inner or outer edge of the black line must be an untrue circle, else the line could not be thicker in one place than another. Hence all "force," as it is called, is gained by falsification of the contours; so that no artist whose eye is true and fine could endure to look at it. It does indeed often happen that a painter, sketching rapidly, and trying again and again for some line which he cannot quite strike, blackens or loads the first line by setting others beside and across it; and then a careless observer supposes it has been thickened on purpose: or, sometimes also, at a place where shade is afterwards to enclose the form, the painter will strike a broad dash of this shade beside his outline at once, looking as if he meant to thicken the out-line; whereas this broad line is only the first instalment of the future shadow, and the outline is really drawn with its inner edge.* And thus, far from good draughtsmen darkening the lines which turn away from the light, the *tendency* with them is rather to darken them towards the light, for it is there in general that shade will ultimately enclose them. The best example of this treatment that I know is Raphael's sketch, in the Louvre, of the head of the

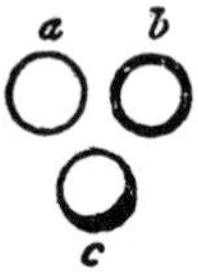

a *b*

c

Fig. 12

---

* See Note 2 in Appendix I. [p. 215].

[1] [For other criticisms of Flaxman's outlines in illustration of Dante, see *Modern Painters,* vol. iv. (Vol. VI. pp. 371–373).]

angel pursuing Heliodorus,[1] the one that shows part of the
left eye; where the dark strong lines which terminate the
nose and forehead towards the light are opposed to tender
and light ones behind the ear, and in other places towards the
shade. You will see in Fig. 11 the same principle variously
exemplified; the principal dark lines, in the head and drapery
of the arms, being on the side turned to the light.

98. All these refinements and ultimate principles, however, do not affect your drawing for the present. You must
try to make your outlines as *equal* as possible; and employ
pure outline only for the two following purposes: either (1.)
to steady your hand, as in Exercise ii., for if you cannot
draw the line itself, you will never be able to terminate
your shadow in the precise shape required, when the line is
absent; or (2.) to give you shorthand memoranda of forms,
when you are pressed for time. Thus the forms of distant
trees in groups are defined, for the most part, by the light
edge of the rounded mass of the nearer one being shown
against the darker part of the rounded mass of a more distant one; and to draw this properly, nearly as much work
is required to round each tree as to round the stone in
Fig. 5. Of course you cannot often get time to do this; but
if you mark the terminal line of each tree as is done by
Dürer in Fig. 13,[2] you will get a most useful memorandum
of their arrangement, and a very interesting drawing. Only
observe in doing this, you must not, because the procedure
is a quick one, hurry that procedure itself. You will find,
on copying that bit of Dürer, that every one of his lines is
firm, deliberate, and accurately descriptive as far as it goes.

[1] [Ruskin had noted this point in studying the drawings in 1856. The entry in his
diary (Paris, September 22) is this :—
    "I find in the Louvre drawings that no great artist *ever* can draw a straight
    line, it is always a little curved—so [a sketch]; if architectural, so [another
    sketch]; and that all the great men incline to draw the dark outline towards
    the light, and light towards dark; though there are many exceptions to this,
    it is clearly the tendency; and *vice versâ* of the inferior men. The clearest
    example is the head of the angel—Raphael's sketch—driving out Heliodorus;
    the one which shows the left eye, and is on the whole the finest drawing.
    The lip and forehead towards the light outlined with black; the ears and
    shadow behind the ear, in the shade quite pale."]
[2] [Part of the distance in Dürer's plate of "The Cannon"; for a further notice
of it, see *Modern Painters*, vol. v. pt. ix. ch. iv. § 7.]

It means a bush of such a size and such a shape, definitely observed and set down; it contains a true "signalement"[1] of every nut-tree, and apple-tree, and higher bit of hedge, all round that village.   If you have not time to draw thus carefully, do not draw at all—you are merely wasting your work and spoiling your taste.   When you have had four or five years' practice you may be able to make useful memoranda at a rapid rate, but not yet; except sometimes of light and shade, in a way of which I will tell you presently.   And

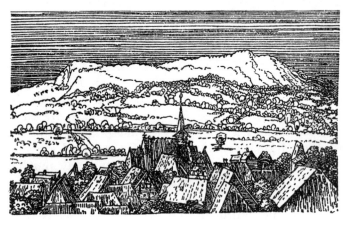

Fig. 13

this use of outline, note farther, is wholly confined to objects which have edges or limits.   You can outline a tree or a stone, when it rises against another tree or stone; but you cannot outline folds in drapery, or waves in water; if these are to be expressed at all, it must be by some sort of shade, and therefore the rule that no good drawing can consist throughout of pure outline remains absolute.   You see, in that woodcut of Dürer's, his reason for even limiting himself so much to outline as he has, in those distant woods and plains, is that he may leave them in bright light, to be thrown out still more by the dark sky and the dark village

[1] [The technical term, in French law and science, for a schedule of particulars serving to identify an individual or a *genus*.]

spire: and the scene becomes real and sunny only by the addition of these shades.

99. Understanding, then, thus much of the use of out-line, we will go back to our question about tree-drawing left unanswered at page 74.[1]

We were, you remember, in pursuit of mystery among the leaves. Now, it is quite easy to obtain mystery and disorder, to any extent; but the diffi-culty is to keep organi-zation in the midst of mystery. And you will never succeed in doing this

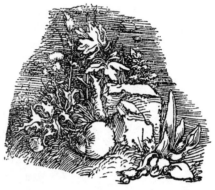

Fig. 14

unless you lean always to the definite side, and allow your-self rarely to become quite vague, at least through all your

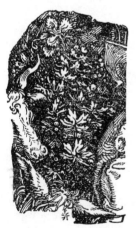

Fig. 15

early practice. So, after your single groups of leaves, your first step must be to conditions like Figs. 14 and 15, which are careful facsimiles of two portions of a beautiful woodcut of Dürer's, the " Flight into Egypt." Copy these carefully,—never mind how little at a time, but thoroughly; then trace the Dürer, and apply it to your drawing, and do not be content till the one fits the other, else your eye is not true enough to carry you safely through meshes of real leaves. And in the course of doing this, you will find that not a line nor dot of Dürer's can be displaced without harm; that all add to the effect, and either express something, or illumine something, or relieve something. If, afterwards,

1 [See also below, p. 111.]

you copy any of the pieces of modern tree-drawing, of which so many rich examples are given constantly in our cheap illustrated periodicals (any of the Christmas numbers of last year's *Illustrated News* or *Times*[1] are full of them), you will see that, though good and forcible general effect is produced, the lines are thrown in by thousands without

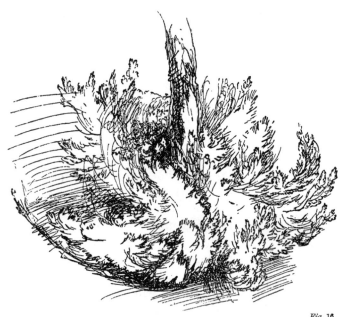

Fig. 16

special intention, and might just as well go one way as another, so only that there be enough of them to produce all together a well-shaped effect of intricacy : and you will find that a little careless scratching about with your pen will bring you very near the same result without an effort ; but that no scratching of pen, nor any fortunate chance, nor anything but downright skill and thought, will imitate so much as one leaf of Dürer's. Yet there is considerable

[1] [The *Illustrated Times Weekly Newspaper*, 1855–1872.]

intricacy and glittering confusion in the interstices of those vine leaves of his, as well as of the grass.

100. When you have got familiarised to his firm manner, you may draw from Nature as much as you like in the same way; and when you are tired of the intense care required for this, you may fall into a little more easy massing of the leaves, as in Fig. 10 (p. 81). This is facsimiled from an engraving after Titian, but an engraving not quite first-rate in manner, the leaves being a little too formal; still, it is a good enough model for your times of rest; and when you cannot carry the thing even so far as this, you may sketch the forms of the masses, as in Fig. 16,* taking care always to have thorough command over your hand; that is, not to let the mass take a free shape because your hand ran glibly over the paper, but because in Nature it has actually a free and noble shape, and you have faithfully followed the same.

101. And now that we have come to questions of noble shape, as well as true shape, and that we are going to draw from Nature at our pleasure, other considerations enter into the business, which are by no means confined to first practice, but extend to all practice; these (as this letter is long enough, I should think, to satisfy even the most exacting of correspondents) I will arrange in a second letter; praying you only to excuse the tiresomeness of this first one—tiresomeness inseparable from directions touching the beginning of any art,—and to believe me, even though I am trying to set you to dull and hard work,

Very faithfully yours,

J. Ruskin.

* This sketch is not of a tree standing on its head, though it looks like it. You will find it explained presently.[1]

---

[1] [See below, § 104, p. 91.]

LETTER II

SKETCHING FROM NATURE

102. My dear Reader, — The work we have already gone through together has, I hope, enabled you to draw with fair success either rounded and simple masses, like stones, or complicated arrangements of form, like those of leaves; provided only these masses or complexities will stay quiet for you to copy, and do not extend into quantity so great as to baffle your patience. But if we are now to go out to the fields, and to draw anything like a complete landscape, neither of these conditions will any more be observed for us. The clouds will not wait while we copy their heaps or clefts; the shadows will escape from us as we try to shape them, each, in its stealthy minute march, still leaving light where its tremulous edge had rested the moment before, and involving in eclipse objects that had seemed safe from its influence; and instead of the small clusters of leaves which we could reckon point by point, embarrassing enough even though numerable, we have now leaves as little to be counted as the sands of the sea, and restless, perhaps, as its foam.

103. In all that we have to do now, therefore, direct imitation becomes more or less impossible. It is always to be aimed at so far as it *is* possible; and when you have time and opportunity, some portions of a landscape may, as you gain greater skill, be rendered with an approximation almost to mirrored portraiture. Still, whatever skill you may reach, there will always be need of judgment to choose, and of speed to seize, certain things that are principal or fugitive; and you must give more and more effort daily

to the observance of characteristic points, and the attainment of concise methods.

104. I have directed your attention early to foliage for two reasons. First, that it is always accessible as a study; and secondly, that its modes of growth present simple examples of the importance of leading or governing lines. It is by seizing these leading lines, when we cannot seize all, that likeness and expression are given to a portrait, and grace and a kind of vital truth to the rendering of every natural form. I call it vital truth, because these chief lines are always expressive of the past history and present action of the thing. They show in a mountain, first, how it was built or heaped up; and secondly, how it is now being worn away, and from what quarter the wildest storms strike it. In a tree, they show what kind of fortune it has had to endure from its childhood: how troublesome trees have come in its way, and pushed it aside, and tried to strangle or starve it; where and when kind trees have sheltered it, and grown up lovingly together with it, bending as it bent; what winds torment it most; what boughs of it behave best, and bear most fruit; and so on. In a wave or cloud, these leading lines show the run of the tide and of the wind, and the sort of change which the water or vapour is at any moment enduring in its form, as it meets shore, or counter-wave, or melting sunshine. Now remember, nothing distinguishes great men from inferior men more than their always, whether in life or in art, *knowing the way things are going*. Your dunce thinks they are standing still, and draws them all fixed; your wise man sees the change or changing in them, and draws them so,—the animal in its motion, the tree in its growth, the cloud in its course, the mountain in its wearing away. Try always, whenever you look at a form, to see the lines in it which have had power over its past fate and will have power over its futurity. Those are its *awful* lines; see that you seize on those, whatever else you miss. Thus, the leafage in Fig. 16 (p. 88) grew round the root of a stone pine, on the brow

of a crag at Sestri near Genoa, and all the sprays of it are
thrust away in their first budding by the great rude root,
and spring out in every direction round it, as water splashes
when a heavy stone is thrown into it. Then, when they
have got clear of the root, they begin to bend up again ;
some of them, being little stone pines themselves, have a
great notion of growing upright, if they can ; and this
struggle of theirs to recover their straight road towards
the sky, after being obliged to grow sideways in their
early years, is the effort that will mainly influence their
future destiny, and determine if they are to be crabbed,
forky pines, striking from that rock of Sestri, whose clefts
nourish them, with bared red lightning of angry arms towards the sea ; or if they are to be goodly and solemn
pines, with trunks like pillars of temples, and the purple
burning of their branches sheathed in deep globes of cloudy
green. Those, then, are their fateful lines ; see that you
give that spring and resilience, whatever you leave un-
given : depend upon it, their chief beauty is in these.

105. So in trees in general, and bushes, large or small,
you will notice that, though the boughs spring irregularly
and at various angles, there is a tendency in all to stoop
less and less as they near the top of the tree. This structure, typified in the simplest possible terms at *c*, Fig. 17, is
common to all trees that I know of, and it gives them a
certain plumy character, and aspect of unity in the hearts
of their branches, which are essential to their beauty. The
stem does not merely send off a wild branch here and there
to take its own way, but all the branches share in one
great fountain-like impulse; each has a curve and a path to
take, which fills a definite place, and each terminates all its
minor branches at its outer extremity, so as to form a great
outer curve, whose character and proportion are peculiar for each species. That is to say, the general type or
idea of a tree is not as *a*, Fig. 17, but as *b*, in which, observe, the boughs all carry their minor divisions right out
to the bounding curve; not but that smaller branches, by

thousands, terminate in the heart of the tree, but the idea and main purpose in every branch are to carry all its child branches well out to the air and light, and let each of them, however small, take its part in filling the united flow of the bounding curve, so that the type of each separate bough is again not *a*, but *b*, Fig. 18 ; approximating, that is to say, so far to the structure of a plant of broccoli as to throw the great mass of spray and leafage out to a rounded sur-

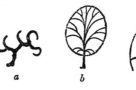

Fig. 17

face.   Therefore beware of getting into a careless habit of drawing boughs with successive sweeps of the pen or brush, one hanging to the other, as in Fig. 19.   If you look at the tree-boughs in any painting of Wilson's you will see this structure, and nearly every other that is to be avoided, in their intensest types.[1]   You will also notice that Wilson never conceives a tree as a round mass, but flat, as if it had been pressed and dried.   Most people in drawing pines seem to fancy, in the same way, that the boughs come out only on two sides of the trunk, instead of all round it:

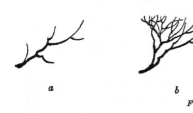

Fig. 18

always, therefore, take more pains in trying to draw the boughs of trees that grow *towards* you than those that go off to the sides ; anybody can draw the latter, but the fore-shortened ones are not so easy.   It will help you in drawing them to observe that in most trees the ramification of each branch, though not of the tree itself, is more or less flattened, and approximates, in its position, to the look of a hand held out to receive something, or shelter something.   If you take a looking-glass, and hold your hand

[1] [For the "two-pronged barbarisms of Wilson," see Vol. XIII. p. 145, and compare *Modern Painters,* vol. iii. ch. ix. (Vol. V. pp. 162 *seq.*).]

before it slightly hollowed, with the palm upwards, and
the fingers open, as if you were going to support the base
of some great bowl, larger than you could easily hold; and
sketch your hand as you see it in the glass with the points
of the fingers towards you; it will materially help you in
understanding the way trees generally hold out their hands:
and if then you will turn yours with its palm downwards,
as if you were going to try to hide something, but with
the fingers expanded, you will get a good type of the action
of the lower boughs in cedars and
such other spreading trees.

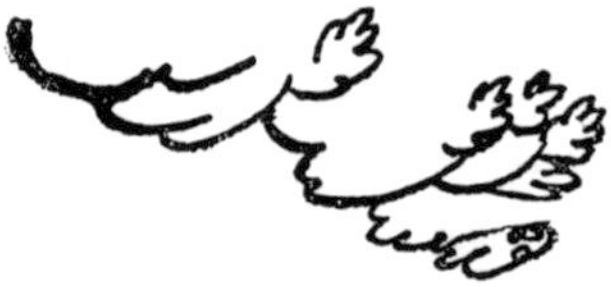

106. Fig. 20 will give you a
good idea of the simplest way in
which these and other such facts
can be rapidly expressed; if you
copy it carefully, you will be sur-
prised to find how the touches all group together, in expressing the plumy toss of the tree branches, and the springing
of the bushes out of the bank, and the undulation of the
ground: note the careful drawing of the footsteps made by
the climbers of the little mound on the left.* It is facsimiléd
from an etching of Turner's, and is as good an example as
you can have of the use of pure and firm lines; it will also
show you how the particular action in foliage, or anything
else to which you wish to direct attention, may be intensi-
fied by the adjuncts. The tall and upright trees are made
to look more tall and upright still, because their line is
continued below by the figure of the farmer with his stick;
and the rounded bushes on the bank are made to look more
rounded because their line is continued in one broad sweep
by the black dog and the boy climbing the wall. These
figures are placed entirely with this object, as we shall see

Fig. 19

* It is meant, I believe, for "Salt Hill." [1]

---

[1] [Fig. 20 is a portion of "Sheep-washing: Windsor from Slough," an unpublished
plate for *Liber Studiorum*: see below, § 109 *n.*, p. 99. The drawing is No. 880 in
the National Gallery. "Salt Hill" was the scene of the Eton "Montem."]

more fully hereafter when we come to talk about composition; but, if you please, we will not talk about that yet

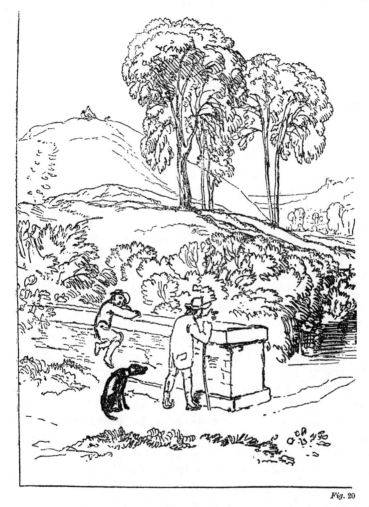

Fig. 20

awhile. What I have been telling you about the beautiful lines and action of foliage has nothing to do with composition, but only with fact, and the brief and expressive representation of fact. But there will be no harm in your

looking forward, if you like to do so, to the account, in
Letter III., of the "Law of Radiation,"[1] and reading what
is said there about tree growth: indeed it would in some
respects have been better to have said it here than there,
only it would have broken up the account of the principles
of composition somewhat awkwardly.

107. Now, although the lines indicative of action are
not always quite so manifest in other things as in trees, a
little attention will soon enable you to see that there are
such lines in everything. In an old house roof, a bad observer and bad draughtsman will only see and draw the
spotty irregularity of tiles or slates all over; but a good
draughtsman will see all the bends of the under timbers,
where they are weakest and the weight is telling on them
most, and the tracks of the run of the water in time of
rain, where it runs off fastest, and where it lies long and
feeds the moss; and he will be careful, however few slates
he draws, to mark the way they bend together towards
those hollows (which have the future fate of the roof in
them), and crowd gradually together at the top of the gable,
partly diminishing in perspective, partly, perhaps, diminished
on purpose (they are so in most English old houses) by the
slate-layer. So in ground, there is always the direction of
the run of the water to be noticed, which rounds the earth
and cuts it into hollows; and, generally, in any bank or
height worth drawing, a trace of bedded or other internal
structure besides. Figure 20 will give you some idea of
the way in which such facts may be expressed by a few
lines. Do you not feel the depression in the ground all
down the hill where the footsteps are, and how the people
always turn to the left at the top, losing breath a little, and
then how the water runs down in that other hollow towards
the valley, behind the roots of the trees?

108. Now, I want you in your first sketches from Nature
to aim exclusively at understanding and representing these

1 [Below, p. 180.]

vital facts of form ; using the pen—not now the steel, but
the quill—firmly and steadily, never scrawling with it, but
saying to yourself before you lay on a single touch,—" *that*
leaf is the main one, *that* bough is the guiding one, and
this touch, *so* long, *so* broad, means that part of it,"—point
or side or knot, as the case may be. Resolve always, as
you look at the thing, what you will take, and what miss
of it, and never let your hand run away with you, or get
into any habit or method of touch. If you want a continuous line, your hand should pass calmly from one end
of it to the other without a tremor ; if you want a shaking
and broken line, your hand should shake, or break off, as
easily as a musician's finger shakes or stops on a note : only
remember this, that there is no general way of doing *any*
thing ; no recipe can be given you for so much as the drawing of a cluster of grass. The grass may be ragged and
stiff, or tender and flowing ; sunburnt and sheep-bitten, or
rank and languid ; fresh or dry ; lustrous or dull : look at
it, and try to draw it as it is, and don't think how somebody "told you to *do* grass." So a stone may be round or
angular, polished or rough, cracked all over like an ill-glazed
teacup, or as united and broad as the breast of Hercules.
It may be as flaky as a wafer, as powdery as a field puff-
ball ; it may be knotted like a ship's hawser, or kneaded
like hammered iron, or knit like a Damascus sabre, or fused
like a glass bottle, or crystallised like hoar-frost, or veined
like a forest leaf : look at it, and don't try to remember
how anybody told you to " do a stone."

109. As soon as you find that your hand obeys you
thoroughly, and that you can render any form with a firmness and truth approaching that of Turner's or Dürer's
work,* you must add a simple but equally careful light and
shade to your pen drawing, so as to make each study as
complete as possible ; for which you must prepare yourself

---

* I do not mean that you can approach Turner or Dürer in their
strength, that is to say, in their imagination or power of design. But you
may approach them, by perseverance, in truth of manner.

thus. Get, if you have the means, a good impression of one plate of Turner's Liber Studiorum; if possible, one of the subjects named in the note below.* If you cannot obtain, or even borrow for a little while, any of these engravings, you must use a photograph instead (how, I will

* The following are the most desirable plates :—

Grande Chartreuse.	Pembury Mill.
Æsacus and Hesperie.	Little Devil's Bridge.
Cephalus and Procris.	River Wye (*not* Wye and Severn).
Source of Arveron.	Holy Island.
Ben Arthur.	Clyde.
Watermill.	Lauffenburg.
Hindhead Hill.	Blair Athol.
Hedging and Ditching.	Alps from Grenoble.
Dunblane Abbey.	Raglan. (Subject with quiet
Morpeth.	brook, trees, and castle on the
Calais Pier.	right.)

If you cannot get one of these, any of the others will be serviceable except only the twelve following, which are quite useless :—

1. Scene in Italy, with goats on a walled road, and trees above.
2. Interior of church.
3. Scene with bridge, and trees above; figures on left, one playing a pipe.
4. Scene with figure playing on tambourine.
5. Scene on Thames with high trees, and a square tower of a church seen through them.
6. Fifth Plague of Egypt.
7. Tenth Plague of Egypt.
8. Rivaulx Abbey.
9. Wye and Severn.
10. Scene with castle in centre, cows under trees on the left.
11. Martello Towers.
12. Calm.

It is very unlikely that you should meet with one of the original etchings; if you should, it will be a drawing-master in itself alone, for it is not only equivalent to a pen-and-ink drawing by Turner, but to a very careful one; only observe, the Source of Arveron, Raglan, and Dunblane were not etched by Turner; and the etchings of those three are not good for separate study, though it is deeply interesting to see how Turner, apparently provoked at the failure of the beginnings in the Arveron and Raglan, took the plates up himself, and either conquered or brought into use the bad etching by his marvellous engraving. The Dunblane was, however, well etched by Mr. Lupton, and beautifully engraved by him. The finest Turner etching is of an aqueduct with a stork standing in a mountain stream, not in the published series; and next to it, are the tell you presently); but, if you can get the Turner, it will be best. You will see that it is composed of a firm etching in line, with mezzotint shadow laid over it. You must first copy the etched part of it accurately; to which end put the print against the window, and trace slowly with the greatest care every black line; retrace this on smooth drawing-paper; and, finally, go over the whole with your pen, looking at the original plate always, so that if you err at all, it may be on the right side, not making a line which is too curved or too straight already in the tracing, more curved or more straight, as you go over it. And in doing this, never work after you are tired, nor to "get the thing done," for if it is badly done, it will be of no use to you. The true zeal and patience of a quarter of an hour are better than the sulky and inattentive labour of a whole day. If you have not made the touches right at the first going over with the pen, retouch them delicately, with little ink in your pen, thickening or reinforcing them as they need: you cannot give too much care to the facsimile. Then keep this etched outline by you in order to study at your ease the way in which Turner uses his line as preparatory for the subsequent shadow; * it is only in getting the two separate that you will be able to reason on this. Next, copy once more, though for the fourth time, any part of this etching which

unpublished etchings of the Via Mala[1] and Crowhurst. Turner seems to have been so fond of these plates that he kept retouching and finishing them, and never made up his mind to let them go. The Via Mala is certainly, in the state in which Turner left it, the finest of the whole series: its etching is, as I said, the best after that of the aqueduct. Figure 20, above, is part of another fine unpublished etching, "Windsor, from Salt Hill." Of the published etchings, the finest are the Ben Arthur, Æsacus, Cephalus, and Stone Pines, with the Girl washing at a Cistern; the three latter are the more generally instructive. Hindhead Hill, Isis, Jason, and Morpeth, are also very desirable.

* You will find more notice of this point in the account of Harding's tree-drawing, a little farther on [p. 113].

[1] [This is the plate more correctly called "Swiss Bridge, Mont St. Gothard": see *Modern Painters*, vol. iv. (Vol. VI. p. 40), and Fig. 1 (which is a representation of a portion of it). See also Vol. XIII. p. 96. The "Stone Pines, etc." is usually called "Nymph at a Well."]

you like, and put on the light and shade with the brush, and any brown colour that matches that of the plate; * working it with the point of the brush as delicately as if you were drawing with pencil, and dotting and cross-hatching as lightly as you can touch the paper, till you get the gradations of Turner's engraving.

110. In this exercise, as in the former one, a quarter of an inch worked to close resemblance of the copy is worth more than the whole subject carelessly done. Not that in drawing afterwards from Nature you are to be obliged to finish every gradation in this way, but that, once having fully accomplished the drawing *something* rightly, you will thenceforward feel and aim at a higher perfection than you could otherwise have conceived, and the brush will obey you, and bring out quickly and clearly the loveliest results, with a submissiveness which it would have wholly refused if you had not put it to severest work. Nothing is more strange in art than the way that chance and materials seem to favour you, when once you have thoroughly conquered them. Make yourself quite independent of chance, get your result in spite of it, and from that day forward all things will somehow fall as you would have them. Show the camel's hair, and the colour in it, that no bending nor blotting is of any use to escape your will; that the touch and the shade *shall* finally be right, if it costs you a year's toil; and from that hour of corrective conviction, said camel's hair will bend itself to all your wishes, and no blot will dare to transgress its appointed border. If you cannot obtain a print from the Liber Studiorum, get a photograph † of some general landscape subject, with high hills and a village or picturesque town, in the middle distance, and some calm water of varied character (a stream with stones in it, if possible), and copy any part

---

* The impressions vary so much in colour that no brown can be specified.

† You had better get such a photograph, even though you have a Liber print as well.

of it you like, in this same brown colour, working, as I have just directed you to do from the Liber, a great deal with the point of the brush. You are under a twofold disadvantage here, however; first, there are portions in every photograph too delicately done for you at present to be at all able to copy; and, secondly, there are portions always more obscure or dark than there would be in the real scene, and involved in a mystery which you will not be able, as yet, to decipher. Both these characters will be advantageous to you for future study, after you have gained experience, but they are a little against you in early attempts at tinting; still you must fight through the difficulty, and get the power of producing delicate gradations with brown or grey, like those of the photograph.

111. Now observe; the perfection of work would be tinted shadow, like photography, without any obscurity or exaggerated darkness; and as long as your effect depends in anywise on visible lines, your art is not perfect, though it may be first-rate of its kind. But to get complete results in tints merely, requires both long time and consummate skill; and you will find that a few well-put pen lines, with a tint dashed over or under them, get more expression of facts than you could reach in any other way, by the same expenditure of time. The use of the Liber Studiorum print to you is chiefly as an example of the simplest shorthand of this kind, a shorthand which is yet capable of dealing with the most subtle natural effects; for the firm etching gets at the expression of complicated details, as leaves, masonry, textures of ground, etc., while the overlaid tint enables you to express the most tender distances of sky, and forms of playing light, mist, or cloud. Most of the best drawings by the old masters are executed on this principle, the touches of the pen being useful also to give a look of transparency to shadows, which could not otherwise be attained but by great finish of tinting; and if you have access to any ordinarily good

public gallery, or can make friends of any printsellers who have folios either of old drawings, or facsimiles of them, you will not be at a loss to find some example of this unity of pen with tinting. Multitudes of photographs also are now taken from the best drawings by the old masters, and I hope that our Mechanics' Institutes, and other societies organised with a view to public instruction, will not fail to possess themselves of examples of these, and to make them accessible to students of drawing in the vicinity; a single print from Turner's Liber, to show the unison of tint with pen etching, and the " St. Catherine," photographed by Thurston Thompson [1] from Raphael's drawing in the Louvre, to show the unity of the soft tinting of the stump with chalk, would be all that is necessary, and would, I believe, be in many cases more serviceable than a larger collection, and certainly than a whole gallery of second-rate prints. Two such examples are peculiarly desirable, because all other modes of drawing, with pen separately, or chalk separately, or colour separately, may be seen by the poorest student in any cheap illustrated book, or in shop windows. But this unity of tinting with line he cannot generally see but by some special enquiry, and in some out of the way places he could not find a single example of it. Supposing that this should be so in your own case, and that you cannot meet with any example of this kind, try to make the matter out alone, thus:

112. Take a small and simple photograph; allow yourself half an hour to express its subjects with the pen only, using some permanent liquid colour instead of ink, outlining its buildings or trees firmly, and laying in the deeper shadows, as you have been accustomed to do in your bolder pen drawings; then, when this etching is dry, take your sepia or grey, and tint it over, getting now the finer gradations of the photograph; and finally taking out the higher lights

[1] [For Thompson, see Vol. XII. p. 7 *n.*; and for the head of St. Catherine, Vol. XII. p. 488.]

with penknife or blotting paper. You will soon find what can be done in this way; and by a series of experiments you may ascertain for yourself how far the pen may be made serviceable to reinforce shadows, mark characters of texture, outline unintelligible masses, and so on. The more time you have, the more delicate you may make the pen drawing, blending it with the tint; the less you have, the more distinct you must keep the two. Practise in this way from one photograph, allowing yourself sometimes only a quarter of an hour for the whole thing, sometimes an hour, sometimes two or three hours; in each case drawing the whole subject in full depth of light and shade, but with such degree of finish in the parts as is possible in the given time. And this exercise, observe, you will do well to repeat frequently, whether you can get prints and drawings as well as photographs, or not.

113. And now at last, when you can copy a piece of Liber Studiorum, or its photographic substitute, faithfully, you have the complete means in your power of working from Nature on all subjects that interest you, which you should do in four different ways.

First. When you have full time, and your subject is one that will stay quiet for you, make perfect light and shade studies, or as nearly perfect as you can, with grey or brown colour of any kind, reinforced and defined with the pen.

114. Secondly. When your time is short, or the subject is so rich in detail that you feel you cannot complete it intelligibly in light and shade, make a hasty study of the effect, and give the rest of the time to a Düreresque expression of the details. If the subject seems to you interesting, and there are points about it which you cannot understand, try to get five spare minutes to go close up to it, and make a nearer memorandum; not that you are ever to bring the details of this nearer sketch into the farther one, but that you may thus perfect your experience of the aspect of things, and know that such and such a look of a

tower or cottage at five hundred yards off means *that* sort
of tower or cottage near; while, also, this nearer sketch
will be useful to prevent any future misinterpretation of
your own work. If you have time, however far your light
and shade study in the distance may have been carried, it
is always well, for these reasons, to make also your Düreresque and your near memoranda; for if your light and
shade drawing be good, much of the interesting detail must
be lost in it, or disguised.

115. Your hasty study of effect may be made most
easily and quickly with a soft pencil, dashed over when
done with one tolerably deep tone of grey, which will fix
the pencil. While this fixing colour is wet, take out the
higher lights with the dry brush; and, when it is quite dry,
scratch out the highest lights with the penknife. Five
minutes, carefully applied, will do much by these means.
Of course the paper is to be white. I do not like studies on
grey paper so well; for you can get more gradation by the
taking off your wet tint, and laying it on cunningly a little
darker here and there, than you can with body-colour white,
unless you are consummately skilful. There is no objec-
tion to your making your Düreresque memoranda on grey
or yellow paper, and touching or relieving them with white;
only, do not depend much on your white touches, nor make
the sketch for their sake.

116. Thirdly. When you have neither time for careful
study nor for Düreresque detail, sketch the outline with
pencil, then dash in the shadows with the brush boldly,
trying to do as much as you possibly can at once, and to
get a habit of expedition and decision; laying more colour
again and again into the tints as they dry, using every expedient which your practice has suggested to you of carrying out your chiaroscuro in the manageable and moist
material, taking the colour off here with the dry brush,
scratching out lights in it there with the wooden handle of
the brush, rubbing it in with your fingers, drying it off
with your sponge, etc. Then, when the colour is in, take

your pen and mark the outline characters vigorously, in the manner of the Liber Studiorum. This kind of study is very convenient for carrying away pieces of effect which depend not so much on refinement as on complexity, strange shapes of involved shadows, sudden effects of sky, etc.; and it is most useful as a safeguard against any too servile or slow habits which the minute copying may induce in you; for although the endeavour to obtain velocity merely for velocity's sake, and dash for display's sake, is as baneful as it is despicable; there *are* a velocity and a dash which not only are compatible with perfect drawing, but obtain certain results which cannot be had otherwise. And it is perfectly safe for you to study occasionally for speed and decision, while your continual course of practice is such as to ensure your retaining an accurate judgment and a tender touch. Speed, under such circumstances, is rather fatiguing than tempting; and you will find yourself always beguiled rather into elaboration than negligence.

117. Fourthly. You will find it of great use, whatever kind of landscape scenery you are passing through, to get into the habit of making memoranda of the shapes of shadows. You will find that many objects of no essential interest in themselves, and neither deserving a finished study, nor a Düreresque one, may yet become of singular value in consequence of the fantastic shapes of their shadows; for it happens often, in distant effect, that the shadow is by much a more important element than the substance. Thus, in the Alpine bridge, Fig. 21, seen within a few yards of it, as in the figure, the arrangement of timbers to which the shadows are owing is perceptible; but at half a mile's distance, in bright sunlight, the timbers would not be seen; and a good painter's expression of the bridge would be merely the large spot, and the crossed bars, of pure grey; wholly without indication of their cause, as in Fig. 22 *a*; and if we saw it at still greater distances, it would appear as in Fig. 22 *b* and *c*, diminishing at last to a strange, unintelligible, spider-like spot of grey on the light hillside.

A perfectly great painter, throughout his distances, continually reduces his objects to these shadow abstracts; and the singular, and to many persons unaccountable, effect of the confused touches in Turner's distances, is owing chiefly to this thorough accuracy and intense meaning of the shadow abstracts.

118. Studies of this kind are easily made, when you are in haste, with an F. or HB. pencil: it requires some hardness of the point to ensure your drawing delicately enough when the forms of the shadows are very subtle; they are

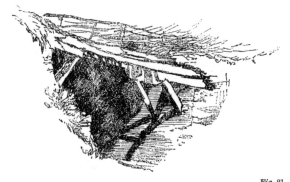

Fig. 21

sure to be so somewhere, and are generally so everywhere. The pencil is indeed a very precious instrument after you are master of the pen and brush, for the pencil, cunningly used, is both, and will draw a line with the precision of the one and the gradation of the other; nevertheless, it is so unsatisfactory to see the sharp touches, on which the best of the detail depends, getting gradually deadened by time, or to find the places where force was wanted look shiny, and like a fire-grate, that I should recommend rather the steady use of the pen, or brush, and colour, whenever time admits of it; keeping only a small memorandum-book in the breast-pocket, with its well-cut, sheathed pencil, ready for notes on passing opportunities: but never being without this.

119. Thus much, then, respecting the manner in which you are at first to draw from Nature. But it may perhaps be serviceable to you, if I also note one or two points respecting your choice of subjects for study, and the best special methods of treating some of them; for one of by no means the least difficulties which you have at first to encounter is a peculiar instinct, common, as far as I have noticed, to all beginners, to fix on exactly the most unmanageable feature in the given scene. There are many things in every landscape which can be drawn, if at all, only by the most accomplished artists; and I have noticed that it is nearly always these which a beginner will dash at; or, if not these, it will be something which, though pleasing to him in itself, is unfit for a picture, and in which, when he has drawn it, he will have little pleasure. As some slight protection against this evil genius of beginners, the following general warnings may be useful:

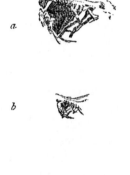

Fig. 22

120. (1.) Do not draw things that you love, on account of their associations; or at least do not draw them because you love them; but merely when you cannot get anything else to draw. If you try to draw places that you love, you are sure to be always entangled amongst neat brick walls, iron railings, gravel walks, greenhouses, and quickset hedges; besides that you will be continually led into some endeavour to make your drawing pretty, or complete, which will be fatal to your progress. You need never hope to get on, if you are the least anxious that the drawing you are actually at work upon should look nice when it is done. All you have to care about is to make it *right*, and to learn as much in doing it as possible. So then, though when you are sitting in your friend's parlour, or in your own, and have nothing else to do, you may draw anything that is

there, for practice; even the fire-irons or the pattern on the carpet: be sure that it *is* for practice, and not because it is a beloved carpet, or a friendly poker and tongs, nor because you wish to please your friend by drawing her room.

121. Also, never make presents of your drawings. Of course I am addressing you as a beginner — a time may come when your work will be precious to everybody; but be resolute not to give it away till you know that it is worth something (as soon as it is worth anything you will know that it is so). If any one asks you for a present of a drawing, send them a couple of cakes of colour and a piece of Bristol board: those materials are, for the present, of more value in that form than if you had spread the one over the other.

The main reason for this rule is, however, that its observance will much protect you from the great danger of trying to make your drawings pretty.

122. (2.) Never, by choice, draw anything polished; especially if complicated in form. Avoid all brass rods and curtain ornaments, chandeliers, plate, glass, and fine steel. A shining knob of a piece of furniture does not matter if it comes in your way; but do not fret yourself if it will not look right, and choose only things that do not shine.

(3.) Avoid all very neat things. They are exceedingly difficult to draw, and very ugly when drawn. Choose rough, worn, and clumsy-looking things as much as possible; for instance, you cannot have a more difficult or profitless study than a newly painted Thames wherry, nor a better study than an old empty coal-barge, lying ashore at low tide: in general, everything that you think very ugly will be good for you to draw.

(4.) Avoid, as much as possible, studies in which one thing is seen through another. You will constantly find a thin tree standing before your chosen cottage, or between you and the turn of the river; its near branches all entangled with the distance. It is intensely difficult to represent this; and though, when the tree *is* there, you must not imaginarily cut it down, but do it as well as you can, yet always look for subjects that fall into definite masses, not into network; that is, rather for a cottage with a dark tree beside it, than for one with a thin tree in front of it, rather for a mass of wood, soft, blue, and rounded, than for a ragged copse, or confusion of intricate stems.

(5.) Avoid, as far as possible, country divided by hedges. Perhaps nothing in the whole compass of landscape is so utterly unpicturesque and unmanageable as the ordinary English patchwork of field and hedge,[1] with trees dotted over it in independent spots, gnawed straight at the cattle line.

Still, do not be discouraged if you find you have chosen ill, and that the subject overmasters you. It is much better that it should, than that you should think you had entirely mastered *it*. But at first, and even for some time, you must be prepared for very discomfortable failure; which, nevertheless, will not be without some wholesome result.

123. As, however, I have told you what most definitely to avoid, I may, perhaps, help you a little by saying what to seek. In general, all banks are beautiful things, and will reward work better than large landscapes. If you live in a lowland country, you must look for places where the ground is broken to the river's edges, with decayed posts, or roots of trees; or, if by great good luck there should be such things within your reach, for remnants of stone quays or steps, mossy mill-dams, etc. Nearly every other mile of road in chalk country will present beautiful bits of broken bank at its sides; better in form and colour than high chalk cliffs. In woods, one or two trunks, with the flowery ground below, are at once the richest and easiest kind of study: a not very thick trunk, say nine inches or a foot in diameter, with ivy running up it sparingly, is an easy, and always a rewarding subject.

---

[1] [Compare *The Poetry of Architecture*, §§ 14, 15 (Vol. I. p. 14), where Ruskin contrasts the "snug" appearance of English landscape "minutely chequered into fields," with the open spaciousness of France—a contrast noted also in *Modern Painters*, vol. iv. ch. i.]

124. Large nests of buildings in the middle distance are always beautiful, when drawn carefully, provided they are not modern rows of pattern cottages, or villas with Ionic and Doric porticoes. Any old English village, or cluster of farm-houses, drawn with all its ins and outs, and haystacks, and palings, is sure to be lovely; much more a French one. French landscape is generally as much superior to English as Swiss landscape is to French; in some respects, the French is incomparable. Such scenes as that avenue on the Seine, which I have recommended you to buy the engraving of,[1] admit no rivalship in their expression of graceful rusticity and cheerful peace, and in the beauty of component lines.

In drawing villages, take great pains with the gardens; a rustic garden is in every way beautiful. If you have time, draw all the rows of cabbages, and hollyhocks, and broken fences, and wandering eglantines, and bossy roses; you cannot have better practice, nor be kept by anything in purer thoughts.

Make intimate friends with all the brooks in your neighbourhood, and study them ripple by ripple.

Village churches in England are not often good subjects; there is a peculiar meanness about most of them and awkwardness of line. Old manor-houses are often pretty. Ruins are usually, with us, too prim, and cathedrals too orderly. I do not think there is a single cathedral in England from which it is possible to obtain *one* subject for an impressive drawing. There is always some discordant civility, or jarring vergerism about them.[2]

125. If you live in a mountain or hill country, your only danger is redundance of subject. Be resolved, in the first place, to draw a piece of rounded rock, with its variegated lichens, quite rightly, getting its complete roundings, and all the patterns of the lichen in true local colour. Till

---

[1] [See above, § 86 *n*. The engraving is "The View on the Seine, between Mantes and Vernon"; the drawing is No. 138 in the National Gallery. For Ruskin's fondness for French landscape, see Vol. III. p. 238.]

[2] [Compare the *Seven Lamps*, Vol. VIII. p. 188, and *Stones of Venice*, vol. ii. (Vol. X. p. 78).]

you can do this, it is of no use your thinking of sketching among hills; but when once you have done this, the forms of distant hills will be comparatively easy.

126. When you have practised for a little time from such of these subjects as may be accessible to you, you will certainly find difficulties arising which will make you wish more than ever for a master's help: these difficulties will vary according to the character of your own mind (one question occurring to one person, and one to another), so that it is impossible to anticipate them all; and it would make this too large a book if I answered all that I *can* anticipate; you must be content to work on, in good hope that Nature will, in her own time, interpret to you much for herself; that farther experience on your own part will make some difficulties disappear; and that others will be removed by the occasional observation of such artists' work as may come in your way. Nevertheless, I will not close this letter without a few general remarks, such as may be useful to you after you are somewhat advanced in power; and these remarks may, I think, be conveniently arranged under three heads, having reference to the drawing of vegetation, water, and skies.

127. And, first, of vegetation. You may think, perhaps, we have said enough about trees already; yet if you have done as you were bid, and tried to draw them frequently enough, and carefully enough, you will be ready by this time to hear a little more of them. You will also recollect that we left our question, respecting the mode of expressing intricacy of leafage, partly unsettled in the first letter.[1] I left it so because I wanted you to learn the real structure of leaves, by drawing them for yourself, before I troubled you with the most subtle considerations as to method in drawing them. And by this time, I imagine, you must have found out two principal things, universal facts, about leaves; namely, that they always, in the main tendencies

---

[1] [See above, pp. 74, 87.]

of their lines, indicate a beautiful divergence of growth, according to the law of radiation, already[1] referred to;* and the second, that this divergence is never formal, but carried out with endless variety of individual line. I must now press both these facts on your attention a little farther.

128. You may, perhaps, have been surprised that I have not yet spoken of the works of J. D. Harding, especially if you happen to have met with the passages referring to them in *Modern Painters*, in which they are highly praised.[2] They are deservedly praised, for they are the only works by a modern draughtsman which express in any wise the energy of trees, and the laws of growth, of which we have been speaking. There are no lithographic sketches which, for truth of general character, obtained with little cost of time, at all rival Harding's. Calame,[3] Robert, and the other lithographic landscape sketchers are altogether inferior in power, though sometimes a little deeper in meaning. But you must not take even Harding for a model, though you may use his works for occasional reference; and if you can afford to buy his Lessons on Trees,† it will be serviceable to you in various ways, and will at present help me to explain the point under consideration. And it is well that I should illustrate this point by reference to Harding's works, because their great influence on young students renders it desirable that their real character should be thoroughly understood.

129. You will find, first, in the title-page of the Lessons

* See the closing letter in this volume.

† If you are not acquainted with Harding's works, (an unlikely supposition, considering their popularity,) and cannot meet with the one in question, the diagrams given here will enable you to understand all that is needful for our purposes.[4]

---

[1] [See above, p. 96.]

[2] [See, for instance, Vol. III. pp. 201, 600.]

[3] [For Calame, see Vol. III. p. 449 *n.*, and Vol. VI. p. 101. The artist next mentioned is Louis Léopold Robert (1794–1835), painter and engraver.]

[4] [The *Lessons on Trees* was published by Bogue in 1850. Plate 1 contains "Lessons" "to afford practice in drawing the forms of stems and branches, and also to show how the character of the bark may be indicated by the simplest means."]

on Trees, a pretty woodcut, in which the tree stems are drawn with great truth, and in a very interesting arrangement of lines. Plate 1 is not quite worthy of Mr. Harding, tending too much to make his pupil, at starting, think everything depends on black dots; still, the main lines are good, and very characteristic of tree growth.   Then, in Plate 2, we come to the point at issue. The first examples in that plate are given to the pupil that he may practise from them till his hand gets into the habit of arranging lines freely in a similar manner; and they are stated by Mr. Harding to be universal in application; " all outlines expressive of foliage," he says, " are but modifications of them." They consist of groups of lines, more or less resembling our Fig. 23 below; and the characters especially insisted upon are, that they " tend at their inner ends to a common centre"; that " their ends terminate in [are enclosed by]¹ ovoid curves"; and that " the outer ends are most emphatic."

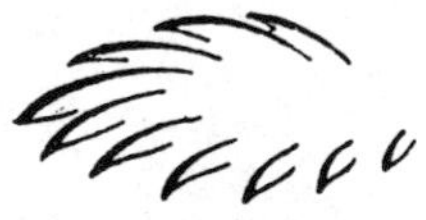

Fig. 23

130. Now, as thus expressive of the great laws of radiation and enclosure, the main principle of this method of execution confirms, in a very interesting way, our conclusions respecting foliage composition. The reason of the last rule, that the outer end of the line is to be most emphatic, does not indeed at first appear; for the line at one end of a natural leaf is not more emphatic than the line at the other; but ultimately, in Harding's method, this darker part of the touch stands more or less for the shade at the outer extremity of the leaf mass; and, as Harding uses these touches, they express as much of tree character as any mere habit of touch *can* express. But, unfortunately, there is another law of tree growth, quite as fixed as the law of radiation, which this and all other conventional modes of execution wholly lose sight of. This second law is, that

¹ [This is an addition made by Ruskin to Harding's text (in the notes on Plate 2 in his book).]

the radiating tendency shall be carried out only as a ruling spirit in reconcilement with perpetual individual caprice on the part of the separate leaves. So that the moment a touch is monotonous, it must be also false, the liberty of the leaf individually being just as essential a truth, as its unity of growth with its companions in the radiating group.

131. It does not matter how small or apparently symmetrical the cluster may be, nor how large or vague. You

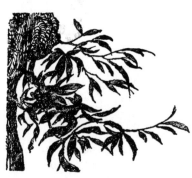

Fig. 24

can hardly have a more formal one than *b* in Fig. 9, p. 72, nor a less formal one than this shoot of Spanish chestnut, shedding its leaves, Fig. 24;[1] but in either of them, even the general reader, unpractised in any of the previously recommended exercises, must see that there are wandering lines mixed with the radiating ones, and radiating lines with the wild ones: and if he takes the pen, and tries to copy either of these examples, he will find that neither play of hand to left nor to right, neither a free touch nor a firm touch, nor any learnable or describable touch whatsoever, will enable him to produce, currently, a resemblance of it; but that he must either draw it slowly

---

[1] [This shoot of Spanish chestnut was drawn by Ruskin at Carrara; the original drawing, here reproduced, was given at vol. i. p. 121 of W. G. Collingwood's *Life and Work of John Ruskin* (1893), under the incorrect title "Olive at Carrara." The drawing (now in the collection of Mr. T. F. Taylor) was shown at the Ruskin Exhibition, Manchester (1904), No. 114, and is here reproduced. Ruskin had intended to contrast his sketch with one of Harding's and to add further illustrations, as appears from the passage (cancelled when the intended illustrations were withdrawn) in the proof-sheets, which reads thus:—

"... its unity of growth with its companions in the radiating group. Let us take an instance. Plate 19, in this work of Harding's [*Lessons on Trees*], is a sketch of a Spanish chestnut, and on the right-hand side, a dark bough of it comes against the sky. The formal habit of the hand, brought into the best possible application to the character of chestnut foliage, results in conditions which, though they of course look better in the soft colour of the chalk than in the black of the woodcut, present in reality no truer profiles against the sky than those in Fig. . Now, here is a spray of real

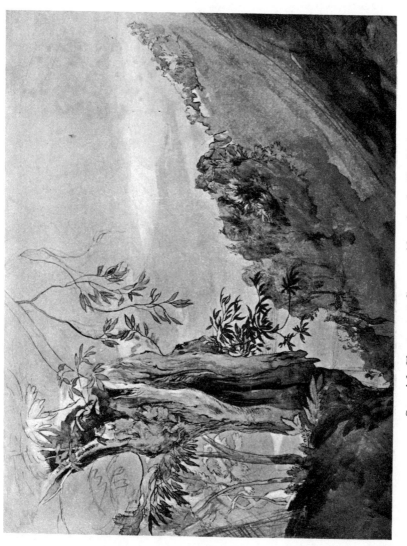

Spanish Chestnut at Carrara (drawing by Ruskin)

or give it up. And (which makes the matter worse still) though gathering the bough, and putting it close to you, or seeing a piece of near foliage against the sky, you may draw the entire outline of the leaves, yet if the spray has light upon it, and is ever so little a way off, you will miss, as we have seen, a point of a leaf here, and an edge there; some of the surfaces will be confused by glitter, and some spotted with shade; and if you look carefully through this confusion for the edges or dark stems which you really *can* see and put only those down, the result will be neither like Fig. 9 nor Fig. 24, but such an interrupted and puzzling piece of work as Fig. 25.*

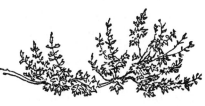

Fig. 25

132. Now, it is in the perfect acknowledgment and expression of these *three* laws that all good drawing of landscape consists. There is, first, the organic unity; the law, whether of radiation, or parallelism, or concurrent action, which rules the masses of herbs and trees, of rocks, and clouds, and waves; secondly,

* I draw this figure (a young shoot of oak) in outline only, it being impossible to express the refinements of shade in distant foliage in a woodcut.

Spanish chestnut, thrown in similarly black profile against the white paper. (It may perhaps add a little to the interest the reader takes in it, if I tell him that it is not a bit of Greenwich Park chestnut, but of one growing, I doubt not to this day, on a projecting crag of sculptors' marble at Massa Carrara.) I have not taken particular pains in drawing it; but I think the reader will feel in a moment that, though there are indeed radiating lines governing the groups, there are other lines, by no means radiating, but wilful and wild, mingling with them continually. And this is just as true of every other tree as it is of chestnut, nor of every tree only but of every herb that grows. It does not matter how formal their arrangement of foliage may at first appear, no regular method of execution will express it. Take a spray of cross-wort madder, for instance, Fig.   . Legal enough it is, certainly, in the stated repetitions of its four crossed leaves, at regular distances on the stalk; yet you cannot express such a leaf as that, when seen a little way off, by any quick crossing touch of pen, as, for instance, *b*. The plant in no way resembles that; it is much more perfect and less regular; every one of its leaves is a little out of law—a little too short or too long, or turned too much down or too much up. And if he takes the pen . . ."]

the individual liberty of the members subjected to these laws of unity; and, lastly, the mystery under which the separate character of each is more or less concealed.

I say, first, there must be observance of the ruling organic law. This is the first distinction between good artists and bad artists. Your common sketcher or bad painter puts his leaves on the trees as if they were moss tied to sticks; he cannot see the lines of action or growth; he scatters the shapeless clouds over his sky, not perceiving the sweeps of associated curves which the real clouds are following as they fly; and he breaks his mountain side into rugged fragments, wholly unconscious of the lines of force with which the real rocks have risen, or of the lines of couch in which they repose. On the contrary it is the main delight of the great draughtsman, to trace these laws of government; and his tendency to error is always in the exaggeration of their authority rather than in its denial.

133. Secondly, I say, we have to show the individual character and liberty of the separate leaves, clouds, or rocks. And herein the great masters separate themselves finally from the inferior ones; for if the men of inferior genius ever express law at all, it is by the sacrifice of individuality. Thus, Salvator Rosa has great perception of the sweep of foliage and rolling of clouds, but never draws a single leaflet or mist wreath accurately.[1] Similarly, Gainsborough, in his landscape, has great feeling for masses of form and harmony of colour; but in the detail gives nothing but meaningless touches; not even so much as the species of tree, much less the variety of its leafage, being ever discernible. Now, although both these expressions of government and individuality are essential to masterly work, the individuality is the *more* essential, and the more difficult of attainment; and, therefore, that attainment separates the great masters *finally* from the inferior ones. It is the more

---

[1] [On these points in Salvator, see *Modern Painters*, vol. i. (Vol. III. p. 375); and in Gainsborough, *ibid*. (Vol. III. p. 190).]

essential, because, in these matters of beautiful arrangement in visible things, the same rules hold that hold in moral things.[1] It is a lamentable and unnatural thing to see a number of men subject to no government, actuated by no ruling principle, and associated by no common affection: but it would be a more lamentable thing still, were it possible, to see a number of men so oppressed into assimilation as to have no more any individual hope or character, no differences in aim, no dissimilarities of passion, no irregularities of judgment; a society in which no man could help another, since none would be feebler than himself; no man admire another, since none would be stronger than himself; no man be grateful to another, since by none he could be relieved; no man reverence another, since by none he could be instructed; a society in which every soul would be as the syllable of a stammerer instead of the word of a speaker, in which every man would walk as in a frightful dream, seeing spectres of himself, in everlasting multiplication, gliding helplessly around him in a speechless darkness. Therefore it is that perpetual difference, play, and change in groups of form are more essential to them even than their being subdued by some great gathering law: the law is needful to them for their perfection and their power, but the difference is needful to them for their life.

134. And here it may be noted in passing, that, if you enjoy the pursuit of analogies and types, and have any ingenuity of judgment in discerning them, you may always accurately ascertain what are the noble characters in a piece of painting by merely considering what are the noble characters of man in his association with his fellows. What grace of manner and refinement of habit are in society, grace of line and refinement of form are in the association of visible objects. What advantage or harm there may be in sharpness, ruggedness, or quaintness in the dealings or conversations of men; precisely that relative degree of

---

[1] [On Ruskin's use of such analogies, see above, Introduction, p. xviii.]

advantage or harm there is in them as elements of pictorial composition. What power is in liberty or relaxation to strengthen or relieve human souls; that power precisely in the same relative degree, play and laxity of line have to strengthen or refresh the expression of a picture. And what goodness or greatness we can conceive to arise in companies of men, from chastity of thought, regularity of life, simplicity of custom, and balance of authority; precisely that kind of goodness and greatness may be given to a picture by the purity of its colour, the severity of its forms, and the symmetry of its masses.

135. You need not be in the least afraid of pushing these analogies too far. They cannot be pushed too far; they are so precise and complete, that the farther you pursue them, the clearer, the more certain, the more useful you will find them. They will not fail you in one particular, or in any direction of enquiry. There is no moral vice, no moral virtue, which has not its *precise* prototype in the art of painting; so that you may at your will illustrate the moral habit by the art, or the art by the moral habit. Affection and discord, fretfulness and quietness, feebleness and firmness, luxury and purity, pride and modesty, and all other such habits, and every conceivable modification and mingling of them, may be illustrated, with mathematical exactness, by conditions of line and colour; and not merely these definable vices and virtues, but also every conceivable shade of human character and passion, from the righteous or unrighteous majesty of the king to the innocent or faultful simplicity of the shepherd boy.

136. The pursuit of this subject belongs properly, however, to the investigation of the higher branches of composition, matters which it would be quite useless to treat of in this book; and I only allude to them here, in order that you may understand how the utmost noblenesses of art are concerned in this minute work, to which I have set you in your beginning of it. For it is only by the closest

attention, and the most noble execution, that it is possible to express these varieties of individual character, on which all excellence of portraiture depends, whether of masses of mankind, or of groups of leaves.

137. Now you will be able to understand, among other matters, wherein consists the excellence, and wherein the shortcoming, of the tree-drawing of Harding. It is excellent in so far as it fondly observes, with more truth than any other work of the kind, the great laws of growth and action in trees: it fails,—and observe, not in a minor, but in the principal point,—because it cannot rightly render any one individual detail or incident of foliage. And in this it fails, not from mere carelessness or incompletion, but of necessity; the true drawing of detail being for evermore impossible to a hand which has contracted a *habit* of execution. The noble draughtsman draws a leaf, and stops, and says calmly,—That leaf is of such and such a character; I will give him a friend who will entirely suit him : then he considers what his friend ought to be, and having determined, he draws his friend. This process may be as quick as lightning when the master is great—one of the sons of the giants; or it may be slow and timid : but the process is always gone through; no touch or form is ever added to another by a good painter without a mental determination and affirmation. But when the hand has got into a habit, leaf No. 1 necessitates leaf No. 2; you cannot stop, your hand is as a horse with the bit in its teeth; or rather is, for the time, a machine, throwing out leaves to order and pattern, all alike. You must stop that hand of yours, however painfully; make it understand that it is not to have its own way any more, that it shall never more slip from one touch to another without orders; otherwise it is not you who are the master, but your fingers. You may therefore study Harding's drawing, and take pleasure in it;*

* His lithographic sketches, those for instance in the *Park and the Forest,* and his various lessons on foliage, possess greater merit than the

and you may properly admire the dexterity which applies the habit of the hand so well, and produces results on the whole so satisfactory : but you must never copy it ; otherwise your progress will be at once arrested. The utmost you can ever hope to do would be a sketch in Harding's manner, but of far inferior dexterity; for he has given his life's toil to gain his dexterity, and you, I suppose, have other things to work at besides drawing. You would also incapacitate yourself from ever understanding what truly great work was, or what Nature was; but, by the earnest and complete study of facts, you will gradually come to understand the one and love the other more and more, whether you can draw well yourself or not.

138. I have yet to say a few words respecting the third law above stated, that of mystery; the law, namely, that nothing is ever seen perfectly, but only by fragments, and under various conditions of obscurity.* This last fact renders the visible objects of Nature complete as a type of the human nature. We have, observe, first, Subordination; secondly, Individuality; lastly, and this not the least essential character, Incomprehensibility; a perpetual lesson, in every serrated point and shining vein which escapes or deceives our sight among the forest leaves, how little we may hope to discern clearly, or judge justly, the rents and veins of the human heart; how much of all that is round us, in men's actions or spirits, which we at first think we understand, a closer and more loving watchfulness would show to be full of mystery, never to be either fathomed or withdrawn.

more ambitious engravings in his *Principles and Practice of Art.*[1] There are many useful remarks, however, dispersed through this latter work.

* On this law you do well, if you can get access to it, to look at the fourth chapter of the fourth volume of *Modern Painters.*

1 [*The Park and the Forest*, by J. D. Harding : London, Thomas Maclean, 1841— a large folio volume containing twenty-six lithographs. For his *Lessons on Trees*, see above, p. 112. *The Principles and Practice of Art* was published by Chapman and Hall in 1845, "with illustrations drawn and engraved by the author."]

139. The expression of this final character in landscape has never been completely reached by any except Turner; nor can you hope to reach it at all until you have given much time to the practice of art. Only try always when you are sketching any object with a view to completion in light and shade, to draw only those parts of it which you really see definitely; preparing for the after development of the forms by chiaroscuro. It is this preparation by isolated touches for a future arrangement of superimposed light and shade which renders the etchings of the Liber Studiorum so inestimable as examples, and so peculiar. The character exists more or less in them exactly in proportion to the pains that Turner has taken. Thus the Æsacus and Hesperie[1] was wrought out with the greatest possible care; and the principal branch on the near tree is etched as in Fig. 26. The work looks at first like a scholar's instead of a master's; but when the light

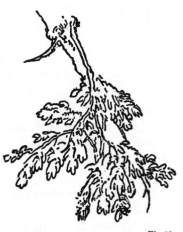

Fig. 26

and shade are added, every touch falls into its place, and a perfect expression of grace and complexity results. Nay, even before the light and shade are added, you ought to be able to see that these irregular and broken lines, especially where the expression is given of the way the stem loses itself in the leaves, are more true than the monotonous though graceful leaf-drawing which, before Turner's time, had been employed, even by the best masters, in their distant masses. Fig. 27 is sufficiently characteristic of the manner of the old woodcuts after Titian; in which, you see, the leaves are too much of one shape, like bunches

---

[1] [Reproduced and referred to in *Lectures on Landscape*, § 73; see also Vol. III. pp. 586, 595 *n.*; Vol. XIII. p. 462.]

of fruit; and the boughs too completely seen, besides being somewhat soft and leathery in aspect, owing to the want of angles in their outline. By great men like Titian,

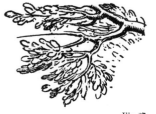

Fig. 27

this somewhat conventional structure was only given in haste to distant masses; and their exquisite delineation of the foreground, kept their conventionalism from degeneracy: but in the drawings of the Carracci [1] and other derivative masters, the conventionalism prevails everywhere, and sinks gradually into scrawled work, like Fig. 28, about the worst which it is possible to get into the habit of using, though an ignorant person might perhaps suppose it more "free," and therefore better than Fig. 26. Note also, that in noble outline drawing, it does not follow that a bough is wrongly drawn, because it looks contracted unnaturally somewhere, as in Fig. 26, just above the foliage. Very often the muscular action which is to be expressed by the line runs into the middle of the branch, and the actual outline of the branch at that place may be dimly seen, or not at all; and it is then only by the future shade that its actual shape, or the cause of its disappearance, will be indicated.

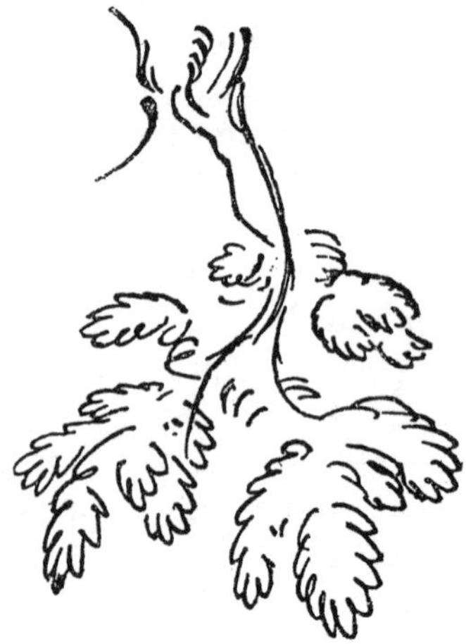

140. One point more remains to be noted about trees, and I have done. In the minds of our

Fig. 28

ordinary water-colour artists a distant tree seems only to be conceived as a flat green blot, grouping pleasantly with other

---

[1] [For another reference to the worthlessness of their landscape, see *Modern Painters,* vol. iii. (Vol. V. p. 400).]

masses, and giving cool colour to the landscape, but differing no wise, in texture, from the blots of other shapes which these painters use to express stones, or water, or figures. But as soon as you have drawn trees carefully a little while, you will be impressed, and impressed more strongly the better you draw them, with the idea of their *softness* of surface. A distant tree is not a flat and even piece of colour, but a more or less globular mass of a downy or bloomy texture, partly passing into a misty vagueness. I find, practically, this lovely softness of far-away trees the most difficult of all characters to reach, because it cannot be got by mere scratching or roughening the surface, but is always associated with such delicate expressions of form and growth as are only imitable by very careful drawing. The pen-knife passed lightly *over* this careful drawing will do a good deal; but you must accustom yourself, from the beginning, to aim much at this softness in the lines of the drawing itself, by crossing them delicately, and more or less effacing and confusing the edges. You must invent, according to the character of tree, various modes of execution adapted to express its texture; but always keep this character of softness in your mind, and in your scope of aim; for in most landscapes it is the intention of Nature that the tenderness and transparent infinitude of her foliage should be felt, even at the far distance, in the most distinct opposition to the solid masses and flat surfaces of rocks or buildings.

141. II. We were, in the second place, to consider a little the modes of representing water, of which important feature of landscape I have hardly said anything yet.

Water is expressed, in common drawings, by conventional lines, whose horizontality is supposed to convey the idea of its surface. In paintings, white dashes or bars of light are used for the same purpose.

But these and all other such expedients are vain and absurd. A piece of calm water always contains a picture in itself, an exquisite reflection of the objects above it. If you give the time necessary to draw these reflections, disturbing them here and there as you see the breeze or current disturb them, you will get the effect of the water; but if you have not patience to draw the reflections, no expedient will give you a true effect. The picture in the pool needs nearly as much delicate drawing as the picture above the pool; except only that if there be the least motion on the water, the horizontal lines of the images will be diffused and broken, while the vertical ones will remain decisive, and the oblique ones decisive in proportion to their steepness.

142. A few close studies will soon teach you this: the only thing you need to be told is to watch carefully the lines of disturbance on the surface, as when a bird swims across it, or a fish rises, or the current plays round a stone, reed, or other obstacle. Take the greatest pains to get the *curves* of these lines true; the whole value of your careful drawing of the reflections may be lost by your admitting a single false curve of ripple from a wild duck's breast. And (as in other subjects) if you are dissatisfied with your result, always try for more unity and delicacy: if your reflections are only soft and gradated enough, they are nearly sure to give you a pleasant effect.* When you are taking pains, work the softer reflections, where they are drawn out by motion in the water, with touches as nearly horizontal as may be; but when you are in a hurry, indicate the place and play of the images with vertical lines. The actual construction of a calm elongated reflection is with horizontal lines: but it is often impossible to draw the descending shades delicately enough with a horizontal touch; and it is best always when you are in a hurry, and sometimes when you are not, to use the vertical touch. When the ripples are large, the reflections become shaken, and must be drawn with bold undulatory descending lines.

143. I need not, I should think, tell you that it is of

---

* See Note 3 in Appendix I. [p. 216].

the greatest possible importance to draw the curves of the shore rightly. Their perspective is, if not more subtle, at least more stringent than that of any other lines in Nature. It will not be detected by the general observer, if you miss the curve of a branch, or the sweep of a cloud, or the perspective of a building;* but every intelligent spectator will feel the difference between a rightly-drawn bend of shore or shingle, and a false one. *Absolutely* right, in difficult river perspectives seen from heights, I believe no one but Turner ever has been yet; and observe, there is NO rule for them. To develop the curve mathematically would require a knowledge of the exact quantity of water in the river, the shape of its bed, and the hardness of the rock or shore; and even with these data, the problem would be one which no mathematician could solve but approximatively. The instinct of the eye can do it; nothing else.

144. If, after a little study from Nature, you get puzzled by the great differences between the aspect of the reflected image and that of the object casting it; and if you wish to know the law of reflection, it is simply this: Suppose all the objects above the water *actually* reversed (not in appearance, but in fact) beneath the water, and precisely the same in form and in relative position, only all topsy-turvy. Then, whatever you could see, from the place in which you stand, of the solid objects so reversed under the water, you will see in the reflection, always in the true perspective of the solid objects so reversed.

If you cannot quite understand this in looking at water, take a mirror, lay it horizontally on the table, put some books and papers upon it, and draw them and their reflections; moving them about, and watching how their reflections alter, and chiefly how their reflected colours and shades differ from their own colours and shades, by being

---

* The student may hardly at first believe that the perspective of buildings is of little consequence; but he will find it so ultimately. See the remarks on this point in the Preface [p. 19].

brought into other oppositions. This difference in chiaroscuro is a more important character in water-painting than mere difference in form.

145. When you are drawing shallow or muddy water, you will see shadows on the bottom, or on the surface, continually modifying the reflections; and in a clear mountain stream, the most wonderful complications of effect resulting from the shadows and reflections of the stones in it, mingling with the aspect of the stones themselves seen through the water. Do not be frightened at the complexity; but, on the other hand, do not hope to render it hastily. Look at it well, making out everything that you see, and distinguishing each component part of the effect. There will be, first, the stones seen through the water, distorted always by refraction, so that, if the general structure of the stone shows straight parallel lines above the water, you may be sure they will be bent where they enter it; then the reflection of the part of the stone above the water crosses and interferes with the part that is seen through it, so that you can hardly tell which is which; and wherever the reflection is darkest, you will see through the water best,* and *vice versâ*. Then the real shadow of the stone crosses both these images, and where that shadow falls, it makes the water more reflective, and where the sunshine falls, you will see more of the surface of the water, and of any dust or motes that may be floating on it: but whether you are to see, at the same spot, most of the bottom of the water, or of the reflection of the objects above, depends on the position of the eye. The more you look down into the water, the better you see objects through it; the more you look along it, the eye being low, the more you see the reflection of objects above it. Hence the colour of a given space of surface in a stream will entirely change while you stand still in the same spot, merely as you stoop or raise your head; and thus the colours with which water

---

* See Note 4 in Appendix I. [p. 216].

is painted are an indication of the position of the spectator, and connected inseparably with the perspective of the shores. The most beautiful of all results that I know in mountain streams is when the water is shallow, and the stones at the bottom are rich reddish-orange and black, and the water is seen at an angle which exactly divides the visible colours between those of the stones and that of the sky, and the sky is of clear, full blue. The resulting purple, obtained by the blending of the blue and the orange-red, broken by the play of innumerable gradations in the stones, is indescribably lovely.

146. All this seems complicated enough already; but if there be a strong colour in the clear water itself, as of green or blue in the Swiss lakes, all these phenomena are doubly involved; for the darker reflections now become of the colour of the water. The reflection of a black gondola, for instance, at Venice, is never black, but pure dark green. And, farther, the colour of the water itself is of three kinds: one, seen on the surface, is a kind of milky bloom; the next is seen where the waves let light through them, at their edges; and the third, shown as a change of colour on the objects seen through the water. Thus, the same wave that makes a white object look of a clear blue, when seen through it, will take a red or violet-coloured bloom on its surface, and will be made pure emerald green by transmitted sunshine through its edges. With all this, however, you are not much concerned at present, but I tell it you partly as a preparation for what we have afterwards to say about colour, and partly that you may approach lakes and streams with reverence,* and study them as carefully as other things, not hoping to express them by a few horizontal dashes of white, or a few tremulous blots.† Not but

* See Note 5 in Appendix I. [p. 216].

† It is a useful piece of study to dissolve some Prussian blue in water, so as to make the liquid definitely blue: fill a large white basin with the solution, and put anything you like to float on it, or lie in it; walnut shells, bits of wood, leaves of flowers, etc. Then study the effects of the reflections,

that much may be done by tremulous blots, when you know precisely what you mean by them, as you will see by many of the Turner sketches, which are now framed at the National Gallery; but you must have painted water many and many a day—yes, and all day long—before you can hope to do anything like those.

147. III. Lastly. You may perhaps wonder why, before passing to the clouds, I say nothing special about *ground.** But there is too much to be said about that to admit of my saying it here. You will find the principal laws of its structure examined at length in the fourth volume of *Modern Painters;*[1] and if you can get that volume, and copy carefully Plate 21, which I have etched after Turner with great pains, it will give you as much help as you need in the linear expression of ground-surface. Strive to get the retirement and succession of masses in irregular ground: much may be done in this way by careful watching of the perspective diminutions of its herbage, as well as by contour; and much also by shadows. If you draw the shadows of leaves and tree trunks on any undulating ground with entire carefulness, you will be surprised to find how much they explain of the form and distance of the earth on which they fall.

148. Passing then to skies, note that there is this great peculiarity about sky subject, as distinguished from earth subject;—that the clouds, not being much liable to man's interference, are always beautifully arranged. You cannot be

and of the stems of the flowers or submerged portions of the floating objects, as they appear through the blue liquid; noting especially how, as you lower your head and look along the surface, you see the reflections clearly; and how, as you raise your head, you lose the reflections, and see the submerged stems clearly.

* Respecting Architectural Drawing, see the notice of the works of Prout in the Appendix [p. 221].

---

[1] [See, in this edition, Vol. VI. Plate 21 in "The Pass of Faido."]

sure of this in any other features of landscape. The rock on which the effect of a mountain scene especially depends is always precisely that which the roadmaker blasts or the landlord quarries; and the spot of green which Nature left with a special purpose by her dark forest sides, and finished with her most delicate grasses, is always that which the farmer ploughs or builds upon. But the clouds, though we can hide them with smoke, and mix them with poison, cannot be quarried nor built over, and they are always therefore gloriously arranged; so gloriously, that unless you have notable powers of memory you need not hope to approach the effect of any sky that interests you. For both its grace and its glow depend upon the united influence of every cloud within its compass: they all move and burn together in a marvellous harmony; not a cloud of them is out of its appointed place, or fails of its part in the choir: and if you are not able to recollect (which in the case of a complicated sky it is impossible you should) precisely the form and position of all the clouds at a given moment, you cannot draw the sky at all; for the clouds will not fit if you draw one part of them three or four minutes before another.

149. You must try therefore to help what memory you have, by sketching at the utmost possible speed the whole range of the clouds; marking, by any shorthand or symbolic work you can hit upon, the peculiar character of each, as transparent, or fleecy, or linear, or undulatory; giving afterwards such completion to the parts as your recollection will enable you to do. This, however, only when the sky is interesting from its general aspect; at other times, do not try to draw all the sky, but a single cloud: sometimes a round cumulus will stay five or six minutes quite steady enough to let you mark out his principal masses; and one or two white or crimson lines which cross the sunrise will often stay without serious change for as long. And in order to be the readier in drawing them, practise occasionally drawing lumps of cotton, which will teach you better

than any other stable thing the kind of softness there is in clouds. For you will find when you have made a few genuine studies of sky, and then look at any ancient or modern painting, that ordinary artists have always fallen into one of two faults : either, in rounding the clouds, they make them as solid and hard-edged as a heap of stones tied up in a sack, or they represent them not as rounded at all, but as vague wreaths of mist or flat lights in the sky ; and think they have done enough in leaving a little white paper between dashes of blue, or in taking an irregular space out with the sponge. Now clouds are not as solid as flour-sacks ; but, on the other hand, they are neither spongy nor flat. They are definite and very beautiful forms of sculptured mist ; sculptured is a perfectly accurate word ; they are not more *drifted* into form than they are *carved* into form, the warm air around them cutting them into shape by absorbing the visible vapour beyond certain limits ; hence their angular and fantastic outlines, as different from a swollen, spherical, or globular formation, on the one hand, as from that of flat films or shapeless mists on the other. And the worst of all is, that while these forms are difficult enough to draw on any terms, especially considering that they never stay quiet, they must be drawn also at greater disadvantage of light and shade than any others, the force of light in clouds being wholly unattainable by art ; so that if we put shade enough to express their form as positively as it is expressed in reality, we must make them painfully too dark on the dark sides. Nevertheless, they are so beautiful, if you in the least succeed with them, that you will hardly, I think, lose courage.

150. Outline them often with the pen, as you can catch them here and there ; one of the chief uses of doing this will be, not so much the memorandum so obtained, as the lesson you will get respecting the softness of the cloud-outlines. You will always find yourself at a loss to see where the outline really is ; and when drawn it will always look hard and false, and will assuredly be either too round

or too square, however often you alter it, merely passing from the one fault to the other and back again, the real cloud striking an inexpressible mean between roundness and squareness in all its coils or battlements. I speak at present, of course, only of the cumulus cloud : the lighter wreaths and flakes of the upper sky cannot be outlined ;—they can only be sketched, like locks of hair, by many lines of the pen. Firmly developed bars of cloud on the horizon are in general easy enough, and may be drawn with decision. When you have thus accustomed yourself a little to the placing and action of clouds, try to work out their light and shade, just as carefully as you do that of other things, looking exclusively for examples of treatment to the vignettes in Rogers's *Italy* and *Poems*, and to the Liber Studiorum, unless you have access to some examples of Turner's own work. No other artist ever yet drew the sky : even Titian's clouds, and Tintoret's, are conventional. The clouds in the " Ben Arthur," " Source of Arveron," and " Calais Pier," are among the best of Turner's storm studies ; and of the upper clouds, the vignettes to Rogers's *Poems* furnish as many examples as you need.

151. And now, as our first lesson was taken from the sky,[1] so, for the present, let our last be. I do not advise you to be in any haste to master the contents of my next letter. If you have any real talent for drawing, you will take delight in the discoveries of natural loveliness, which the studies I have already proposed will lead you into, among the fields and hills ; and be assured that the more quietly and single-heartedly you take each step in the art, the quicker, on the whole, will your progress be. I would rather, indeed, have discussed the subjects of the following letter at greater length, and in a separate work addressed to more advanced students ; but as there are one or two things to be said on composition which may set the young artist's mind somewhat more at rest, or furnish him with

---

[1] [See above, § 14, pp. 34–35.]

defence from the urgency of ill-advisers, I will glance over the main heads of the matter here; trusting that my doing so may not beguile you, my dear reader, from your serious work, or lead you to think me, in occupying part of this book with talk not altogether relevant to it, less entirely or

Faithfully yours,

J. RUSKIN.

LETTER III

ON COLOUR AND COMPOSITION[1]

152. MY DEAR READER,—If you have been obedient, and have hitherto done all that I have told you, I trust it has not been without much subdued remonstrance, and some serious vexation. For I should be sorry if, when you were led by the course of your study to observe closely such things as are beautiful in colour,[2] you had not longed to paint them, and felt considerable difficulty in complying with your restriction to the use of black, or blue, or grey. You *ought* to love colour, and to think nothing quite beautiful or perfect without it; and if you really do love it, for its own sake, and are not merely desirous to colour because you think painting a finer thing than drawing, there is some chance you may colour well. Nevertheless, you need not hope ever to produce anything more than pleasant helps to memory, or useful and suggestive sketches in colour, unless you mean to be wholly an artist. You may, in the time which other vocations leave at your disposal, produce finished, beautiful, and masterly drawings in light and shade. But to colour well, requires your life. It cannot be done cheaper. The difficulty of doing right is increased—not twofold nor threefold, but a thousandfold, and more—by the addition of colour to your work. For the

---

[1] [§§ 152–154 here were reprinted as §§ 1–4 in ch. viii. of *The Laws of Fésole:* see below, p. 432. The notes and modifications there introduced are here given in footnotes.]

[2] [In *The Laws of Fésole* Ruskin here introduced the words "(feathers, and the like, not to say rocks and clouds)," and appended the following footnote:—

"The first four paragraphs of this chapter, this connecting parenthesis excepted, are reprinted from *The Elements of Drawing.* Read, however, carefully, the modifying notes."]

chances are more than a thousand to one against your being right both in form and colour with a given touch: it is difficult enough to be right in form, if you attend to that only; but when you have to attend, at the same moment, to a much more subtle thing than the form, the difficulty is strangely increased, — and multiplied almost to infinity by this great fact, that, while form is absolute, so that you can say at the moment you draw any line that it is either right or wrong, colour is wholly *relative*.[1] Every hue throughout your work is altered by every touch that you add in other places; so that what was warm[2] a minute ago, becomes cold when you have put a hotter colour in another place, and what was in harmony when you left it, becomes discordant as you set other colours beside it; so that every touch must be laid, not with a view to its effect at the time, but with a view to its effect in futurity, the result upon it of all that is afterwards to be done being previously considered. You may easily understand that, this being so, nothing but the devotion of life, and great genius besides, can make a colourist.

153. But though you cannot produce finished coloured drawings of any value, you may give yourself much pleasure,

---

[1] [In *The Laws of Fésole* Ruskin bracketed the word "wholly," and appended the following note :—
  "No, not 'wholly' by any means. This is one of the over-hasty statements which render it impossible for me to republish, without more correction than they are worth, the books I wrote before the year 1860. Colour is no less positive than line, considered as a representation of fact; and you either match a given colour, or do not, as you either draw a given ellipse or square, or do not. Nor, on the other hand, are lines, in their grouping, destitute of relative influence; they exalt or depress their individual powers by association; and the necessity for the correction of the above passage in this respect was pointed out to me by Miss Hill, many and many a year ago, when she was using the *Elements* in teaching design for glass. But the influence of lines on each other is restricted within narrow limits, while the sequences of colour are like those of sound, and susceptible of all the complexity and passion of the most accomplished music."
Miss Octavia Hill was at this time (1856 onwards) assisting Ruskin's work in various ways; see, for instance, *Modern Painters*, vol. v., Preface, § 6 n.]
  [2] [Here in *The Laws of Fésole* Ruskin appended the following note :—
  "I assumed in *The Elements of Drawing* the reader's acquaintance with this and other ordinary terms of art. But see § 30 of the last chapter :"
in *The Laws of Fésole* (below, p. 430).]

and be of great use to other people, by occasionally sketching with a view to colour only ; and preserving distinct statements of certain colour facts—as that the harvest moon at rising was of such and such a red, and surrounded by clouds of such and such a rosy grey; that the mountains at evening were in truth so deep in purple ; and the waves by the boat's side were indeed of that incredible green. This only, observe, if you have an eye for colour ; but you may presume that you have this, if you enjoy colour.

154. And, though of course you should always give as much form to your subject as your attention to its colour will admit of, remember that the whole value of what you are about depends, in a coloured sketch, on the colour merely. If the colour is wrong, everything is wrong : just as, if you are singing, and sing false notes, it does not matter how true the words are. If you sing at all, you must sing sweetly ; and if you colour at all, you must colour rightly. Give up all the form, rather than the slightest part of the colour : just as, if you felt yourself in danger of a false note, you would give up the word, and sing a meaningless sound, if you felt that so you could save the note. Never mind though your houses are all tumbling down,—though your clouds are mere blots, and your trees mere knobs, and your sun and moon like crooked sixpences,—so only that trees, clouds, houses, and sun or moon, are of the right colours. Of course,[1] the discipline you have gone through will enable you to hint something of form, even in the fastest sweep of the brush ; but do not let the thought of form hamper you in the least, when you begin to make coloured memoranda. If you want the form of the subject, draw it in black and white. If you want its colour, take its colour, and be sure you *have* it, and not a spurious, treacherous, half-measured

---

[1] [In *The Laws of Fésole* Ruskin made a new section here, and thus revised :—
   " 4. Of course, the collateral discipline to which you are submitting— (if you are)—will soon enable you . . ."]

piece of mutual concession, with the colours all wrong, and the forms still anything but right. It is best to get into the habit of considering the coloured work merely as supplementary to your other studies; making your careful drawings of the subject first, and then a coloured memorandum separately, as shapeless as you like, but faithful in hue, and entirely minding its own business. This principle, however, bears chiefly on large and distant subjects: in foregrounds and near studies, the colour cannot be had without a good deal of definition of form. For if you do not map[1] the mosses on the stones accurately, you will not have the right quantity of colour in each bit of moss pattern, and then none of the colours will look right; but it always simplifies the work much if you are clear as to your point of aim, and satisfied, when necessary, to fail of all but that.

155. Now, of course, if I were to enter into detail respecting colouring, which is the beginning and end of a painter's craft, I should need to make this a work in three volumes instead of three letters, and to illustrate it in the costliest way. I only hope, at present, to set you pleasantly and profitably to work, leaving you, within the tethering of certain leading-strings, to gather what advantages you can from the works of art of which every year brings a greater number within your reach;—and from the instruction which, every year, our rising artists will be more ready to give kindly, and better able to give wisely.

156. And, first, of materials. Use hard cake colours,[2] not moist colours: grind a sufficient quantity of each on your palette every morning, keeping a separate plate, large and deep, for colours to used in broad washes, and wash both plate and palette every evening, so as to be able always to get good and pure colour when you need it; and force yourself into cleanly and orderly habits about your colours. The two best colourists of modern times, Turner

[1] [In *The Laws of Fésole* Ruskin altered "map" to "shape."]
[2] [But see note on p. 42, above.]

and Rossetti,* afford us, I am sorry to say, no confirmation of this precept by their practice. Turner was, and Rossetti is, as slovenly in all their procedures as men can well be; but the result of this was, with Turner, that the colours have altered in all his pictures, and in many of his drawings; and the result of it with Rossetti is, that though his colours are safe, he has sometimes to throw aside work that was half done, and begin over again. William Hunt, of the Old Water-colour, is very neat in his practice; so, I believe, is Mulready; so is John Lewis; and so are the leading Pre-Raphaelites, Rossetti only excepted. And there can be no doubt about the goodness of the advice, if it were only for this reason, that the more particular you are about your colours the more you will get into a deliberate and methodical habit in using them, and all true speed in colouring comes of this deliberation.

157. Use Chinese white, well ground, to mix with your colours in order to pale them, instead of a quantity of water. You will thus be able to shape your masses more quietly, and play the colours about with more ease; they will not damp your paper so much, and you will be able to go on continually, and lay forms of passing cloud and other fugitive or delicately shaped lights, otherwise unattainable except by time.

158. This mixing of white with the pigments, so as to render them opaque, constitutes body-colour drawing as opposed to transparent-colour drawing, and you will, perhaps, have it often said to you that this body-colour is

* I give Rossetti this preëminence, because, though the leading Pre-Raphaelites have all about equal power over colour in the abstract, Rossetti and Holman Hunt are distinguished above the rest for rendering colour under effects of light; and of these two, Rossetti composes with richer fancy, and with a deeper sense of beauty, Hunt's stern realism leading him continually into harshness. Rossetti's carelessness, to do him justice, is only in water-colour, never in oil.[1]

[1] [For Rossetti and Holman Hunt as colourists, see *Art of England*, Lecture i. "Rossetti's carelessness" is the subject of admonitions in letters to the artist (see a later volume).]

"illegitimate." It is just as legitimate as oil-painting, being, so far as handling is concerned, the same process, only without its uncleanliness, its unwholesomeness, or its inconvenience; for oil will not dry quickly, nor carry safely, nor give the same effects of atmosphere without tenfold labour. And if you hear it said that the body-colour looks chalky or opaque, and, as is very likely, think so yourself, be yet assured of this, that though certain effects of glow and transparencies of gloom are not to be reached without transparent colour, those glows and glooms are *not* the noblest aim of art. After many years' study of the various results of fresco and oil painting in Italy, and of body-colour and transparent colour in England, I am now entirely convinced that the greatest things that are to be done in art must be done in dead colour. The habit of depending on varnish or on lucid tints for transparency, makes the painter comparatively lose sight of the nobler translucence which is obtained by breaking various colours amidst each other: and even when, as by Correggio, exquisite play of hue is joined with exquisite transparency, the delight in the depth almost always leads the painter into mean and false chiaroscuro; it leads him to like dark backgrounds instead of luminous ones,* and to enjoy, in

---

* All the degradation of art which was brought about, after the rise of the Dutch school, by asphaltum, yellow varnish, and brown trees [1] would have been prevented, if only painters had been forced to work in dead colour. Any colour will do for some people, if it is browned and shining; but fallacy in dead colour is detected on the instant. I even believe that whenever a painter begins to *wish* that he could touch any portion of his work with gum, he is going wrong.

It is necessary, however, in this matter, carefully to distinguish between translucency and lustre. Translucency, though, as I have said above, a dangerous temptation, is, in its place, beautiful; but lustre or *shininess* is always, in painting, a defect. Nay, one of my best painter-friends (the "best" being understood to attach to both divisions of that awkward compound word), tried the other day to persuade me that lustre was an ignobleness in anything; and it was only the fear of treason to ladies' eyes, and to mountain streams, and to morning dew, which kept me from yielding the

---

[1] [For the " brown tree," see Vol. III. p. 45.]

general, quality of colour more than grandeur of composition, and confined light rather than open sunshine: so that the really greatest thoughts of the greatest men have always, so far as I remember, been reached in dead colour, and the noblest oil pictures of Tintoret and Veronese are those which are likest frescoes.

159. Besides all this, the fact is, that though sometimes a little chalky and coarse-looking body-colour is, in a sketch, infinitely liker Nature than transparent colour: the bloom and mist of distance are accurately and instantly represented by the film of opaque blue (*quite* accurately, I think, by nothing else); and for ground, rocks, and buildings, the earthy and solid surface is, of course, always truer than the most finished and carefully wrought work in transparent tints can ever be.

160. Against one thing, however, I must steadily caution you. All kinds of colour are equally illegitimate, if you think they will allow you to alter at your pleasure, or blunder at your ease. There is *no* vehicle or method of colour which admits of alteration or repentance; you must be right at once, or never; and you might as well hope to catch a rifle bullet in your hand, and put it straight, when it was going wrong, as to recover a tint once spoiled. The secret of all good colour in oil, water, or anything else, lies primarily in that sentence spoken to me by Mulready: " Know what you have to do." [1] The process may be a long one, perhaps: you may have to ground with one colour; to touch it with fragments of a second; to crumble a third into the interstices; a fourth into the interstices of the third; to glaze the whole with a fifth; and to reinforce

point to him. One is apt always to generalise too quickly in such matters; but there can be no question that lustre is destructive of loveliness in colour, as it is of intelligibility in form. Whatever may be the pride of a young beauty in the knowledge that her eyes shine (though perhaps even eyes are most beautiful in dimness), she would be sorry if her cheeks did; and which of us would wish to polish a rose?

[1] [See *Seven Lamps of Architecture*, Vol. VIII. p. 19.]

in points with a sixth: but whether you have one, or ten, or twenty processes to go through, you must go *straight* through them knowingly and foreseeingly all the way; and if you get the thing once wrong, there is no hope for you but in washing or scraping boldly down to the white ground, and beginning again.

161. The drawing in body-colour will tend to teach you all this, more than any other method, and above all it will prevent you from falling into the pestilent habit of sponging to get texture; a trick which has nearly ruined our modern water-colour school of art.   There are sometimes places in which a skilful artist will roughen his paper a little to get certain conditions of dusty colour with more ease than he could otherwise; and sometimes a skilfully rased piece of paper will, in the midst of transparent tints, answer nearly the purpose of chalky body-colour in representing the surfaces of rocks or building.   But artifices of this kind are always treacherous in a tyro's hands, tempting him to trust in them: and you had better always work on white or grey paper as smooth as silk;* and never disturb the surface of your colour or paper, except finally to scratch out the very highest lights if you are using transparent colours.

162. I have said above that body-colour drawing will teach you the use of colour better than working with merely transparent tints; but this is not because the process is an easier one, but because it is a more complete one, and also because it involves some working with transparent tints in the best way.   You are not to think that because you use body-colour you may make any kind of mess that you like, and yet get out of it.   But you are to avail yourself of the characters of your material, which enable you

---

* But not shiny or greasy.   Bristol board, or hot-pressed imperial, or grey paper that feels slightly adhesive to the hand, is best.   Coarse, gritty, and sandy papers are fit only for blotters and blunderers; no good draughtsman would lay a line on them.   Turner worked much on a thin tough paper, dead in surface; rolling up his sketches in tight bundles that would go deep into his pockets.

most nearly to imitate the processes of Nature. Thus,
suppose you have a red rocky cliff to sketch, with blue
clouds floating over it. You paint your cliff first firmly,
then take your blue, mixing it to such a tint (and here is
a great part of the skill needed) that when it is laid over
the red, in the thickness required for the effect of the mist,
the warm rock-colour showing through the blue cloud-
colour, may bring it to exactly the hue you want (your
upper tint, therefore, must be mixed colder than you want
it); then you lay it on, varying it as you strike it, getting the forms of the mist at once, and, if it be rightly
done, with exquisite quality of colour, from the warm tint's
showing through and between the particles of the other.
When it is dry, you may add a little colour to retouch
the edges where they want shape, or heighten the lights
where they want roundness, or put another tone over the
whole: but you can take none away. If you touch or
disturb the surface, or by any untoward accident mix the
under and upper colours together, all is lost irrecoverably.
Begin your drawing from the ground again if you like, or
throw it into the fire if you like. But do not waste time
in trying to mend it.*

163. This discussion of the relative merits of transparent and opaque colour has, however, led us a little beyond the point where we should have begun; we must go
back to our palette, if you please. Get a cake of each of
the hard colours named in the note below † and try experiments on their simple combinations, by mixing each colour
with every other. If you like to do it in an orderly way,
you may prepare a squared piece of pasteboard, and put
the pure colours in columns at the top and side; the mixed

---

* I insist upon this unalterability of colour the more because I address
you as a beginner, or an amateur: a great artist can sometimes get out of a
difficulty with credit, or repent without confession. Yet even Titian's altera-
tions usually show as stains on his work.

† It is, I think, a piece of affectation to try to work with few colours:
it saves time to have enough tints prepared without mixing, and you may
at once allow yourself these twenty-four. If you arrange them in your

tints being given at the intersections, thus (the letters standing for colours):

	b	c	d	e	f	etc.
a	a b	a c	a d	a e	a f	
b	—	b c	b d	b e	b f	
c	—	—	c d	c e	c f	
d	—	—	—	d e	d f	
e	—	—	—	—	e f	
etc.						

This will give you some general notion of the characters of mixed tints of two colours only, and it is better in practice to confine yourself as much as possible to these, and to get more complicated colours, either by putting the third *over* the first blended tint, or by putting the third into its interstices. Nothing but watchful practice will teach you the effects that colours have on each other when thus put over, or beside, each other.

164. When you have got a little used to the principal colour-box in the order I have set them down, you will always easily put your finger on the one you want.

Cobalt	Smalt	Antwerp blue	Prussian blue
Black	Gamboge	Emerald green	Hooker's green
Lemon yellow	Cadmium yellow	Yellow ochre	Roman ochre
Raw sienna	Burnt sienna	Light red	Indian red
Mars orange	Extract of vermilion	Carmine	Violet carmine
Brown madder	Burnt umber	Vandyke brown	Sepia

Antwerp blue and Prussian blue are not very permanent colours, but you need not care much about permanence in your work as yet, and they are both beautiful; while Indigo is marked by Field as more fugitive still, and is very ugly. Hooker's green is a mixed colour, put in the box merely to save you loss of time in mixing gamboge and Prussian blue. No. 1 is the best tint of it. Violet carmine is a noble colour for laying broken shadows with, to be worked into afterwards with other colours.

If you wish to take up colouring seriously you had better get Field's *Chromatography*[1] at once; only do not attend to anything it says about principles or harmonies of colour; but only to its statements of practical serviceableness in pigments, and of their operations on each other when mixed, etc.

---

[1] [For this book, see Vol. IV. p. 362.]

combinations, place yourself at a window which the sun
does not shine in at,[1] commanding some simple piece of
landscape : outline this landscape roughly ; then take a piece
of white cardboard, cut out a hole in it about the size of
a large pea ; and supposing ʀ is the room, *a d* the window,
and you are sitting at *a*, Fig. 29, hold this
cardboard a little outside of the window,
upright, and in the direction *b d*, parallel to
the side of the window, or a little turned,
so as to catch more light, as at *a d*, never
turned as at *c d*, or the paper will be dark.
Then you will see the landscape, bit by
bit, through the circular hole. Match the
colours of each important bit as nearly as

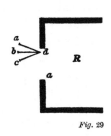

Fig. 29

you can, mixing your tints with white, beside the aperture.
When matched, put a touch of the same tint at the top of
your paper, writing under it: "dark tree colour," "hill
colour," "field colour," as the case may be. Then wash
the tint away from beside the opening, and the cardboard
will be ready to match another piece of the landscape.*
When you have got the colours of the principal masses
thus indicated, lay on a piece of each in your sketch in
its right place, and then proceed to complete the sketch in
harmony with them, by your eye.

165. In the course of your early experiments, you will
be much struck by two things : the first, the inimitable
brilliancy of light in sky and in sun-lighted things ; and the
second, that among the tints which you can imitate, those

---

* A more methodical, though under general circumstances uselessly
prolix way, is to cut a square hole, some half an inch wide, in the sheet
of cardboard, and a series of small circular holes in a slip of cardboard an
inch wide. Pass the slip over the square opening, and match each colour
beside one of the circular openings. You will thus have no occasion to
wash any of the colours away. But the first rough method is generally
all you want, as, after a little practice, you only need to *look* at the
hue through the opening in order to be able to transfer it to your drawing at once.

---

[1] [Compare the passage from Leonardo cited above, p. 49.]

which you thought the darkest will continually turn out
to be in reality the lightest. Darkness of objects is esti-
mated by us, under ordinary circumstances, much more by
knowledge than by sight; thus, a cedar or Scotch fir, at
200 yards off, will be thought of darker green than an elm
or oak near us; because we know by experience that the
peculiar colour they exhibit, at that distance, is the *sign* of
darkness of foliage. But when we try them through the
cardboard, the near oak will be found, indeed, rather dark
green, and the distant cedar, perhaps, pale grey-purple.[1]
The quantity of purple and grey in Nature is, by the way,
another somewhat surprising subject of discovery.

166. Well, having ascertained thus your principal tints,
you may proceed to fill up your sketch; in doing which
observe these following particulars:

(1.) Many portions of your subject appeared through
the aperture in the paper brighter than the paper, as sky,
sun-lighted grass, etc. Leave these portions, for the present,
white; and proceed with the parts of which you can match
the tints.

(2.) As you tried your subject with the cardboard, you
must have observed how many changes of hue took place
over small spaces. In filling up your work, try to educate
your eye to perceive these differences of hue without the
help of the cardboard, and lay them deliberately, like a
mosaic-worker, as separate colours, preparing each carefully on your palette, and laying it as if it were a patch
of coloured cloth, cut out, to be fitted neatly by its edge
to the next patch; so that the *fault* of your work may be,
not a slurred or misty look, but a patched bed-cover look,
as if it had all been cut out with scissors. For instance,
in drawing the trunk of a birch tree, there will be probably white high lights, then a pale rosy grey round them
on the light side, then a (probably greenish) deeper grey on
the dark side, varied by reflected colours, and, over all,

[1] [On the colour of distant trees, compare *Modern Painters*, vol. iv. (Vol. VI.
p. 421 and *n*.).]

rich black strips of bark and brown spots of moss. Lay first the rosy grey, leaving white for the high lights *and for the spots of moss*, and not touching the dark side. Then lay the grey for the dark side, fitting it well up to the rosy grey of the light, leaving also in this darker grey the white paper in the places for the black and brown moss; then prepare the moss colours separately for each spot, and lay each in the white place left for it. Not one grain of white, except that purposely left for the high lights, must be visible when the work is done, even through a magnifying-glass, so cunningly must you fit the edges to each other. Finally, take your background colours, and put them on each side of the tree trunk, fitting them carefully to its edge.

167. Fine work you would make of this, wouldn't you, if you had not learned to draw first, and could not now draw a good outline for the stem, much less terminate a colour mass in the outline you wanted?

Your work will look very odd for some time, when you first begin to paint in this way, and before you can modify it, as I shall tell you presently how;[1] but never mind; it is of the greatest possible importance that you should practise this separate laying on of the hues, for all good colouring finally depends on it. It is, indeed, often necessary, and sometimes desirable, to lay one colour and form boldly over another: thus, in laying leaves on blue sky, it is impossible always in large pictures, or when pressed for time, to fill in the blue through the interstices of the leaves; and the great Venetians constantly lay their blue ground first, and then, having let it dry, strike the golden brown over it in the form of the leaf, leaving the under blue to shine through the gold, and subdue it to the olive-green they want. But in the most precious and perfect work each leaf is inlaid, and the blue worked round it; and, whether you use one or other mode of getting

---

[1] [Below, p. 201.]

your result, it is equally necessary to be absolute and decisive in your laying the colour. Either your ground must be laid firmly first, and then your upper colour struck upon it in perfect form, for ever, thenceforward, unalterable; or else the two colours must be individually put in their places, and led up to each other till they meet at their appointed border, equally, thenceforward, unchangeable. Either process, you see, involves absolute decision. If you once begin to slur, or change, or sketch, or try this way and that with your colour, it is all over with it and with you. You will continually see bad copyists trying to imitate the Venetians, by daubing their colours about, and retouching, and finishing, and softening: when every touch and every added hue only lead them farther into chaos. There is a dog between two children in a Veronese in the Louvre,[1] which gives the copyists much employment. He has a dark ground behind him, which Veronese has painted first, and then when it was dry, or nearly so, struck the locks of the dog's white hair over it with some half-dozen curling sweeps of his brush, right at once, and for ever. Had one line or hair of them gone wrong, it would have been wrong for ever; no retouching could have mended it. The poor copyists daub in first some background, and then some dog's hair; then retouch the background, then the hair; work for hours at it, expecting it always to come right to-morrow—" when it is finished." They *may* work for centuries at it, and they will never do it. If they can do it with Veronese's allowance of work, half a dozen sweeps of the hand over the dark background, well; if not, they may ask the dog himself whether it will ever come right, and get true answer from him—on Launce's conditions: " If he say 'ay,' it will; if he say 'no,' it will; if he shake his tail and say nothing, it will."[2]

168. (3.) Whenever you lay on a mass of colour, be sure

---

[1] [The group is in the picture of "The Supper at Emmaus": see "Notes on the Louvre," § 8, Vol. XII. p. 451.]

[2] [*Two Gentlemen of Verona*, ii. 5.]

that however large it may be, or however small, it shall be
gradated.   No colour exists in Nature under ordinary circumstances without gradation. If you do not see this, it
is the fault of your inexperience : you will see it in due
time, if you practise enough.   But in general you may see
it at once.   In the birch trunk, for instance, the rosy grey
must be gradated by the roundness of the stem till it meets
the shaded side ; similarly the shaded side is gradated by
reflected light. Accordingly, whether by adding water, or
white paint, or by unequal force of touch (this you will do
at pleasure, according to the texture you wish to produce),
you must, in every tint you lay on, make it a little paler
at one part than another, and get an even gradation between the two depths.   This is very like laying down a
formal law or recipe for you ; but you will find it is merely
the assertion of a natural fact.   It is not indeed physically
impossible to meet with an ungradated piece of colour,
but it is so supremely improbable, that you had better get
into the habit of asking yourself invariably, when you are
going to copy a tint—not " Is that gradated ? " but " Which
way is that gradated ? " and at least in ninety-nine out of a
hundred instances, you will be able to answer decisively
after a careful glance, though the gradation may have been
so subtle that you did not see it at first.   And it does not
matter how small the touch of colour may be, though not
larger than the smallest pin's head, if one part of it is not
darker than the rest, it is a bad touch ; for it is not merely
because the natural fact is so, that your colour should be
gradated ; the preciousness and pleasantness of the colour
itself depends more on this than on any other of its qualities, for gradation is to colours just what curvature is to
lines, both being felt to be beautiful by the pure instinct of
every human mind, and both, considered as types, expressing the law of gradual change and progress in the human
soul itself.   What the difference is in mere beauty between
a gradated and ungradated colour, may be seen easily by
laying an even tint of rose-colour on paper, and putting a

rose leaf beside it.   The victorious beauty of the rose as
compared with other flowers, depends wholly on the delicacy
and quantity of its colour gradations,[1] all other flowers being
either less rich in gradation, not having so many folds of
leaf; or less tender, being patched and veined instead of
flushed.

169. (4.) But observe, it is not enough in general that
colour should be gradated by being made merely paler or
darker at one place than another.   Generally colour changes
as it diminishes, and is not merely darker at one spot, but
also purer at one spot than anywhere else.   It does not in
the least follow that the darkest spot should be the purest;
still less so that the lightest should be the purest.   Very
often the two gradations more or less cross each other, one
passing in one direction from paleness to darkness, another
in another direction from purity to dulness, but there will
almost always be both of them, however reconciled; and
you must never be satisfied with a piece of colour until you
have got both: that is to say, every piece of blue that
you lay on must be *quite* blue only at some given spot,
nor that a large spot; and must be gradated from that into
less pure blue,—greyish blue, or greenish blue, or purplish
blue,—over all the rest of the space it occupies.   And this
you must do in one of three ways: either, while the colour
is wet, mix with it the colour which is to subdue it, adding
gradually a little more and a little more; or else, when
the colour is quite dry, strike a gradated touch of another
colour over it, leaving only a point of the first tint visible;
or else, lay the subduing tints on in small touches, as in
the exercise of tinting the chess-board.   Of each of these
methods I have something to tell you separately; but that
is distinct from the subject of gradation, which I must not
quit without once more pressing upon you the preëminent
necessity of introducing it everywhere.   I have profound
dislike of anything like habit of hand, and yet, in this one

---

[1] [Compare *Modern Painters,* vol. iv. (Vol. VI. p. 62).]

instance, I feel almost tempted to encourage you to get into a habit of never touching paper with colour, without securing a gradation. You will not, in Turner's largest oil pictures, perhaps six or seven feet long by four or five high, find one spot of colour as large as a grain of wheat ungradated : and you will find in practice, that brilliancy of hue, and vigour of light, and even the aspect of transparency in shade, are essentially dependent on this character alone ; hardness, coldness, and opacity resulting far more from *equality* of colour than from nature of colour. Give me some mud off a city crossing, some ochre out of a gravel pit, a little whitening, and some coal-dust, and I will paint you a luminous picture, if you give me time to gradate my mud, and subdue my dust : but though you had the red of the ruby, the blue of the gentian, snow for the light, and amber for the gold, you cannot paint a luminous picture, if you keep the masses of those colours unbroken in purity, and unvarying in depth.

170. (5.) Next, note the three processes by which gradation and other characters are to be obtained:

A. Mixing while the colour is wet.

You may be confused by my first telling you to lay on the hues in separate patches, and then telling you to mix hues together as you lay them on: but the separate masses are to be laid, when colours distinctly oppose each other at a given limit; the hues to be mixed, when they palpitate one through the other, or fade one into the other. It is better to err a little on the distinct side. Thus I told you to paint the dark and light sides of the birch trunk separately, though, in reality, the two tints change, as the trunk turns away from the light, gradually one into the other; and, after being laid separately on, will need some farther touching to harmonise them : but they do so in a very narrow space, marked distinctly all the way up the trunk, and it is easier and safer, therefore, to keep them separate at first. Whereas it often happens that the whole beauty of two colours will depend on the one being continued well through the other, and playing in the midst of it: blue and green often do so in water; blue and grey, or purple and scarlet, in sky: in hundreds of such instances the most beautiful and truthful results may be obtained by laying one colour into the other while wet; judging wisely how far it will spread, or blending it with the brush in somewhat thicker consistence of wet body-colour; only observe, never mix in this way two *mixtures ;* let the colour you lay into the other be always a simple, not a compound tint.

171. B. Laying one colour over another.

If you lay on a solid touch of vermilion, and after it is quite dry, strike a little very wet carmine quickly over it, you will obtain a much more brilliant red than by mixing the carmine and vermilion. Similarly, if you lay a dark colour first, and strike a little blue or white body-colour lightly over it, you will get a more beautiful grey than by mixing the colour and the blue or white. In very perfect painting, artifices of this kind are continually used; but I would not have you trust much to them: they are apt to make you think too much of quality of colour. I should like you to depend on little more than the dead colours, simply laid on, only observe always this, that the *less* colour you do the work with, the better it will always be:* so that if you had laid a red colour, and you want a purple one above, do not mix the purple on your palette and lay it on so thick as to overpower the red, but take a little thin blue from your palette, and lay it lightly over the red, so as to let the red be seen through, and thus produce the required purple; and if you want a green hue over a blue one, do not lay a quantity of green on the blue, but a *little* yellow, and so on, always bringing the under colour into

---

* If colours were twenty times as costly as they are, we should have many more good painters. If I were Chancellor of the Exchequer I would lay a tax of twenty shillings a cake on all colours except black, Prussian blue, Vandyke brown, and Chinese white, which I would leave for students. I don't say this jestingly; I believe such a tax would do more to advance real art than a great many schools of design.

service as far as you possibly can. If, however, the colour beneath is wholly opposed to the one you have to lay on, as, suppose, if green is to be laid over scarlet, you must either remove the required parts of the under colour daintily first with your knife, or with water; or else, lay solid white over it massively, and leave that to dry, and then glaze the white with the upper colour. This is better, in general, than laying the upper colour itself so thick as to conquer the ground, which, in fact, if it be a transparent colour, you cannot do. Thus, if you have to strike warm boughs and leaves of trees over blue sky, and they are too intricate to have their places left for them in laying the blue, it is better to lay them first in solid white, and then glaze with sienna and ochre, than to mix the sienna and white; though, of course, the process is longer and more troublesome. Nevertheless, if the forms of touches required are very delicate, the after glazing is impossible. You must then mix the warm colour thick at once, and so use it: and this is often necessary for delicate grasses, and such other fine threads of light in foreground work.

172. C. Breaking one colour in small points through or over another.

This is the most important of all processes in good modern * oil and water-colour painting, but you need not hope to attain very great skill in it. To do it well is very laborious, and requires such skill and delicacy of hand as can only be acquired by unceasing practice. But you will find advantage in noting the following points:

173. (a.) In distant effects of rich subject, wood, or rippled water, or broken clouds, much may be done by touches or crumbling dashes of rather dry colour, with other colours afterwards put cunningly into the interstices. The more you practise this, when the subject evidently calls

---

* I say *modern*, because Titian's quiet way of blending colours, which is the perfectly right one, is not understood now by any artist. The best colour we reach is got by stippling; but this is not quite right.

for it, the more your eye will enjoy the higher qualities of colour. The process is, in fact, the carrying out of the principle of separate colours to the utmost possible refinement; using atoms of colour in juxtaposition, instead of large spaces. And note, in filling up minute interstices of this kind, that if you want the colour you fill them with to show brightly, it is better to put a rather positive point of it, with a little white left beside or round it in the interstice, than to put a pale tint of the colour over the whole interstice. Yellow or orange will hardly show, if pale, in small spaces; but they show brightly in firm touches, however small, with white beside them.

174. (*b*.) If a colour is to be darkened by superimposed portions of another, it is, in many cases, better to lay the uppermost colour in rather vigorous small touches, like finely chopped straw, over the under one, than to lay it on as a tint, for two reasons: the first, that the play of the two colours together is pleasant to the eye; the second, that much expression of form may be got by wise administration of the upper dark touches. In distant mountains they may be made pines of, or broken crags, or villages, or stones, or whatever you choose; in clouds they may indicate the direction of the rain, the roll and outline of the cloud masses; and in water, the minor waves. All noble effects of dark atmosphere are got in good water-colour drawing by these two expedients, interlacing the colours, or retouching the lower one with fine darker drawing in an upper. Sponging and washing for dark atmospheric effect is barbarous, and mere tyro's work, though it is often useful for passages of delicate atmospheric light.

175. (*c*.) When you have time, practise the production of mixed tints by interlaced touches of the pure colours out of which they are formed, and use the process at the parts of your sketches where you wish to get rich and luscious effects. Study the works of William Hunt,[1] of the Old

---

[1] [See also Vol. XIV. p. 384, where Ruskin refers to William Hunt as the best model in water-colour painting. Compare § 68 above, p. 64.]

Water-colour Society, in this respect, continually, and make frequent memoranda of the variegations in flowers; not painting the flower completely, but laying the ground colour of one petal, and painting the spots on it with studious precision: a series of single petals of lilies, geraniums, tulips, etc., numbered with proper reference to their position in the flower, will be interesting to you on many grounds besides those of art. Be careful to get the gradated distribution of the spots well followed in the calceolarias, foxgloves, and the like; and work out the odd, indefinite hues of the spots themselves with minute grains of pure interlaced colour, otherwise you will never get their richness or bloom. You will be surprised to find as you do this, first, the universality of the law of gradation we have so much insisted upon; secondly, that Nature is just as economical of *her* fine colours as I have told you to be of yours. You would think, by the way she paints, that her colours cost her something enormous; she will only give you a single pure touch, just where the petal turns into light; but down in the bell all is subdued, and under the petal all is subdued, even in the showiest flower. What you thought was bright blue is, when you look close, only dusty grey, or green, or purple, or every colour in the world at once, only a single gleam or streak of pure blue in the centre of it. And so with all her colours. Sometimes I have really thought her miserliness intolerable: in a gentian, for instance, the way she economises her ultramarine down in the bell is a little too bad.*

176. Next, respecting general tone. I said, just now, that, for the sake of students, my tax should not be laid on black or on white pigments; but if you mean to be a colourist, you must lay a tax on them yourself when you begin to use true colour; that is to say, you must use them little, and make of them much. There is no better test of your colour tones being good, than your having

---

* See Note 6 in Appendix I. [p. 217].

made the white in your picture precious, and the black conspicuous.[1]

177. I say, first, the white precious. I do not mean merely glittering or brilliant: it is easy to scratch white sea-gulls out of black clouds, and dot clumsy foliage with chalky dew; but when white is well managed, it ought to be strangely delicious,—tender as well as bright,—like inlaid mother of pearl, or white roses washed in milk. The eye ought to seek it for rest, brilliant though it may be; and to feel it as a space of strange, heavenly paleness in the midst of the flushing of the colours. This effect you can only reach by general depth of middle tint, by absolutely refusing to allow any white to exist except where you need it, and by keeping the white itself subdued by grey, except at a few points of chief lustre.

178. Secondly, you must make the black conspicuous. However small a point of black may be, it ought to catch the eye, otherwise your work is too heavy in the shadow. All the ordinary shadows should be of some *colour*,— never black, nor approaching black, they should be evidently and always of a luminous nature, and the black should look strange among them; never occurring except in a black object, or in small points indicative of intense shade in the very centre of masses of shadow. Shadows of absolutely negative grey, however, may be beautifully used with white, or with gold; but still though the black thus, in subdued strength, becomes spacious, it should always be conspicuous; the spectator should notice this grey neutrality with some wonder, and enjoy, all the more intensely on account of it, the gold colour and the white which it relieves. Of all the great colourists Velasquez is the greatest master of the black chords. His black is more precious than most other people's crimson.

179. It is not, however, only white and black which you must make valuable; you must give rare worth to

---

[1] [Compare *Lectures on Landscape*, § 73, where Ruskin repeats and illustrates this "testing rule for good colour," and *Lectures on Art*, § 138.]

every colour you use; but the white and black ought to separate themselves quaintly from the rest, while the other colours should be continually passing one into the other, being all evidently companions in the same gay world; while the white, black, and neutral grey should stand monkishly aloof in the midst of them. You may melt your crimson into purple, your purple into blue, and your blue into green, but you must not melt any of them into black. You should, however, try, as I said, to give preciousness to all your colours; and this especially by never using a grain more than will just do the work, and giving each hue the highest value by opposition. All fine colouring, like fine drawing, is delicate; and so delicate that if, at last, you *see* the colour you are putting on, you are putting on too much. You ought to feel a change wrought in the general tone, by touches of colour which individually are too pale to be seen; and if there is one atom of any colour in the whole picture which is unnecessary to it, that atom hurts it.[1]

180. Notice also that nearly all good compound colours are *odd* colours. You shall look at a hue in a good painter's work ten minutes before you know what to call it. You thought it was brown, presently you feel that it is red; next that there is, somehow, yellow in it; presently afterwards that there is blue in it. If you try to copy it you will always find your colour too warm or too cold—no colour in the box will seem to have an affinity with it; and yet it will be as pure as if it were laid at a single touch with a single colour.

181. As to the choice and harmony of colours in general, if you cannot choose and harmonise them by instinct, you will never do it at all. If you need examples of utterly harsh and horrible colour, you may find plenty given in treatises upon colouring, to illustrate the laws of harmony;

---

[1] [On this subject, of delicacy in art, see above, pp. 14, 37, and compare *Lectures on Colour*, § 35, Vol. XII. p. 503; and see Vol. XIII. p. 336, where this passage is quoted and illustrated.]

and if you want to colour beautifully, colour as best pleases yourself at *quiet times*, not so as to catch the eye, nor look as if it were clever or difficult to colour in that way, but so that the colour may be pleasant to you when you are happy or thoughtful. Look much at the morning and evening sky, and much at simple flowers—dog-roses, wood-hyacinths, violets, poppies, thistles, heather, and such like,—as Nature arranges them in the woods and fields. If ever any scientific person tells you that two colours are "discordant," make a note of the two colours, and put them together whenever you can. I have actually heard people say that blue and green were discordant; the two colours which Nature seems to intend never to be separated, and never to be felt, either of them, in its full beauty without the other!—a peacock's neck, or a blue sky through green leaves, or a blue wave with green lights through it, being precisely the loveliest things, next to clouds at sunrise, in this coloured world of ours. If you have a good eye for colours, you will soon find out how constantly Nature puts purple and green together, purple and scarlet, green and blue, yellow and neutral grey, and the like; and how she strikes these colour-concords for general tones, and then works into them with innumerable subordinate ones; and you will gradually come to like what she does, and find out new and beautiful chords of colour in her work every day. If you enjoy them, depend upon it you will paint them to a certain point right: or, at least, if you do not enjoy them, you are certain to paint them wrong. If colour does not give you intense pleasure, let it alone; depend upon it, you are only tormenting the eyes and senses of people who feel colour, whenever you touch it; and that is unkind and improper.

182. You will find, also, your power of colouring depend much on your state of health and right balance of mind; when you are fatigued or ill you will not see colours well, and when you are ill-tempered you will not choose them well: thus, though not infallibly a test of character in

individuals, colour power is a great sign of mental health in nations;[1] when they are in a state of intellectual decline, their colouring always gets dull.* You must also take great care not to be misled by affected talk about colours from people who have not the gift of it: numbers are eager and voluble about it who probably never in all their lives received one genuine colour-sensation. The modern religionists of the school of Overbeck are just like people who eat slate-pencil and chalk, and assure everybody that they are nicer and purer than strawberries and plums.[2]

183. Take care also never to be misled into any idea that colour can help or display *form;* colour † always disguises form, and is meant to do so.

184. It is a favourite dogma among modern writers on colour that " warm colours" (reds and yellows) "approach," or express nearness, and "cold colours" (blue and grey) "retire," or express distance.[3] So far is this from being the case, that no expression of distance in the world is so great as that of the gold and orange in twilight sky. Colours,

---

* The worst general character that colour can possibly have is a prevalent tendency to a dirty yellowish green, like that of a decaying heap of vegetables; this colour is *accurately* indicative of decline or paralysis in missal-painting.

† That is to say, local colour inherent in the object. The gradations of colour in the various shadows belonging to various lights exhibit form, and therefore no one but a colourist can ever draw *forms* perfectly (see *Modern Painters,* vol. iv. chap. iii. at the end [4]); but all notions of explaining form by superimposed colour, as in architectural mouldings, are absurd. Colour adorns form, but does not interpret it. An apple is prettier because it is striped, but it does not look a bit rounder; and a cheek is prettier because it is flushed, but you would see the form of the cheek bone better if it were not. Colour may, indeed, detach one shape from another, as in grounding a bas-relief, but it always diminishes the appearance of projection, and whether you put blue, purple, red, yellow, or green, for your ground, the bas-relief will be just as clearly or just as imperfectly relieved, as long as the colours are of equal depth. The blue ground will not retire the hundredth part of an inch more than the red one.

---

[1] [Compare Vol. X. p. 173.]

[2] [For Overbeck, see Vol. V. p. 50; and for the "muddy" German school, Vol. III. p. 351.]

[3] [See Vol. XIII. p. 218, where Ruskin illustrates the argument here from Turner's sketch, No. 73 in the National Gallery.]

[4] [In this edition, Vol. VI. pp. 71.]

as such, are ABSOLUTELY inexpressive respecting distance. It is their quality (as depth, delicacy, etc.) which expresses distance, not their tint. A blue bandbox set on the same shelf with a yellow one will not look an inch farther off, but a red or orange cloud, in the upper sky, will always appear to be beyond a blue cloud close to us, as it is in reality. It is quite true that in certain objects, blue is a *sign* of distance; but that is not because blue is a retiring colour, but because the mist in the air is blue, and therefore any warm colour which has not strength of light enough to pierce the mist is lost or subdued in its blue: but blue is no more, on this account, a "retiring colour," than brown is a retiring colour, because, when stones are seen through brown water, the deeper they lie the browner they look; or than yellow is a retiring colour, because, when objects are seen through a London fog, the farther off they are the yellower they look. Neither blue, nor yellow, nor red, can have, as such, the smallest power of expressing either nearness or distance: they express them only under the peculiar circumstances which render them at the moment, or in that place, *signs* of nearness or distance. Thus, vivid orange in an orange is a sign of nearness, for if you put the orange a great way off, its colour will not look so bright; but vivid orange in sky is a sign of distance, because you cannot get the colour of orange in a cloud near you. So purple in a violet or a hyacinth is a sign of nearness, because the closer you look at them the more purple you see. But purple in a mountain is a sign of distance, because a mountain close to you is not purple, but green or grey. It may, indeed, be generally assumed that a tender or pale colour will more or less express distance, and a powerful or dark colour nearness; but even this is not always so. Heathery hills will usually give a pale and tender purple near, and an intense and dark purple far away; the rose colour of sunset on snow is pale on the snow at your feet, deep and full on the snow in the distance; and the green of a Swiss lake is pale in the clear waves on the beach, but intense as an emerald in the sunstreak six miles from shore. And in any case, when the foreground is in strong light, with much water about it, or white surface, casting intense reflections, all its colours may be perfectly delicate, pale, and faint; while the distance, when it is in shadow, may relieve the whole foreground with intense darks of purple, blue green, or ultramarine blue. So that, on the whole, it is quite hopeless and absurd to expect any help from laws of " aërial perspective." [1] Look for the natural effects, and set them down as fully as you can, and as faithfully, and *never* alter a colour because it won't look in its right place. Put the colour strong, if it be strong, though far off; faint, if it be faint, though close to you. Why should you suppose that Nature always means you to know exactly how far one thing is from another? She certainly intends you always to enjoy her colouring, but she does not wish you always to measure her space. You would be hard put to it, every time you painted the sun setting, if you had to express his 95,000,000 miles of distance in " aërial perspective."

185. There is, however, I think, one law about distance, which has some claims to be considered a constant one: namely, that dulness and heaviness of colour are more or less indicative of nearness. All distant colour is *pure* colour: it may not be bright, but it is clear and lovely, not opaque nor soiled; for the air and light coming between us and any earthy or imperfect colour, purify or harmonise it; hence a bad colourist is peculiarly incapable of expressing distance. I do not of course mean that you are to use bad colours in your foreground by way of making it come forward; but only that a failure in colour, there, will not put it out of its place; while a failure in colour in the distance will at once do away with its remoteness; your dull-coloured foreground will still be a foreground, though ill-painted; but your ill-painted distance will not be merely a dull distance,—it will be no distance at all.

---

[1] [On this subject, see Vol. III. p. 260, Vol. XI. pp. 59–60.]

186. I have only one thing more to advise you, namely, never to colour petulantly or hurriedly. You will not, indeed, be able, if you attend properly to your colouring, to get anything like the quantity of form you could in a chiaroscuro sketch; nevertheless, if you do not dash or rush at your work, nor do it lazily, you may always get enough form to be satisfactory. An extra quarter of an hour, distributed in quietness over the course of the whole study, may just make the difference between a quite intelligible drawing, and a slovenly and obscure one. If you determine well beforehand what outline each piece of colour is to have, and, when it is on the paper, guide it without nervousness, as far as you can, into the form required; and then, after it is dry, consider thoroughly what touches are needed to complete it, before laying one of them on; you will be surprised to find how masterly the work will soon look, as compared with a hurried or ill-considered sketch. In no process that I know of—least of all in sketching—can time be really gained by precipitation. It is gained only by caution; and gained in all sorts of ways; for not only truth of form, but force of light, is always added by an intelligent and shapely laying of the shadow colours. You may often make a simple flat tint, rightly gradated and edged, express a complicated piece of subject without a single retouch. The two Swiss cottages, for instance, with their balconies, and glittering windows, and general character of shingly eaves, are expressed in Fig. 30 with one tint of grey, and a few dispersed spots and lines of it; all of which you ought to be able to lay on without more than thrice dipping your brush, and without a single touch after the tint is dry.

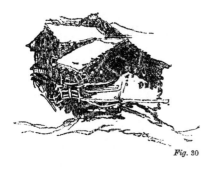

Fig. 30

187. Here, then, for I cannot without coloured illustrations tell you more, I must leave you to follow out the subject for yourself, with such help as you may receive from the water-colour drawings accessible to you ; or from any of the little treatises on their art which have been published lately[1] by our water-colour painters.* But do not trust much to works of this kind. You may get valuable hints from them as to mixture of colours; and here and there you will find a useful artifice or process explained; but nearly all such books are written only to help idle amateurs to a meretricious skill, and they are full of precepts and principles which may, for the most part, be interpreted by their *precise* negatives, and then acted upon with advantage. Most of them praise boldness,[2] when the only safe attendant spirit of a beginner is caution;—advise velocity, when the first condition of success is deliberation; —and plead for generalisation, when all the foundations of power must be laid in knowledge of speciality.

188. And now, in the last place, I have a few things to tell you respecting that dangerous nobleness of consummate art,—COMPOSITION. For though it is quite unnecessary for you yet awhile to attempt it, and it *may* be inexpedient for you to attempt it at all, you ought to know what it means, and to look for and enjoy it in the art of others.

Composition means, literally and simply, putting several things together, so as to make *one* thing out of them ; the nature and goodness of which they all have a share in producing. Thus a musician composes an air, by putting notes together in certain relations; a poet composes a poem, by putting thoughts and words in pleasant order ; and a

---

* See, however, at the close of this letter, the notice of one more point connected with the management of colour, under the head " Law of Harmony " [p. 200].

---

[1] [Such as the works of Harding and Prout already referred to; also *On Painting in Oil and Water Colours*, by T. H. Fielding (brother of Copley Fielding), 1839, and *A Treatise on Landscape Painting and Effect in Water Colours*, by David Cox, 1841.]

[2] [See above, § 16, p. 36.]

painter a picture, by putting thoughts, forms, and colours in pleasant order.

In all these cases, observe, an intended unity must be the result of composition. A paviour cannot be said to compose the heap of stones which he empties from his cart, nor the sower the handful of seed which he scatters from his hand. It is the essence of composition that everything should be in a determined place, perform an intended part, and act, in that part, advantageously for everything that is connected with it.

189. Composition, understood in this pure sense, is the type, in the arts of mankind, of the Providential government of the world.* It is an exhibition, in the order given to notes, or colours, or forms, of the advantage of perfect fellowship, discipline, and contentment. In a well-composed air, no note, however short or low, can be spared, but the least is as necessary as the greatest : no note, however prolonged, is tedious ; but the others prepare for, and are benefited by, its duration : no note, however high, is tyrannous ; the others prepare for, and are benefited by, its exaltation : no note, however low, is overpowered ; the others prepare for, and sympathise with, its humility : and the result is, that each and every note has a value in the position assigned to it, which, by itself, it never possessed, and of which, by separation from the others, it would instantly be deprived.

190. Similarly, in a good poem, each word and thought enhances the value of those which precede and follow it ; and every syllable has a loveliness which depends not so much on its abstract sound as on its position. Look at the same word in a dictionary, and you will hardly recognise it.

Much more in a great picture ; every line and colour is so arranged as to advantage the rest. None are inessential, however slight ; and none are independent, however forcible.

* See farther, on this subject, *Modern Painters*, vol. iv. chap. viii. § 6 [Vol. VI. p. 132].

It is not enough that they truly represent natural objects; but they must fit into certain places, and gather into certain harmonious groups: so that, for instance, the red chimney of a cottage is not merely set in its place as a chimney, but that it may affect, in a certain way pleasurable to the eye, the pieces of green or blue in other parts of the picture; and we ought to see that the work is masterly, merely by the positions and quantities of these patches of green, red, and blue, even at a distance which renders it perfectly impossible to determine what the colours represent: or to see whether the red is a chimney, or an old woman's cloak; and whether the blue is smoke, sky, or water.

191. It seems to be appointed, in order to remind us, in all we do, of the great laws of Divine government and human polity, that composition in the arts should strongly affect every order of mind, however unlearned or thoughtless. Hence the popular delight in rhythm and metre, and in simple musical melodies. But it is also appointed that *power* of composition in the fine arts should be an exclusive attribute of great intellect. All men can more or less copy what they see, and, more or less, remember it: powers of reflection and investigation are also common to us all, so that the decision of inferiority in these rests only on questions of *degree*. A. has a better memory than B., and C. reflects more profoundly than D. But the gift of composition is not given *at all* to more than one man in a thousand; in its highest range, it does not occur above three or four times in a century.

192. It follows, from these general truths, that it is impossible to give rules which will enable you to compose. You might much more easily receive rules to enable you to be witty. If it were possible to be witty by rule, wit would cease to be either admirable or amusing: if it were possible to compose melody by rule, Mozart and Cimarosa need not have been born: if it were possible to compose pictures by rule, Titian and Veronese would be ordinary

men. The essence of composition lies precisely in the fact of its being unteachable, in its being the operation of an individual mind of range and power exalted above others.[1]

But though no one can *invent* by rule, there are some simple laws of arrangement which it is well for you to know, because, though they will not enable you to produce a good picture, they will often assist you to set forth what goodness may be in your work in a more telling way than you could have done otherwise; and by tracing them in the work of good composers, you may better understand the grasp of their imagination, and the power it possesses over their materials. I shall briefly state the chief of these laws.

1. THE LAW OF PRINCIPALITY.

193. The great object of composition being always to secure unity; that is, to make out of many things one whole; the first mode in which this can be effected is, by determining that *one* feature shall be more important than all the rest, and that the others shall group with it in subordinate positions.

This is the simplest law of ordinary ornamentation. Thus the group of two leaves, *a*, Fig. 31, is unsatisfactory,

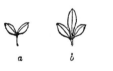

because it has no leading leaf; but that at *b is* prettier, because it has a head or master leaf; and *c* more satisfactory still, because the subordination of the other members to this head leaf is made more manifest by their gradual loss of size as they fall back from it. Hence part of the pleasure we have in the Greek honeysuckle ornament,[2] and such others.

a   b   c

Fig. 31

194. Thus, also, good pictures have always one light larger and brighter than the other lights, or one figure

---

[1] [Compare Vol. V. pp. 118–122.]
[2] [For which see *Stones of Venice*, vol. i. (Vol. IX. pp. 267, 368, 369).]

more prominent than the other figures, or one mass of colour dominant over all the other masses; and in general you will find it much benefit your sketch if you manage that there shall be one light on the cottage wall, or one blue cloud in the sky, which may attract the eye as leading light, or leading gloom, above all others. But the observance of the rule is often so cunningly concealed by the great composers, that its force is hardly at first traceable; and you will generally find they are vulgar pictures in which the law is strikingly manifest.

195. This may be simply illustrated by musical melody: for instance, in such phrases as this—

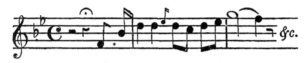

one note (here the upper G) rules the whole passage, and has the full energy of it concentrated in itself. Such passages, corresponding to completely subordinated compositions in painting, are apt to be wearisome if often repeated. But, in such a phrase as this—

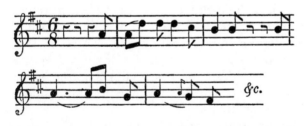

it is very difficult to say which is the principal note.[1] The A in the last bar is slightly dominant, but there is a very equal current of power running through the whole; and such passages rarely weary. And this principle holds through vast scales of arrangement; so that in the grandest

---

[1] [The former phrase is from Bellini's *Somnambula:* "Ah! perchè non posso"; the latter, from Mozart's *Don Juan:* "Horch auf den Klang der Zither."]

compositions, such as Paul Veronese's Marriage in Cana, or Raphael's Disputa,[1] it is not easy to fix at once on the principal figure; and very commonly the figure which is really chief does not catch the eye at first, but is gradually felt to be more and more conspicuous as we gaze. Thus in Titian's grand composition of the Cornaro Family,[2] the figure meant to be principal is a youth of fifteen or sixteen, whose portrait it was evidently the

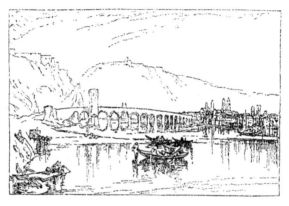

Fig. 32

painter's object to make as interesting as possible. But a grand Madonna, and a St. George with a drifting banner, and many figures more, occupy the centre of the picture, and first catch the eye; little by little we are led away from them to a gleam of pearly light in the lower corner, and find that, from the head which it shines upon, we can turn our eyes no more.

196. As, in every good picture, nearly all laws of design are more or less exemplified, it will, on the whole, be an easier way of explaining them to analyse one composition

---

[1] [For the "Marriage in Cana," see Vol. XII. pp. 451, 452, etc.; for the "Disputa," A Joy for Ever, § 147, and Two Paths, § 21 (Vol. XVI. p. 134); Eagle's Nest, § 46; and Mornings in Florence, § 75 n.]

[2] [A slip of the pen for "Pesaro Family"; the picture is in the Frari, at Venice (see Vol. XI. p. 380); there is a reproduction of it in Claude Phillips' Earlier Work of Titian, p. 92.]

thoroughly, than to give instances from various works. I shall therefore take one of Turner's simplest; which will allow us, so to speak, easily to decompose it, and illustrate each law by it as we proceed.

Fig. 32 is a rude sketch of the arrangement of the whole subject; the old bridge over the Moselle at Coblentz, the town of Coblentz on the right, Ehrenbreitstein on the left.[1] The leading or master feature is, of course, the tower on the bridge. It is kept from being *too* principal by an important group on each side of it; the boats, on the right, and Ehrenbreitstein beyond. The boats are large in mass, and more forcible in colour, but they are broken into small divisions, while the tower is simple, and therefore it still leads. Ehrenbreitstein is noble in its mass, but so reduced by aërial perspective of colour that it cannot contend with the tower, which therefore holds the eye, and becomes the key of the picture. We shall see presently how the very objects which seem at first to contend with it for the mastery are made, occultly, to increase its preëminence.

2. THE LAW OF REPETITION.

197. Another important means of expressing unity is to mark some kind of sympathy among the different objects, and perhaps the pleasantest, because most surprising, kind of sympathy, is when one group imitates or repeats another; not in the way of balance or symmetry, but subordinately, like a far-away and broken echo of it. Prout has insisted much on this law in all his writings on composition;[2] and I think it is even more authoritatively present in the minds

---

[1] [This drawing of Coblentz was in Ruskin's collection: see his *Notes on his Drawings by Turner*, No. 62 (Vol. XIII. p. 454).]

[2] [See, for instance, the remarks on Plate I. in his *Hints on Light and Shadow, Composition, etc.*: "In No. 1, the boat and figures nearly occupy the centre; some object, equally *dark* and *light*, therefore was necessary, *in a less quantity*, to prevent the principal group from appearing as if by itself and unconnected with the whole." In the same work he gives other illustrations of the same law.]

of most great composers than the law of principality.* It is quite curious to see the pains that Turner sometimes takes to echo an important passage of colour; in the Pembroke Castle, for instance,[1] there are two fishing-boats, one with a red, and another with a white sail. In a line with them, on the beach, are two fish in precisely the same relative positions; one red and one white. It is observable that he uses the artifice chiefly in pictures where he wishes to obtain an expression of repose: in my notice of the plate of Scarborough, in the series of the *Harbours of England,* I have already had occasion to dwell on this point; and I extract in the note † one or two sentences which explain the principle. In the composition I have chosen for our illustration, this reduplication is employed to a singular extent. The tower, or leading feature, is first repeated by the low echo of it to the left; put your finger over this lower tower, and see how the picture is spoiled. Then the spires of Coblentz are all arranged in couples (how they are arranged in reality does not matter; when we are composing a great picture, we must play the towers about till they come right, as fearlessly as if they were chessmen instead of cathedrals). The dual arrangement of these towers would have been too easily seen, were it not for the little one which pretends to make a triad of the last group on the right, but is so faint as hardly to be discernible; it just takes off the attention from the artifice, helped in doing so

---

* See Note 7 in Appendix I. [p. 217].

† "In general, throughout Nature, reflection and repetition are peaceful things, associated with the idea of quiet succession in events; that one day should be like another day, or one history the repetition of another history, being more or less results of quietness, while dissimilarity and non-succession are results of interference and disquietude. Thus, though an echo actually increases the quantity of sound heard, its repetition of the note or syllable gives an idea of calmness attainable in no other way; hence also the feeling of calm given to a landscape by the voice of a cuckoo."[2]

---

[1] [In No. 12 of *England and Wales.*]
[2] [Vol. XIII. pp. 73, 74.]

by the mast at the head of the boat, which, however, has instantly its own duplicate put at the stern.* Then there is the large boat near, and its echo beyond it. That echo is divided into two again, and each of those two smaller boats has two figures in it; while two figures are also sitting together on the great rudder that lies half in the water, and half aground. Then, finally, the great mass of Ehrenbreitstein, which appears at first to have no answering form, has almost its *facsimile* in the bank on which the girl is sitting; this bank is as absolutely essential to the completion of the picture as any object in the whole series. All this is done to deepen the effect of repose.

198. Symmetry, or the balance of parts or masses in nearly equal opposition, is one of the conditions of treatment under the law of Repetition. For the opposition, in a symmetrical object, is of like things reflecting each other: it is not the balance of contrary natures (like that of day and night), but of like natures or like forms; one side of a leaf being set like the reflection of the other in water.

Symmetry in Nature is, however, never formal nor accurate. She takes the greatest care to secure some difference between the corresponding things or parts of things; and an approximation to accurate symmetry is only permitted in animals, because their motions secure perpetual difference between the balancing parts. Stand before a mirror; hold your arms in precisely the same position at each side, your head upright, your body straight; divide your hair exactly in the middle and get it as nearly as you can into exactly the same shape over each ear; and you will see the effect of accurate symmetry: you will see, no less, how all grace and power in the human form result from the interference of motion and life with symmetry, and from the reconciliation of its balance with its changefulness.

* This is obscure in the rude woodcut, the masts being so delicate that they are confused among the lines of reflection. In the original they have orange light upon them, relieved against purple behind.

Your position, as seen in the mirror, is the highest type of symmetry as understood by modern architects.

199. In many sacred compositions, living symmetry, the balance of harmonious opposites, is one of the profoundest sources of their power: almost any works of the early painters, Angelico, Perugino, Giotto, etc., will furnish you with notable instances of it. The Madonna of Perugino in the National Gallery, with the angel Michael on one side and Raphael on the other, is as beautiful an example as you can have.[1]

In landscape, the principle of balance is more or less carried out, in proportion to the wish of the painter to express disciplined calmness. In bad compositions, as in bad architecture, it is formal, a tree on one side answering a tree on the other; but in good compositions, as in graceful statues, it is always easy and sometimes hardly traceable. In the Coblentz, however, you cannot have much difficulty in seeing how the boats on one side of the tower and the figures on the other are set in nearly equal balance; the tower, as a central mass, uniting both.

3. THE LAW OF CONTINUITY.

200. Another important and pleasurable way of expressing unity, is by giving some orderly succession to a number of objects more or less similar. And this succession is most interesting when it is connected with some gradual change in the aspect or character of the objects. Thus the succession of the pillars of a cathedral aisle is most interesting when they retire in perspective, becoming more and more obscure in distance: so the succession of mountain promontories one behind another, on the flanks of a valley; so the succession of clouds, fading farther and farther towards the horizon; each promontory and each cloud being of different shape, yet all evidently following in a calm and appointed

---

[1] [No. 288. For other references by Ruskin to the picture, see Vol. XIII. p. 173 *n.*, and Vol. XIV. p. 344.]

order. If there be no change at all in the shape or size of the objects, there is no continuity; there is only repetition —monotony. It is the change in shape which suggests the idea of their being individually free, and able to escape, if they liked, from the law that rules them, and yet submitting to it.

201. I will leave our chosen illustrative composition for a moment to take up another, still more expressive of this

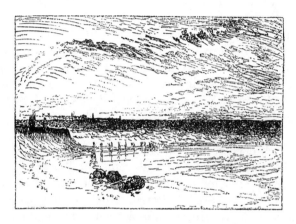

Fig. 33

law. It is one of Turner's most tender studies, a sketch on Calais Sands at sunset;[1] so delicate in the expression of wave and cloud, that it is of no use for me to try to reach it with any kind of outline in a woodcut; but the rough sketch, Fig. 33, is enough to give an idea of its arrangement. The aim of the painter has been to give the intensest expression of repose, together with the enchanted, lulling, monotonous motion of cloud and wave. All the clouds are moving in innumerable ranks after the sun, meeting towards that point in the horizon where he has set; and the tidal waves gain in winding currents upon the sand, with that stealthy haste in which they cross each other so

---

[1] [The editors are unable to trace this sketch.]

quietly, at their edges; just folding one over another as they meet, like a little piece of ruffled silk, and leaping up a little as two children kiss and clap their hands, and then going on again, each in its silent hurry, drawing pointed arches on the sand as their thin edges intersect in parting. But all this would not have been enough expressed without the line of the old pier-timbers, black with weeds, strained and bent by the storm waves, and now seeming to stoop in following one another, like dark ghosts escaping slowly from the cruelty of the pursuing sea.

202. I need not, I hope, point out to the reader the illustration of this law of continuance in the subject chosen for our general illustration.   It was simply that gradual succession of the retiring arches of the bridge which induced Turner to paint the subject at all; and it was this same principle which led him always to seize on subjects including long bridges wherever he could find them; but especially, observe, unequal bridges, having the highest arch at one side rather than at the centre.   There is a reason for this, irrespective of general laws of composition, and connected with the nature of rivers, which I may as well stop a minute to tell you about, and let you rest from the study of composition.

203. All rivers, small or large, agree in one character, they like to lean a little on one side: they cannot bear to have their channels deepest in the middle, but will always, if they can, have one bank to sun themselves upon, and another to get cool under; one shingly shore to play over, where they may be shallow, and foolish, and childlike, and another steep shore, under which they can pause, and purify themselves, and get their strength of waves fully together for due occasion.   Rivers in this way are just like wise men, who keep one side of their life for play, and another for work; and can be brilliant, and chattering, and transparent, when they are at ease, and yet take deep counsel on the other side when they set themselves to their main purpose.   And rivers are just in this divided, also, like

wicked and good men: the good rivers have serviceable deep places all along their banks, that ships can sail in; but the wicked rivers go scooping irregularly under their banks until they get full of strangling eddies, which no boat can row over without being twisted against the rocks; and pools like wells, which no one can get out of but the water-kelpie that lives at the bottom; but, wicked or good, the rivers all agree in having two kinds of sides. Now the natural way in which a village stone-mason therefore throws a bridge over a strong stream is, of course, to build a great door to let the cat through, and little doors to let the kittens through; a great arch for the great current, to give it room in flood time, and little arches for the little currents along the shallow shore. This, even without any prudential respect for the floods of the great current, he would do in simple economy of work and stone; for the smaller your arches are, the less material you want on their flanks. Two arches over the same span of river, supposing the butments are at the same depth, are cheaper than one, and that by a great deal; so that, where the current is shallow, the village mason makes his arches many and low: as the water gets deeper, and it becomes troublesome to build his piers up from the bottom, he throws his arches wider; at last he comes to the deep stream, and, as he cannot build at the bottom of that, he throws his largest arch over it with a leap, and with another little one or so gains the opposite shore. Of course as arches are wider they must be higher, or they will not stand; so the roadway must rise as the arches widen. And thus we have the general type of bridge, with its highest and widest arch towards one side, and a train of minor arches running over the flat shore on the other: usually a steep bank at the river-side next the large arch; always, of course, a flat shore on the side of the small ones: and the bend of the river assuredly concave towards this flat, cutting round, with a sweep into the steep bank; or, if there is no steep bank, still assuredly cutting into the shore at the steep end of the bridge.

Now this kind of bridge, sympathising, as it does, with the spirit of the river, and marking the nature of the thing it has to deal with and conquer, is the ideal of a bridge; and all endeavours to do the thing in a grand engineer's manner, with a level roadway and equal arches, are barbarous; not only because all monotonous forms are ugly in themselves, but because the mind perceives at once that there has been cost uselessly thrown away for the sake of formality.*

204. Well, to return to our continuity. We see that the Turnerian bridge in Fig. 32 is of the absolutely perfect type, and is still farther interesting by having its main arch crowned by a watch-tower. But as I want you to note especially what perhaps was not the case in the real bridge, but is entirely Turner's doing, you will find that though the arches diminish gradually, not one is *regularly* diminished—they are all of different shapes and sizes: you cannot see this clearly in Fig. 32, but in the larger diagram, Fig. 34, opposite, you will with ease. This is indeed also part of the ideal of a bridge, because the lateral currents near the shore are of course irregular in size, and a simple

---

* The cost of art in getting a bridge level is *always* lost, for you must get up to the height of the central arch at any rate, and you only can make the whole bridge level by putting the hill farther back, and pretending to have got rid of it when you have not, but have only wasted money in building an unnecessary embankment. Of course, the bridge should not be difficultly or dangerously steep, but the necessary slope, whatever it may be, should be in the bridge itself, as far as the bridge can take it, and not pushed aside into the approach, as in our Waterloo road; the only rational excuse for doing which is that when the slope must be long it is inconvenient to put on a drag at the top of the bridge, and that any restiveness of the horse is more dangerous on the bridge than on the embankment. To this I answer: first, it is not more dangerous in reality, though it looks so, for the bridge is always guarded by an effective parapet, but the embankment is sure to have no parapet, or only a useless rail; and secondly, that it is better to have the slope on the bridge and make the roadway wide in proportion, so as to be quite safe, because a little waste of space on the river is no loss, but your wide embankment at the side loses good ground; and so my picturesque bridges are right as well as beautiful, and I hope to see them built again some day instead of the frightful straight-backed things which we fancy are fine, and accept from the pontifical rigidities of the engineering mind.

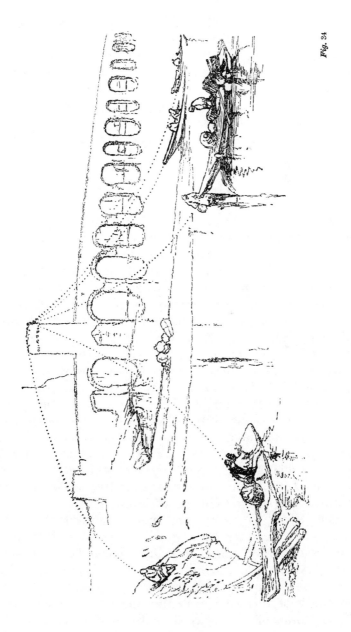

Fig. 34

builder would naturally vary his arches accordingly; and also, if the bottom was rocky, build his piers where the rocks came. But it is not as a part of bridge ideal, but as a necessity of all noble composition, that this irregularity is introduced by Turner. It at once raises the object thus treated from the lower or vulgar unity of rigid law to the greater unity of clouds, and waves, and trees, and human souls, each different, each obedient, and each in harmonious service.

4. THE LAW OF CURVATURE.

205. There is, however, another point to be noticed in this bridge of Turner's. Not only does it slope away unequally at its sides, but it slopes in a gradual though very subtle curve. And if you substitute a straight line for this curve (drawing one with a rule from the base of the tower on each side to the ends of the bridge, in Fig. 34, and effacing the curve), you will instantly see that the design has suffered grievously. You may ascertain, by experiment, that all beautiful objects whatsoever are thus terminated by delicately curved lines, except where the straight line is indispensable to their use or stability; and that when a complete system of straight lines, throughout the form, is necessary to that stability, as in crystals, the beauty, if any exists, is in colour and transparency, not in form. Cut out the shape of any crystal you like, in white wax or wood, and put it beside a white lily, and you will feel the force of the curvature in its purity, irrespective of added colour, or other interfering elements of beauty.

206. Well, as curves are more beautiful than straight lines, it is necessary to a good composition that its continuities of object, mass, or colour should be, if possible, in curves, rather than straight lines or angular ones. Perhaps one of the simplest and prettiest examples of a graceful continuity of this kind is in the line traced at any moment by the corks of a net as it is being drawn: nearly every

person is more or less attracted by the beauty of the dotted line. Now, it is almost always possible, not only to secure such a continuity in the arrangement or boundaries of objects which, like these bridge arches or the corks of the net, are actually connected with each other, but—and this is a still more noble and interesting kind of continuity—among features which appear at first entirely separate. Thus the

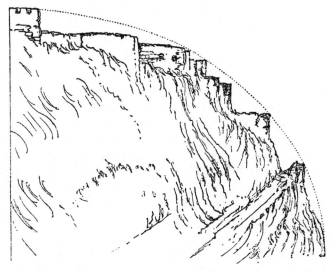

Fig. 35

towers of Ehrenbreitstein, on the left, in Fig. 32, appear at first independent of each other; but when I give their profile, on a larger scale, Fig. 35, the reader may easily perceive that there is a subtle cadence and harmony among them. The reason of this is, that they are all bounded by one grand curve, traced by the dotted line; out of the seven towers, four precisely touch this curve, the others only falling back from it here and there to keep the eye from discovering it too easily.

207. And it is not only always possible to obtain continuities of this kind: it is, in drawing large forest or

mountain forms, essential to truth.   The towers of Ehrenbreitstein might or might not in reality fall into such a
curve, but assuredly the basalt rock on which they stand
did; for all mountain forms not cloven into absolute pre-
cipice, nor covered by straight slopes of shales, are more
or less governed by these great curves, it being one of the
aims of Nature in all her work to produce them.   The
reader must already know this, if he has been able to
sketch at all among mountains; if not, let him merely
draw for himself, carefully, the outlines of any low hills
accessible to him, where they are tolerably steep, or of
the woods which grow on them.   The steeper shore of the
Thames at Maidenhead, or any of the downs at Brighton
or Dover, or, even nearer, about Croydon (as Addington
Hills), is easily accessible to a Londoner; and he will soon
find not only how constant, but how graceful the curvature is.   Graceful curvature is distinguished from ungraceful
by two characters; first in its moderation, that is to say,
its close approach to straightness in some part of its course; *
and, secondly, by its variation, that is to say, its never re-
maining equal in degree at different parts of its course.

208. This variation is itself twofold in all good curves.

A. There is, first, a steady change through the whole
line, from less to more curvature, or more to less, so that

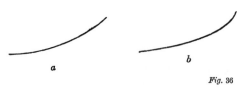

Fig. 36

no part of the line is a
segment of a circle, or
can be drawn by com-
passes in any way what-
ever.   Thus, in Fig. 36,
a is a bad curve be-
cause it is part of a circle, and is therefore monotonous
throughout; but *b* is a good curve, because it continually
changes its direction as it proceeds.

* I cannot waste space here by reprinting what I have said in other
books; but the reader ought, if possible, to refer to the notices of this
part of our subject in *Modern Painters*, vol. iv. chap. xvii.; and *Stones of
Venice*, vol. iii. chap. i. § 8. [Vol. VI. pp. 322 *seq.*, Vol. XI. p. 8.]

The *first* difference between good and bad drawing of tree boughs consists in observance of this fact. Thus, when I put leaves on the line *b*, as in Fig. 37, you can immediately feel the springiness of character dependent on the changefulness of the curve. You may put leaves on the other line for yourself, but

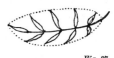

Fig. 37

you will find you cannot make a right tree spray of it. For *all* tree boughs, large or small, as well as all noble

Fig. 38

natural lines whatsoever, agree in this character; and it is a point of primal necessity that your eye should always seize and your hand trace it. Here are two more portions of good curves, with leaves put on them at the extremities instead of the flanks, Fig. 38; and two showing the arrangement of masses of foliage seen a little farther off, Fig. 39, which you may in like manner amuse yourself by turning into segments of circles— you will see with what result. I hope however you have beside you, by this time, many good studies of tree boughs carefully made, in which you may study variations of curvature in their most complicated and lovely forms.*

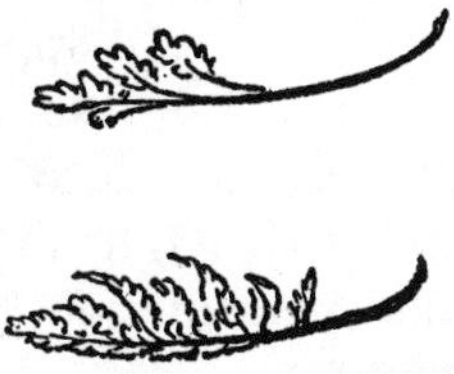

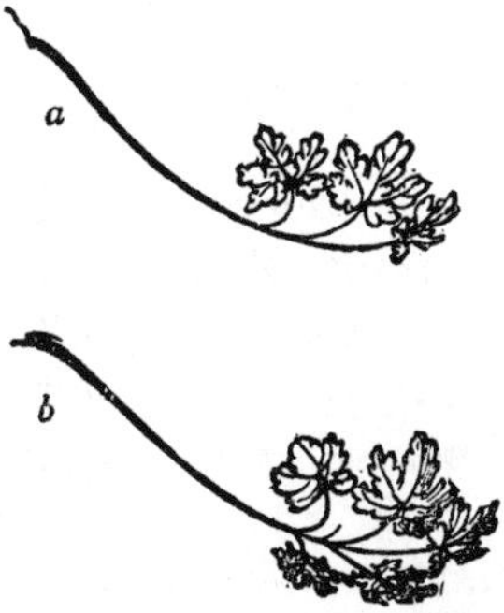

209. B. Not only does every good curve vary in general tendency, but it is modulated, as it proceeds, by myriads of subordinate curves. Thus the outlines of a tree trunk are never as at *a*, Fig. 40, but as at *b*. So also in waves, clouds, and all other nobly

Fig. 39

---

* If you happen to be reading at this part of the book, without having gone through any previous practice, turn back to the sketch of the ramification of stone pine, Fig. 4, p. 41, and examine the curves of its boughs one by one, trying them by the conditions here stated under the heads A and B.

formed masses. Thus another essential difference between good and bad drawing, or good and bad sculpture, depends on the quantity and refinement of minor curvatures carried, by good work, into the great lines. Strictly speaking, however, this is not variation in large curves, but composition of large curves out of small ones; it is an increase in the quantity of the beautiful element, but not a change in its nature.

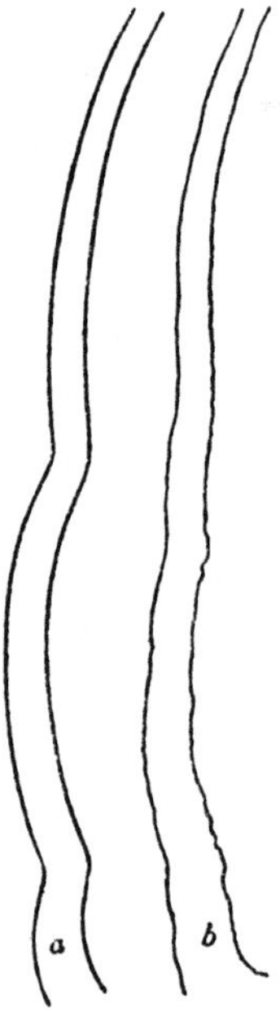

5. THE LAW OF RADIATION.[1]

210. We have hitherto been concerned only with the binding of our various objects into beautiful lines or processions. The next point we have to consider is, how we may unite these lines or processions themselves, so as to make groups of *them*.

Now, there are two kinds of harmonies of lines. One in which, moving more or less side by side, they variously, but evidently with consent, retire from or approach each other, intersect or oppose each other; currents of melody in music, for different voices, thus approach and cross, fall and rise, in harmony; so the waves of the sea, as they approach the shore, flow into one another or cross, but with a great unity through all; and so various lines of composition often flow harmoniously through and across each other in a picture. But the most simple and perfect connexion of lines is by radiation; that is, by their all springing from one point, or closing towards it; and this harmony is often, in Nature almost always, united with the other; as the boughs of trees, though they intersect and play amongst

Fig. 40

---

[1] [On the subject of radiant curvature, compare *Modern Painters*, vol. iv. (Vol. VI. p. 248).]

each other irregularly, indicate by their general tendency their origin from one root.   An essential part of the beauty of all vegetable form is in this radiation; it is seen most simply in a single flower or leaf, as in a convolvulus bell, or chestnut leaf; but more beautifully in the complicated arrangements of the large boughs and sprays.   For a leaf is only a flat piece of radiation; but the tree throws its branches on all sides, and even in every profile view of it, which presents a radiation more or less correspondent to that of its leaves, it is more beautiful, because varied by the freedom of the separate branches.   I believe it has been ascertained that, in all trees, the angle at which, in their leaves, the lateral ribs are set on their central rib is approximately the same at which the branches leave the great stem; and thus each section of the tree would present a kind of magnified view of its own leaf, were it not for the interfering force of gravity on the masses of foliage.   This force in proportion to their age, and the lateral leverage upon them, bears them downwards at

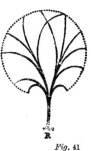

Fig. 41

the extremities, so that, as before noticed, the lower the bough grows on the stem, the more it droops (Fig. 17, p. 93); besides this, nearly all beautiful trees have a tendency to divide into two or more principal masses, which give a prettier and more complicated symmetry than if one stem ran all the way up the centre.   Fig. 41 may thus be considered the simplest type of tree radiation, as opposed to leaf radia-tion.   In this figure, however, all secondary ramification is unrepresented, for the sake of simplicity; but if we take one half of such a tree, and merely give two secondary branches to each main branch (as represented in the general branch structure shown at *b*, Fig. 18, p. 93), we shall have the form Fig. 42.   This I consider the perfect general type of tree structure; and it is curiously connected with certain forms of Greek, Byzantine, and Gothic ornamentation, into the discussion of which, however, we must not enter here.

It will be observed, that both in Figs. 41 and 42 all the branches so spring from the main stem as very nearly to suggest their united radiation from the root R. This is by no means universally the case; but if the branches do not

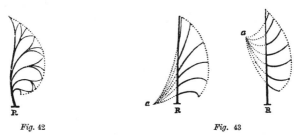

Fig. 42   Fig. 43

bend towards a point in the root, they at least converge to some point or other. In the examples in Fig. 43, the mathematical centre of curvature, a, is thus, in one case, on the ground, at some distance from the root, and in the other, near the top of the tree.   Half, only, of each tree is given, for the sake of clearness: Fig. 44 gives both sides of another example, in which the origins of curvature are below the root. As the positions of such points may be varied without end, and as the arrangement of the lines is also farther complicated by the fact of the boughs springing for the most part in a spiral order round the tree, and at proportionate distances, the systems of curvature which regulate the form of vegetation are quite infinite.   Infinite is a word easily said, and easily written, and people do not always mean it when they say it; in this case I *do* mean it: the number of systems is incalculable, and even to furnish anything like a representative number of types, I should have to give several hundreds of figures such as Fig. 44.*

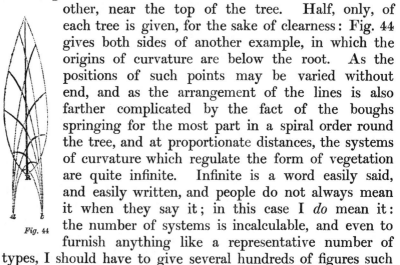

Fig. 44

* The reader, I hope, observes always that every line in these figures is itself one of varying curvature, and cannot be drawn by compasses.

211. Thus far, however, we have only been speaking of the great relations of stem and branches. The forms of the branches themselves are regulated by still more subtle laws, for they occupy an intermediate position between the form of the tree and of the leaf. The leaf has a flat ramification; the tree a completely rounded one; the bough is neither rounded nor flat, but has a structure exactly balanced between the two, in a half-flattened, half-rounded flake, closely resembling in shape one of the thick leaves of an artichoke or the flake of a fir cone; by combination forming the solid mass of the tree, as the leaves compose the artichoke head. I have before pointed out to you the general resemblance of these branch flakes to an extended hand;[1] but they may be more accurately represented by the ribs of a boat. If you can imagine a very broad-headed and flattened boat applied by its keel to the end of a main branch,* as in Fig. 45, the lines which its ribs will take, supposing them out-

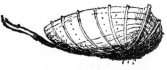

Fig. 45

side of its timbers instead of inside, and the general contour of it, as seen in different directions, from above and below, will give you the closest approximation to the perspectives and foreshortenings of a well-grown branch-flake. Fig. 25 above, p. 115, is an unharmed and unrestrained shoot of healthy young oak; and, if you compare it with Fig. 45, you will understand at once the action of the lines of leafage; the boat only failing as a type in that its ribs are too nearly parallel to each other at the sides, while the bough sends all its ramification well forwards, rounding

---

* I hope the reader understands that these woodcuts are merely facsimiles of the sketches I make at the side of my paper to illustrate my meaning as I write—often sadly scrawled if I want to get on to something else. This one is really a little too careless; but it would take more time and trouble to make a proper drawing of so odd a boat than the matter is worth. It will answer the purpose well enough as it is.

[1] [See above, p. 93.]

to the head, that it may accomplish its part in the outer form of the whole tree, yet always securing the compliance with the great universal law that the branches nearest the root bend most back; and, of course, throwing *some* always back as well as forwards; the appearance of reversed action being much increased, and rendered more striking and beautiful, by perspective. Fig. 25 shows the perspective of such a bough as it is seen from below; Fig. 46 gives rudely the look it would have from above.

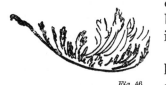

Fig. 46

212. You may suppose, if you have not already discovered, what subtleties of perspective and light and shade are involved in the drawing of these branch-flakes, as you see them in different directions and actions; now raised, now depressed: touched on the edges by the wind, or lifted up and bent back so as to show all the white under surfaces of the leaves shivering in light, as the bottom of a boat rises white with spray at the surge-crest; or drooping in quietness towards the dew of the grass beneath them in windless mornings, or bowed down under oppressive grace of deep-charged snow. Snow time, by the way, is one of the best for practice in the placing of tree masses; but you will only be able to understand them thoroughly by beginning with a single bough and a few leaves placed tolerably even, as in Fig. 38, p. 179. First one with three leaves, a central and two lateral ones, as at *a ;* then with five, as at *b,* and so on; directing your whole attention to the expression, both by contour and light and shade, of the boat-like arrangements, which, in your earlier studies, will have been a good deal confused, partly owing to your inexperience, and partly to the depth of shade, or absolute blackness of mass required in those studies.

213. One thing more remains to be noted, and I will let you out of the wood. You see that in every generally representative figure I have surrounded the radiating branches with a dotted line: such lines do indeed terminate

every vegetable form; and you see that they are themselves beautiful curves, which, according to their flow, and
the width or narrowness of the spaces they enclose, char-
acterise the species of tree or leaf, and express its free or
formal action, its grace of youth or weight of age.   So
that, throughout all the freedom of her wildest foliage,
Nature is resolved on expressing an encompassing limit;
and marking a unity in the whole tree, caused not only
by the rising of its branches from a common root, but by
their joining in one work, and being bound by a common
law.   And having ascertained this, let us turn back for a
moment to a point in leaf structure which, I doubt not,
you must already have observed in your earlier studies,
but which it is well to state here, as connected with the
unity of the branches in the great trees.   You must have
noticed, I should think, that whenever a leaf is compound,
—that is to say, divided into other leaflets which in any
way repeat or imitate the form of the whole leaf,—those
leaflets are not symmetrical, as the whole leaf is, but always
smaller on the side towards the point of the great leaf, so
as to express their subordination to it, and show, even
when they are pulled off, that they are not small independent leaves, but members of one large leaf.[1]

214. Fig. 47, which is a block-plan of a leaf of colum-
bine, without its minor divisions on the edges, will illustrate
the principle clearly.   It is composed of a central large
mass, A, and two lateral ones, of which the one on the
right only is lettered, B.   Each of these masses is again
composed of three others, a central and two lateral ones;
but observe, the minor one, a of A, is balanced equally
by its opposite; but the minor b 1 of B is larger than its
opposite b 2.   Again, each of these minor masses is divided
into three; but while the central mass, A of A, is symmetrically divided, the B of B is unsymmetrical, its largest
side-lobe being lowest.   Again, in b 2, the lobe c 1 (its

_____
[1] [On this subject, compare *Modern Painters*, vol. v. pt. iv. ch. iv. § 6.]

lowest lobe in relation to B) is larger than *c* **2**; and so also in *b* **1**. So that universally one lobe of a lateral leaf is always larger than the other, and the smaller lobe is that which is nearer the central mass; the lower leaf, as it were by courtesy, subduing some of its own dignity or power, in the immediate presence of the greater or captain

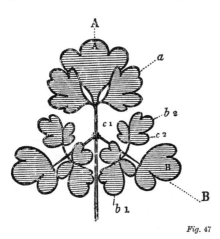

Fig. 47

leaf, and always expressing, therefore, its own subordination and secondary character. This law is carried out even in single leaves. As far as I know, the upper half, towards the point of the spray, is always the smaller; and a slightly different curve, more convex at the springing, is used for the lower side, giving an exquisite variety to the form of the whole leaf; so that one of the chief elements in the beauty of every subordinate leaf throughout the tree is made to depend on its confession of its own lowliness and subjection.

215. And now, if we bring together in one view the principles we have ascertained in trees, we shall find they may be summed under four great laws; and that all perfect * vegetable form is appointed to express these four laws in noble balance of authority.

1. Support from one living root.

2. Radiation, or tendency of force from some one given point, either in the root, or in some stated connection with it.

---

* Imperfect vegetable form I consider that which is in its nature dependent, as in runners and climbers; or which is susceptible of continual injury without materially losing the power of giving pleasure by its aspect, as in the case of the smaller grasses. I have not, of course, space here to explain these minor distinctions, but the laws above stated apply to all the more important trees and shrubs likely to be familiar to the student.

3. Liberty of each bough to seek its own livelihood and happiness according to its needs, by irregularities of action both in its play and its work, either stretching out to get its required nourishment from light and rain, by finding some sufficient breathing-place among the other branches, or knotting and gathering itself up to get strength for any load which its fruitful blossoms may lay upon it, and for any stress of its storm-tossed luxuriance of leaves; or playing hither and thither as the fitful sunshine may tempt its young shoots, in their undecided states of mind about their future life.

4. Imperative requirement of each bough to stop within certain limits, expressive of its kindly fellowship and fraternity with the boughs in its neighbourhood; and to work with them according to its power, magnitude, and state of health, to bring out the general perfectness of the great curve, and circumferent stateliness of the whole tree.

216. I think I may leave you, unhelped, to work out the moral analogies of these laws; you may, perhaps, however, be a little puzzled to see the meaning of the second one. It typically expresses that healthy human actions should spring radiantly (like rays) from some single heart motive; the most beautiful systems of action taking place when this motive lies at the root of the whole life, and the action is clearly seen to proceed from it; while also many beautiful secondary systems of action taking place from motives not so deep or central, but in some beautiful subordinate connection with the central or life motive.

The other laws, if you think over them, you will find equally significative; and as you draw trees more and more in their various states of health and hardship, you will be every day more struck by the beauty of the types they present of the truths most essential for mankind to know; *

* There is a very tender lesson of this kind in the shadows of leaves upon the ground; shadows which are the most likely of all to attract attention, by their pretty play and change. If you examine them, you will find that the shadows do not take the forms of the leaves, but that, through each interstice,

and you will see what this vegetation of the earth, which is necessary to our life, first, as purifying the air for us and then as food, and just as necessary to our joy in all places of the earth,—what these trees and leaves, I say, are meant to teach us as we contemplate them, and read or hear their lovely language, written or spoken for us, not in frightful black letters nor in dull sentences, but in fair green and shadowy shapes of waving words, and blossomed brightness of odoriferous wit, and sweet whispers of unintrusive wisdom, and playful morality.

217. Well, I am sorry myself to leave the wood, whatever my reader may be; but leave it we must, or we shall compose no more pictures to-day.

This law of radiation, then, enforcing unison of action in arising from, or proceeding to, some given point, is perhaps, of all principles of composition, the most influential in producing the beauty of groups of form. Other laws make them forcible or interesting, but this generally is chief in rendering them beautiful. In the arrangement of masses in pictures, it is constantly obeyed by the great composers; but, like the law of principality, with careful concealment of its imperativeness, the point to which the lines of main curvature are directed being very often far away out of the picture. Sometimes, however, a system of curves will be employed definitely to exalt, by their concurrence, the value of some leading object, and then the law becomes traceable enough.

218. In the instance before us, the principal object being,

the light falls, at a little distance, in the form of a round or oval spot; that is to say, it produces the image of the sun itself, cast either vertically or obliquely, in circle or ellipse according to the slope of the ground. Of course the sun's rays produce the same effect, when they fall through any small aperture: but the openings between leaves are the only ones likely to show it to an ordinary observer, or to attract his attention to it by its frequency, and lead him to think what this type may signify respecting the greater Sun; and how it may show us that, even when the opening through which the earth receives light is too small to let us see the Sun Himself, the ray of light that enters, if it comes straight from Him, will still bear with it His image.

as we have seen, the tower on the bridge, Turner has determined that his system of curvature should have its origin in the top of this tower. The diagram Fig. 34, p. 175, compared with Fig. 32, p. 166, will show how this is done. One curve joins the two towers, and is continued by the back of the figure sitting on the bank into the piece of bent timber. This is a limiting curve of great importance, and Turner has drawn a considerable part of it with the edge of the timber very carefully, and then led the eye up to the sitting girl by some white spots and indications of a ledge in the bank; then the passage to the tops of the towers cannot be missed.

219. The next curve is begun and drawn carefully for half an inch of its course by the rudder; it is then taken up by the basket and the heads of the figures, and leads accurately to the tower angle. The gunwales of both the boats begin the next two curves, which meet in the same point; and all are centralised by the long reflection which continues the vertical lines.

220. Subordinated to this first system of curves there is another, begun by the small crossing bar of wood inserted in the angle behind the rudder; continued by the bottom of the bank on which the figure sits, interrupted forcibly beyond it,* but taken up again by the water-line leading to the bridge foot, and passing on in delicate shadows under the arches, not easily shown in so rude a diagram, towards the other extremity of the bridge. This is a most important curve, indicating that the force and sweep of the river have indeed been in old times under the large arches; while the antiquity of the bridge is told us by a long tongue of land, either of carted rubbish, or washed down by some minor

---

* In the smaller figure (32), it will be seen that this interruption is caused by a cart coming down to the water's edge; and this object is serviceable as beginning another system of curves leading out of the picture on the right, but so obscurely drawn as not to be easily represented in outline. As it is unnecessary to the explanation of our point here, it has been omitted in the larger diagram, the direction of the curve it begins being indicated by the dashes only.

stream, which has interrupted this curve, and is now used as a landing-place for the boats, and for embarkation of merchandise, of which some bales and bundles are laid in a heap, immediately beneath the great tower. A common composer would have put these bales to one side or the other, but Turner knows better; he uses them as a foundation for his tower, adding to its importance precisely as the sculptured base adorns a pillar; and he farther increases the aspect of its height by throwing the reflection of it far down in the nearer water. All the great composers have this same feeling about sustaining their vertical masses: you will constantly find Prout using the artifice most dexterously (see, for instance, the figure with the wheelbarrow under the great tower, in the sketch of St. Nicholas, at Prague, and the white group of figures under the tower in the sketch of Augsburg *); and Veronese, Titian, and Tintoret continually put their principal figures at bases of pillars. Turner found out their secret very early, the most prominent instance of his composition on this principle being the drawing of Turin from the Superga, in Hakewill's Italy.[1] I chose Fig. 20, already given to illustrate foliage drawing, chiefly because, being another instance of precisely the same arrangement, it will serve to convince you of its being intentional. There, the vertical, formed by the larger tree, is continued by the figure of the farmer, and that of one of the smaller trees by his stick. The lines of the interior mass of the bushes radiate, under the law of radiation, from a point behind the farmer's head; but their outline curves are carried on and repeated, under the law of continuity, by the curves of the dog and boy—by the way, note the remarkable instance in these of the use of darkest lines towards the light—all more or less guiding the eye up to the right, in order to bring it finally to the Keep of Windsor, which is the central object

* Both in the *Sketches in Flanders and Germany.*

---

[1] [No. 17 in Ruskin's *Notes on his Drawings by Turner* (Vol. XIII. p. 423). The drawing is reproduced in Vol. XVI. (Plate vi.).]

of the picture, as the bridge tower is in the Coblentz. The wall on which the boy climbs answers the purpose of contrasting, both in direction and character, with these greater curves; thus corresponding as nearly as possible to the minor tongue of land in the Coblentz. This, however, introduces us to another law, which we must consider separately.

6. THE LAW OF CONTRAST.

221. Of course the character of everything is best manifested by Contrast. Rest can only be enjoyed after labour; sound to be heard clearly, must rise out of silence; light is exhibited by darkness, darkness by light; and so on in all things. Now in art every colour has an opponent colour, which, if brought near it, will relieve it more completely than any other; so, also, every form and line may be made more striking to the eye by an opponent form or line near them; a curved line is set off by a straight one, a massy form by a slight one, and so on; and in all good work nearly double the value, which any given colour or form would have uncombined, is given to each by contrast.*

In this case again, however, a too manifest use of the artifice vulgarises a picture. Great painters do not commonly, or very visibly, admit violent contrast. They introduce it by stealth, and with intermediate links of tender change; allowing, indeed, the opposition to tell upon the mind as a surprise, but not as a shock.†

222. Thus in the rock of Ehrenbreitstein, Fig. 35, the main current of the lines being downwards, in a convex

---

* If you happen to meet with the plate of Dürer's representing a coat-of-arms with a skull in the shield,[1] note the value given to the concave curves and sharp point of the helmet by the convex leafage carried round it in front; and the use of the blank white part of the shield in opposing the rich folds of the dress.

† Turner hardly ever, as far as I remember, allows a strong light to oppose a full dark, without some intervening tint. His suns never set behind dark mountains without a film of cloud above the mountain's edge.

---

[1] [For this plate, see *Stones of Venice*, vol. iii. (Vol. XI. p. 172).]

swell, they are suddenly stopped at the lowest tower by a counter series of beds, directed nearly straight across them. This adverse force sets off and relieves the great curvature, but it is reconciled to it by a series of radiating lines below, which at first sympathise with the oblique bar, then gradually get steeper, till they meet and join in the fall of the great curve. No passage, however intentionally monotonous, is ever introduced by a good artist without *some* slight counter current of this kind; so much, indeed, do the great composers feel the necessity of it, that they will even do things purposely ill or unsatisfactorily, in order to give greater value to their well-doing in other places. In a skilful poet's versification the so-called bad or inferior lines are not inferior because he could not do them better, but because he feels that if all were equally weighty, there would be no real sense of weight anywhere; if all were equally melodious, the melody itself would be fatiguing; and he purposely introduces the labouring or discordant verse, that the full ring may be felt in his main sentence, and the finished sweetness in his chosen rhythm.*   And continually in painting, inferior artists destroy their work by giving too much of all that they think is good, while the great painter gives just enough to be enjoyed, and passes to an opposite kind of enjoyment, or to an inferior state of enjoyment: he gives a passage of rich, involved, exquisitely wrought colour, then passes away into slight, and pale, and simple colour; he paints for a minute or two with intense decision, then suddenly becomes, as the spectator thinks, slovenly; but he is not slovenly: you could not have *taken* any more decision from him just then; you have had as much as is good for you: he paints over a

---

* " A prudent chief not always must display
His powers in equal ranks and fair array,
But with the occasion and the place comply,
Conceal his force; nay, seem sometimes to fly.
Those oft are stratagems which errors seem,
Nor is it Homer nods, but we that dream."
Essay on Criticism [i. 172–177].

great space of his picture forms of the most rounded and
melting tenderness, and suddenly, as you think by a freak,
gives you a bit as jagged and sharp as a leafless black-
thorn. Perhaps the most exquisite piece of subtle contrast
in the world of painting is the arrow point, laid sharp
against the white side and among the flowing hair of Correggio's Antiope.[1] It is quite singular how very little contrast will sometimes serve to make an entire group of forms
interesting which would otherwise have been valueless.
There is a good deal of picturesque material, for instance,

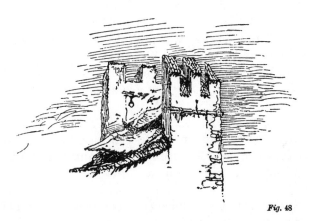

Fig. 48

in this top of an old tower, Fig. 48, tiles and stones and
sloping roof not disagreeably mingled; but all would have
been unsatisfactory if there had not happened to be that
iron ring on the inner wall, which by its vigorous black
circular line precisely opposes all the square and angular
characters of the battlements and roof. Draw the tower
without the ring, and see what a difference it will make.

223. One of the most important applications of the law
of contrast is in association with the law of continuity,
causing an unexpected but gentle break in a continuous
series. This artifice is perpetual in music, and perpetual

---

[1] [For other references to this picture, see Vol. V. p. 93 *n*, (*Modern Painters*,
vol. iii.), and Vol. XII. p. 472.]

also in good illumination; the way in which little surprises of change are prepared in any current borders, or chains of ornamental design, being one of the most subtle characteristics of the work of the good periods. We take, for instance, a bar of ornament between two written columns of an early fourteenth century MS., and at the first glance we suppose it to be quite monotonous all the way up, composed of a winding tendril, with alternately a blue leaf and a scarlet bud. Presently, however, we see that, in order to observe the law of principality, there is one large scarlet leaf instead of a bud, nearly half-way up, which forms a centre to the whole rod; and when we begin to examine the order of the leaves, we find it varied carefully. Let A stand for scarlet bud, *b* for blue leaf, *c* for two blue leaves on one stalk, *s* for a stalk without a leaf, and R for the large red leaf. Then, counting from the ground, the order begins as follows:

b, *b*, A; *b*, *s*, *b*, A; *b*, *b*, A; *b*, *b*, A; and we think we shall have two *b*'s and an A all the way, when suddenly it becomes *b*, A; *b*, R; *b*, A; *b*, A; *b*, A; and we think we are going to have *b*, A continued; but no: here it becomes *b*, *s*; *b*, *s*; *b*, A; *b*, *s*; *b*, *s*; *c*, *s*; *b*, *s*; *b*, *s*; and we think we are surely going to have *b*, *s* continued, but behold it runs away to the end with a quick *b*, *b*, A; *b*, *b*, *b*, *b*!* Very often, however, the designer is satisfied with *one* surprise, but I never saw a good illuminated border without one at least; and no series of any kind was ever introduced by a great composer in a painting without a snap somewhere. There is a pretty one in Turner's drawing of Rome with the large balustrade for a foreground in the Hakewill's Italy series:[1] the single baluster struck out of the line, and showing the street below through the gap, simply makes

---

* I am describing from an MS., *circa* 1300, of Gregory's Decretalia, in my own possession.

---

[1] [The plate referred to is "Rome from the Farnese Gardens:" No. x. in *A Picturesque Tour of Italy, from Drawings made in* 1816–1817. By James Hakewill, Architect. 1820.]

the whole composition right, when otherwise it would have been stiff and absurd.

224. If you look back to Fig. 48 you will see, in the arrangement of the battlements, a simple instance of the use of such variation. The whole top of the tower, though actually three sides of a square, strikes the eye as a continuous series of five masses. The first two, on the left, somewhat square and blank, then the next two higher and richer, the tiles being seen on their slopes. Both these groups being couples, there is enough monotony in the series to make a change pleasant; and the last battlement, therefore, is a little higher than the first two,—a little lower than the second two,—and different in shape from either. Hide it with your finger, and see how ugly and formal the other four battlements look.

225. There are in this figure several other simple illustrations of the laws we have been tracing. Thus the whole shape of the walls' mass being square, it is well, still for the sake of contrast, to oppose it not only by the element of curvature, in the ring, and lines of the roof below, but by that of sharpness; hence the pleasure which the eye takes in the projecting point of the roof. Also, because the walls are thick and sturdy, it is well to contrast their strength with weakness; therefore we enjoy the evident decrepitude of this roof as it sinks between them. The whole mass being nearly white, we want a contrasting shadow somewhere; and get it, under our piece of decrepitude. This shade, with the tiles of the wall below, forms another pointed mass, necessary to the first by the law of repetition. Hide this inferior angle with your finger, and see how ugly the other looks. A sense of the law of symmetry, though you might hardly suppose it, has some share in the feeling with which you look at the battlements; there is a certain pleasure in the opposed slopes of their top, on one side down to the left, on the other to the right. Still less would you think the law of radiation had anything to do with the matter: but if you take the extreme point of

the black shadow on the left for a centre, and follow first the low curve of the eaves of the wall, it will lead you, if you continue it, to the point of the tower cornice; follow the second curve, the top of the tiles of the wall, and it will strike the top of the right-hand battlement; then draw a curve from the highest point of the angled battlement on the left, through the points of the roof and its dark echo; and you will see how the whole top of the tower radiates from this lowest dark point. There are other curvatures crossing these main ones, to keep them from being too conspicuous. Follow the curve of the upper roof, it will take you to the top of the highest battlement; and the stones indicated at the right-hand side of the tower are more extended at the bottom, in order to get some less direct expression of sympathy, such as irregular stones may be capable of, with the general flow of the curves from left to right.

226. You may not readily believe, at first, that all these laws are indeed involved in so trifling a piece of composition. But, as you study longer, you will discover that these laws, and many more, are obeyed by the powerful composers in every *touch:* that literally, there is never a dash of their pencil which is not carrying out appointed purposes of this kind in twenty various ways at once; and that there is as much difference, in way of intention and authority, between one of the great composers ruling his colours, and a common painter confused by them, as there is between a general directing the march of an army, and an old lady carried off her feet by a mob.

7. THE LAW OF INTERCHANGE.

227. Closely connected with the law of contrast is a law which enforces the unity of opposite things, by giving to each a portion of the character of the other. If, for instance, you divide a shield into two masses of colour, all

the way down—suppose blue and white, and put a bar, or figure of an animal, partly on one division, partly on the other, you will find it pleasant to the eye if you make the part of the animal blue which comes upon the white half, and white which comes upon the blue half. This is done in heraldry, partly for the sake of perfect intelligibility, but yet more for the sake of delight in interchange of colour, since, in all ornamentation whatever, the practice is continual, in the ages of good design.

228. Sometimes this alternation is merely a reversal of contrasts; as that, after red has been for some time on one side, and blue on the other, red shall pass to blue's side and blue to red's. This kind of alternation takes place simply in four-quartered shields; in more subtle pieces of treatment, a little bit only of each colour is carried into the other, and they are as it were dovetailed together. One of the most curious facts which will impress itself upon you, when you have drawn some time carefully from Nature in light and shade, is the appearance of intentional artifice with which contrasts of this alternate kind are produced by her; the artistry with which she will darken a tree trunk as long as it comes against light sky, and throw sunlight on it precisely at the spot where it comes against a dark hill, and similarly treat all her masses of shade and colour, is so great, that if you only follow her closely, every one who looks at your drawing with attention will think that you have been inventing the most artificially and unnaturally delightful interchanges of shadow that could possibly be devised by human wit.

229. You will find this law of interchange insisted upon at length by Prout in his Lessons on Light and Shade :[1] it seems of all his principles of composition to be the one he is most conscious of; many others he obeys by instinct, but this he formally accepts and forcibly declares.

[1] [For another reference to this book, see above, § 197. In the remarks on Plate I. Prout notes that "in Nos. 6 and 7 (of the figures there given) light and shadow are respectively interchanged by way of contrast, but in similar proportions." He illustrates the same law in the notes on other plates (especially Plate VI.).]

The typical purpose of the law of interchange is, of course, to teach us how opposite natures may be helped and strengthened by receiving each, as far as they can, some impress or reflection, or imparted power, from the other.

8. THE LAW OF CONSISTENCY.

230. It is to be remembered, in the next place, that while contrast exhibits the *characters* of things, it very often neutralises or paralyses their *power*. A number of white things may be shown to be clearly white by opposition of a black thing, but if we want the full power of their gathered light, the black thing may be seriously in our way. Thus, while contrast displays things, it is unity and sympathy which employ them, concentrating the power of several into a mass. And, not in art merely, but in all the affairs of life, the wisdom of man is continually called upon to reconcile these opposite methods of exhibiting, or using, the materials in his power. By change he gives them pleasantness, and by consistency value; by change he is refreshed, and by perseverance strengthened.

231. Hence many compositions address themselves to the spectator by aggregate force of colour or line, more than by contrasts of either; many noble pictures are painted almost exclusively in various tones of red, or grey, or gold, so as to be instantly striking by their breadth of flush, or glow, or tender coldness, these qualities being exhibited only by slight and subtle use of contrast. Similarly as to form; some compositions associate massive and rugged forms, others slight and graceful ones, each with few interruptions by lines of contrary character. And, in general, such compositions possess higher sublimity than those which are more mingled in their elements. They tell a special tale, and summon a definite state of feeling, while the grand compositions merely please the eye.

232. This unity or breadth of character generally attaches

most to the works of the greatest men; their separate pictures have all separate aims. We have not, in each, grey colour set against sombre, and sharp forms against soft, and loud passages against low: but we have the bright picture, with its delicate sadness; the sombre picture, with its single ray of relief; the stern picture, with only one tender group of lines; the soft and calm picture, with only one rock angle at its flank; and so on. Hence the variety of their work, as well as its impressiveness. The principal bearing of this law, however, is on the separate masses or divisions of a picture: the character of the whole composition may be broken or various, if we please, but there must certainly be a tendency to consistent assemblage in its divisions. As an army may act on several points at once, but can only act effectually by having somewhere formed and regular masses, and not wholly by skirmishers; so a picture may be various in its tendencies, but must be somewhere united and coherent in its masses. Good composers are always associating their colours in great groups; binding their forms together by encompassing lines, and securing, by various dexterities of expedient, what they themselves call "breadth": that is to say, a large gathering of each kind of thing into one place; light being gathered to light, darkness to darkness, and colour to colour. If, however, this be done by introducing false lights or false colours, it is absurd and monstrous; the skill of a painter consists in obtaining breadth by rational arrangement of his objects, not by forced or wanton treatment of them. It is an easy matter to paint one thing all white, and another all black or brown; but not an easy matter to assemble all the circumstances which will naturally produce white in one place, and brown in another. Generally speaking, however, breadth will result in sufficient degree from fidelity of study: Nature is always broad; and if you paint her colours in true relations, you will paint them in majestic masses. If you find your work look broken and scattered, it is, in all probability, not only ill composed, but untrue.

233. The opposite quality to breadth, that of division or scattering of light and colour, has a certain contrasting charm, and is occasionally introduced with exquisite effect by good composers.* Still it is never the mere scattering, but the order discernible through this scattering, which is the real source of pleasure; not the mere multitude, but the constellation of multitude. The broken lights in the work of a good painter wander like flocks upon the hills, not unshepherded, speaking of life and peace: the broken lights of a bad painter fall like hailstones, and are capable only of mischief, leaving it to be wished they were also of dissolution.

9. THE LAW OF HARMONY.

234. This last law is not, strictly speaking, so much one of composition as of truth, but it must guide composition, and is properly, therefore, to be stated in this place.

Good drawing is, as we have seen, an *abstract* of natural facts; you cannot represent all that you would, but must continually be falling short, whether you will or no, of the force, or quantity, of Nature. Now, suppose that your means and time do not admit of your giving the depth of colour in the scene, and that you are obliged to paint it paler. If you paint all the colours proportionately paler, as if an equal quantity of tint had been washed away from each of them, you still obtain a harmonious, though not an equally forcible, statement of natural fact. But if you take away the colours unequally, and leave some tints nearly as deep as they are in Nature, while others are much subdued, you have no longer a true statement. You

---

* One of the most wonderful compositions of Tintoret in Venice is little more than a field of subdued crimson, spotted with flakes of scattered gold.[1] The upper clouds in the most beautiful skies owe great part of their power to infinitude of division; order being marked through this division.

[1] ["The Circumcision" in the Scuola di San Rocco; see Vol. XI. p. 409.]

cannot say to the observer, "Fancy all those colours a little deeper, and you will have the actual fact." However he adds in imagination, or takes away, something is sure to be still wrong. The picture is out of harmony.

235. It will happen, however, much more frequently, that you have to darken the whole system of colours, than to make them paler. You remember, in your first studies of colour from Nature,[1] you were to leave the passages of light which were too bright to be imitated, as white paper. But, in completing the picture, it becomes necessary to put colour into them; and then the other colours must be made darker, in some fixed relation to them. If you deepen all proportionately, though the whole scene is darker than reality, it is only as if you were looking at the reality in a lower light: but if, while you darken some of the tints, you leave others undarkened, the picture is out of harmony, and will not give the impression of truth.

236. It is not, indeed, possible to deepen *all* the colours so much as to relieve the lights in their natural degree, you would merely sink most of your colours, if you tried to do so, into a broad mass of blackness: but it is quite possible to lower them harmoniously, and yet more in some parts of the picture than in others, so as to allow you to show the light you want in a visible relief. In well-harmonised pictures this is done by gradually deepening the tone of the picture towards the lighter parts of it, without materially lowering it in the very dark parts; the tendency in such pictures being, of course, to include large masses of middle tints. But the principal point to be observed in doing this, is to deepen the individual tints without dirtying or obscuring them. It is easy to lower the tone of the picture by washing it over with grey or brown; and easy to see the effect of the landscape, when its colours are thus universally polluted with black, by using the black convex mirror, one of the most pestilent inventions for falsifying Nature and degrading art which ever was put into

----

[1] [Above, p. 145.]

an artist's hand.* For the thing required is not to darken
pale yellow by mixing grey with it, but to deepen the pure
yellow; not to darken crimson by mixing black with it,
but by making it deeper and richer crimson: and thus the
required effect could only be seen in Nature, if you had
pieces of glass of the colour of every object in your landscape, and of every minor hue that made up those colours,
and then could see the real landscape through this deep
gorgeousness of the varied glass. You cannot do this with
glass, but you can do it for yourself as you work; that is
to say, you can put deep blue for pale blue, deep gold for
pale gold, and so on, in the proportion you need; and then
you may paint as forcibly as you choose, but your work
will still be in the manner of Titian, not of Caravaggio or
Spagnoletto,[1] or any other of the black slaves of painting.†

237. Supposing those scales of colour, which I told you
to prepare in order to show you the relations of colour to
grey, were quite accurately made, and numerous enough,
you would have nothing more to do, in order to obtain a
deeper tone in any given mass of colour, than to substitute
for each of its hues the hue as many degrees deeper in the
scale as you wanted, that is to say, if you wanted to
deepen the whole two degrees, substituting for the yellow
No. 5 the yellow No. 7, and for the red No. 9 the red
No. 11, and so on: but the hues of any object in Nature
are far too numerous, and their degrees too subtle, to
admit of so mechanical a process. Still, you may see the
principle of the whole matter clearly by taking a group of

---

* I fully believe that the strange grey gloom, accompanied by considerable power of effect, which prevails in modern French art, must be owing
to the use of this mischievous instrument; the French landscape always
gives me the idea of Nature seen carelessly in the dark mirror, and painted
coarsely, but scientifically, through the veil of its perversion.

† Various other parts of this subject are entered into, especially in their
bearing on the ideal of painting, in *Modern Painters,* vol. iv. chap. iii.

---

[1] [For other references in a similar sense to Caravaggio, see Vol. X. p. 223 ; to
Spagnoletto, Vol. IV. p. 137.]

colours out of your scale, arranging them prettily, and then washing them all over with grey: that represents the treatment of Nature by the black mirror.   Then arrange the same group of colours, with the tints five or six degrees deeper in the scale; and that will represent the treatment of Nature by Titian.

238. You can only, however, feel your way fully to the right of the thing by working from Nature.

The best subject on which to begin a piece of study of this kind is a good thick tree trunk, seen against blue sky with some white clouds in it.   Paint the clouds in true and tenderly gradated white; then give the sky a bold full blue, bringing them well out; then paint the trunk and leaves grandly dark against all, but in such glowing dark green and brown as you see they will bear.   Afterwards proceed to more complicated studies, matching the colours carefully first by your old method; then deepening each colour with its own tint, and being careful, above all things, to keep truth of equal change when the colours are connected with each other, as in dark and light sides of the same object.   Much more aspect and sense of harmony are gained by the precision with which you observe the relation of colours in dark sides and light sides, and the influence of modifying reflections, than by mere accuracy of added depth in independent colours.

239. This harmony of tone, as it is generally called, is the most important of those which the artist has to regard. But there are all kinds of harmonies in a picture, according to its mode of production.   There is even a harmony of touch.   If you paint one part of it very rapidly and forcibly, and another part slowly and delicately, each division of the picture may be right separately, but they will not agree together: the whole will be effectless and valueless, out of harmony.   Similarly, if you paint one part of it by a yellow light in a warm day, and another by a grey light in a cold day, though both may have been sunlight, and both may be well toned, and have their relative

shadows truly cast, neither will look like light; they will destroy each other's power, by being out of harmony. These are only broad and definable instances of discordance; but there is an extent of harmony in all good work much too subtle for definition; depending on the draughtsman's carrying everything he draws up to just the balancing and harmonious point, in finish, and colour, and depth of tone, and intensity of moral feeling, and style of touch, all considered at once; and never allowing himself to lean too emphatically on detached parts, or exalt one thing at the expense of another, or feel acutely in one place and coldly in another. If you have got some of Cruikshank's etchings, you will be able, I think, to feel the nature of harmonious treatment in a simple kind, by comparing them with any of Richter's illustrations to the numerous German story-books lately published at Christmas,[1] with all the German stories spoiled. Cruikshank's work is often incomplete in character and poor in incident, but, as drawing, it is *perfect* in harmony. The pure and simple effects of daylight which he gets by his thorough mastery of treatment in this respect, are quite unrivalled, as far as I know, by any other work executed with so few touches. His vignettes to Grimm's German stories, already recommended,[2] are the most remarkable in this quality. Richter's illustrations, on the contrary, are of a very high stamp as respects understanding of human character, with infinite playfulness and tenderness of fancy; but, as drawings, they are almost unendurably out of harmony, violent blacks in one place being continually opposed to trenchant white in another; and, as is almost sure to be the case with bad harmonists, the local colour hardly felt anywhere. All German work is apt to be out of harmony, in consequence of its too frequent conditions of affectation, and its wilful refusals of fact; as well as by reason of a feverish kind of excitement, which dwells violently on particular points, and

---

[1] [For Richter, see below, p. 224; for Cruikshank, p. 222.]
[2] [See above, p. 79.]

makes all the lines of thought in the picture to stand on end, as it were, like a cat's fur electrified; while good work is always as quiet as a couchant leopard, and as strong.

240. I have now stated to you all the laws of composition which occur to me as capable of being illustrated or defined; but there are multitudes of others which, in the present state of my knowledge, I cannot define, and others which I never hope to define; and these the most important, and connected with the deepest powers of the art. I hope, when I have thought of them more, to be able to explain some of the laws which relate to nobleness and ignobleness; that ignobleness especially which we commonly call "vulgarity," and which, in its essence, is one of the most curious subjects of inquiry connected with human feeling.[1] Others I never hope to explain, laws of expression, bearing simply on simple matters; but, for that very reason, more influential than any others. These are, from the first, as inexplicable as our bodily sensations are; it being just as impossible, I think, to show, finally, why one succession of musical notes * shall be lofty and pathetic, and such as might have been sung by Casella to Dante,[2] and why another succession is base and ridiculous, and would be fit only for the reasonably good ear of Bottom,[3] as to explain why we like sweetness, and dislike bitterness. The best part of every great work is always

---

* In all the best arrangements of colour, the delight occasioned by their mode of succession is entirely inexplicable, nor can it be reasoned about; we like it just as we like an air in music, but cannot reason any refractory person into liking it, if they do not: and yet there is distinctly a right and a wrong in it, and a good taste and bad taste respecting it, as also in music.

---

[1] [Ruskin returned to the subject in *Modern Painters*, vol. v. pt. ix. ch. vii. ("Of Vulgarity"), and compare Vol. XIV. p. 243.]

[2] [See *Purgatorio*, ii. 107 *seq.*, and Milton's "Sonnet to Henry Lawes":—

"Dante shall give fame leave to set thee higher
Than his Casella, whom he wooed to sing,
Met in the milder shades of Purgatory."]

[3] [*Midsummer Night's Dream*, iv. i. 31.]

inexplicable : it is good because it is good ; and innocently gracious, opening as the green of the earth, or falling as the dew of heaven.

241. But though you cannot explain them, you may always render yourself more and more sensitive to these higher qualities by the discipline which you generally give to your character, and this especially with regard to the choice of incidents ; a kind of composition in some sort easier than the artistical arrangements of lines and colours, but in every sort nobler, because addressed to deeper feelings.

242. For instance, in the " Datur Hora Quieti," the last vignette to Rogers's *Poems*, the plough in the foreground has three purposes.[1]   The first purpose is to meet the stream of sunlight on the river, and make it brighter by opposition ; but any dark object whatever would have done this. Its second purpose is, by its two arms, to repeat the cadence of the group of the two ships, and thus give a greater expression of repose ; but two sitting figures would have done this.   Its third and chief, or pathetic, purpose is, as it lies abandoned in the furrow (the vessels also being moored, and having their sails down), to be a type of human labour closed with the close of day.   The parts of it on which the hand leans are brought most clearly into sight ; and they are the chief dark of the picture, because the tillage of the ground is required of man as a punishment: but they make the soft light of the setting sun brighter, because rest is sweetest after toil.   These thoughts may never occur to us as we glance carelessly at the design ; and yet their undercurrent assuredly affects the feelings, and increases, as the painter meant it should, the impression of melancholy, and of peace.

243. Again, in the " Lancaster Sands," which is one of the plates I have marked as most desirable for your possession,[2] the stream of light which falls from the setting sun on the advancing tide stands similarly in need of some force

---

[1] [Compare *Modern Painters*, vol. i. (Vol. III. p. 265), and vol. v. pt. viii. ch. ii. § 5.]
[2] [See above, p. 75 *n.*   For another reference to the plate, see Vol. XIII. p. 495.]

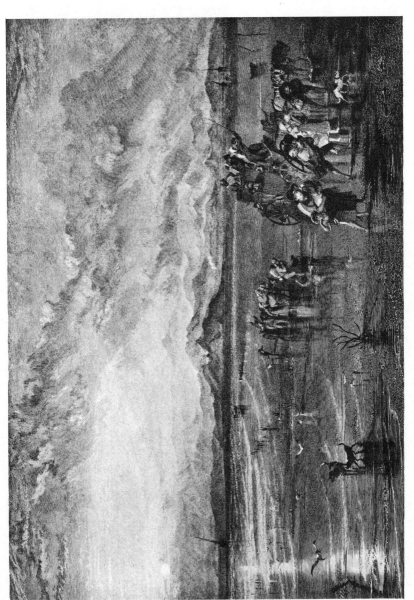

Lancaster Sands (engraving after drawing by Turner)

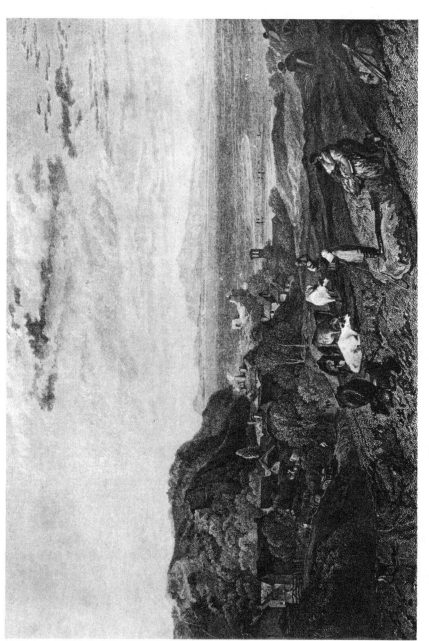

Heysham (engraving after drawing by Turner)

of near object to relieve its brightness. But the incident which Turner has here adopted is the swoop of an angry sea-gull at a dog, who yelps at it, drawing back as the wave rises over his feet, and the bird shrieks within a foot of his face. Its unexpected boldness is a type of the anger of its ocean element, and warns us of the sea's advance just as surely as the abandoned plough told us of the ceased labour of the day.

244. It is not, however, so much in the selection of single incidents of this kind, as in the feeling which regulates the arrangement of the whole subject, that the mind of a great composer is known. A single incident may be suggested by a felicitous chance, as a pretty motto might be for the heading of a chapter. But the great composers so arrange *all* their designs that one incident illustrates another, just as one colour relieves another. Perhaps the "Heysham," of the Yorkshire series,[1] which, as to its locality, may be considered a companion to the last drawing we have spoken of, the "Lancaster Sands," presents as interesting an example as we could find of Turner's feeling in this respect. The subject is a simple north-country village, on the shore of Morecambe Bay; not in the common sense a picturesque village; there are no pretty bow-windows, or red roofs, or rocky steps of entrance to the rustic doors, or quaint gables; nothing but a single street of thatched and chiefly clay-built cottages, ranged in a somewhat monotonous line, the roofs so green with moss that at first we hardly discern the houses from the fields and trees. The village street is closed at the end by a wooden gate, indicating the little traffic there is on the road through it, and giving it something the look of a large farmstead, in which a right of way lies through the yard. The road which leads to this gate is full of ruts, and winds down a bad bit of hill between two broken banks of moor ground, succeeding immediately to the few enclosures which surround the village; they can

[1] [Published in vol. ii. of Whitaker's *Richmondshire*. The drawing was in Ruskin's collection : see *Notes on his Drawings by Turner*, No. 25 (Vol. XIII. p. 429).]

hardly be called gardens: but a decayed fragment or two of fencing fill the gaps in the bank; a clothes-line, with some clothes on it, striped blue and red, and a smock-frock, is stretched between the trunks of some stunted willows; a *very* small haystack and pig-stye being seen at the back of the cottage beyond.   An empty, two-wheeled, lumbering cart, drawn by a pair of horses with huge wooden collars, the driver sitting lazily in the sun, sideways on the leader, is going slowly home along the rough road, it being about country dinner-time.   At the end of the village there is a better house, with three chimneys and a dormer window in its roof, and the roof is of stone shingle instead of thatch, but very rough.   This house is no doubt the clergyman's: there is some smoke from one of its chimneys, none from any other in the village; this smoke is from the lowest chimney at the back, evidently that of the kitchen, and it is rather thick, the fire not having been long lighted.   A few hundred yards from the clergyman's house, nearer the shore, is the church, discernible from the cottages only by its low two-arched belfry, a little neater than one would expect in such a village; perhaps lately built by the Puseyite incumbent:* and beyond the church, close to the sea, are two fragments of a border war-tower, standing on their circular mound, worn on its brow deep into edges and furrows by the feet of the village children.   On the bank of moor, which forms the foreground, are a few cows, the carter's dog barking at a vixenish one: the milkmaid is feeding another, a gentle white one, which turns its head to her, expectant of a handful of fresh hay, which she has brought for it in her blue apron, fastened up round her waist; she stands with her pail on her head, evidently the

* "Puseyism" was unknown in the days when this drawing was made; but the kindly and helpful influences of what may be called ecclesiastical sentiment, which, in a morbidly exaggerated condition, forms one of the principal elements of "Puseyism,"—I use this word regretfully, no other existing which will serve for it,—had been known and felt in our wild northern districts long before.[1]

---

[1] [For Ruskin's dislike of Puseyism, see Vol. XII. pp. 533, 550.]

village coquette, for she has a neat bodice, and pretty striped petticoat under the blue apron, and red stockings. Nearer us, the cowherd, barefooted, stands on a piece of the limestone rock (for the ground is thistly and not pleasurable to bare feet);—whether boy or girl we are not sure: it may be a boy, with a girl's worn-out bonnet on, or a girl with a pair of ragged trowsers on; probably the first, as the old bonnet is evidently useful to keep the sun out of our eyes when we are looking for strayed cows among the moorland hollows, and helps us at present to watch (holding the bonnet's edge down) the quarrel of the vixenish cow with the dog, which, leaning on our long stick, we allow to proceed without any interference. A little to the right the hay is being got in, of which the milkmaid has just taken her apronful to the white cow; but the hay is very thin, and cannot well be raked up because of the rocks; we must glean it like corn, hence the smallness of our stack behind the willows; and a woman is pressing a bundle of it hard together, kneeling against the rock's edge, to carry it safely to the hay-cart without dropping any. Beyond the village is a rocky hill, deep set with brushwood, a square crag or two of limestone emerging here and there, with pleasant turf on their brows, heaved in russet and mossy mounds against the sky, which, clear and calm, and as golden as the moss, stretches down behind it towards the sea. A single cottage just shows its roof over the edge of the hill, looking seawards: perhaps one of the village shepherds is a sea captain now, and may have built it there, that his mother may first see the sails of his ship whenever it runs into the bay. Then under the hill, and beyond the border tower, is the blue sea itself, the waves flowing in over the sand in long curved lines slowly; shadows of cloud, and gleams of shallow water on white sand alternating—miles away; but no sail is visible, not one fisher-boat on the beach, not one dark speck on the quiet horizon. Beyond all are the Cumberland mountains, clear in the sun, with rosy light on all their crags.

245. I should think the reader cannot but feel the kind of harmony there is in this composition; the entire purpose of the painter to give us the impression of wild, yet gentle, country life, monotonous as the succession of the noiseless waves, patient and enduring as the rocks; but peaceful, and full of health and quiet hope, and sanctified by the pure mountain air and baptismal dew of heaven, falling softly between days of toil and nights of innocence.

246. All noble composition of this kind can be reached only by instinct; you cannot set yourself to arrange such a subject; you may see it, and seize it, at all times, but never laboriously invent it. And your power of discerning what is best in expression, among natural subjects, depends wholly on the temper in which you keep your own mind; above all, on your living so much alone as to allow it to become acutely sensitive in its own stillness. The noisy life of modern days is wholly incompatible with any true perception of natural beauty. If you go down into Cumberland by the railroad, live in some frequented hotel, and explore the hills with merry companions, however much you may enjoy your tour or their conversation, depend upon it you will never choose so much as one pictorial subject rightly; you will not see into the depth of any. But take knapsack and stick, walk towards the hills by short day's journeys,—ten or twelve miles a day—taking a week from some starting-place sixty or seventy miles away: sleep at the pretty little wayside inns, or the rough village ones; then take the hills as they tempt you, following glen or shore as your eye glances or your heart guides, wholly scornful of local fame or fashion, and of everything which it is the ordinary traveller's duty to see, or pride to do. Never force yourself to admire anything when you are not in the humour; but never force yourself away from what you feel to be lovely, in search of anything better; and gradually the deeper scenes of the natural world will unfold themselves to you in still increasing fulness of passionate power; and your difficulty will be no more to seek

or to compose subjects, but only to choose one from among the multitude of melodious thoughts with which you will be haunted, thoughts which will of course be noble or original in proportion to your own depth of character and general power of mind; for it is not so much by the consideration you give to any single drawing, as by the previous discipline of your powers of thought, that the character of your composition will be determined. Simplicity of life will make you sensitive to the refinement and modesty of scenery, just as inordinate excitement and pomp of daily life will make you enjoy coarse colours and affected forms. Habits of patient comparison and accurate judgment will make your art precious, as they will make your actions wise; and every increase of noble enthusiasm in your living spirit will be measured by the reflection of its light upon the works of your hands.—Faithfully yours,

J. RUSKIN.

APPENDIX

I

ILLUSTRATIVE NOTES

Note 1, p. 69.—"Principle of the Stereoscope."

247. I am sorry to find a notion current among artists, that they can, in some degree, imitate in a picture the effect of the stereoscope, by confusion of lines. There are indeed one or two artifices by which, as stated in the text, an appearance of retirement or projection may be obtained, so that they partly supply the place of the stereoscopic effect, but they do not imitate that effect. The principle of the human sight is simply this:—by means of our two eyes we literally see everything from two places at once; and, by calculated combination, in the brain, of the facts of form so seen, we arrive at conclusions respecting the distance and shape of the object, which we could not otherwise have reached. But it is just as vain to hope to paint at once the two views of the object as seen from these two places, though only an inch and a half distant from each other, as it would be if they were a mile and a half distant from each other. With the right eye you see one view of a given object, relieved against one part of the distance; with the left eye you see another view of it, relieved against another part of the distance. You may paint whichever of those views you please; you cannot paint both. Hold your finger upright, between you and this page of the book, about six inches from your eyes, and three from the book; shut the right eye, and hide the words "inches from," in the second line above this, with your finger; you will then see "six" on one side of it, and "your," on the other. Now shut the left eye and open the right without moving your finger, and you will see "inches," but not "six." You may paint the finger with "inches" beyond it, or with "six" beyond it, but not with both. And this principle holds for any object and any distance. You might just as well try to paint St. Paul's at once from both ends of London Bridge as to realise any stereoscopic effect in a picture.

Note 2, p. 84.—"Dark Lines turned to the Light."

248. It ought to have been farther observed, that the enclosure of the light by future shadow is by no means the only reason for the dark lines which great masters often thus introduce. It constantly happens that a local colour will show its own darkness most on the light side, by projecting

into and against masses of light in that direction; and then the painter will indicate this future force of the mass by his dark touch. Both the monk's head in Fig. 11 and dog in Fig. 20 are dark towards the light for this reason.

NOTE 3, p. 124.—"SOFTNESS OF REFLECTIONS."

249. I have not quite insisted enough on the extreme care which is necessary in giving the tender evanescence of the edges of the reflections, when the water is in the least agitated; nor on the decision with which you may reverse the object, when the water is quite calm. Most drawing of reflections is at once confused and hard; but Nature's is at once intelligible and tender. Generally, at the edge of the water, you ought not to see where reality ceases and reflection begins; as the image loses itself you ought to keep all its subtle and varied veracities, with the most exquisite softening of its edge. Practise as much as you can from the reflections of ships in calm water, following out all the reversed rigging, and taking, if anything, more pains with the reflection than with the ship.

NOTE 4, p. 126.—"WHERE THE REFLECTION IS DARKEST, YOU WILL SEE THROUGH THE WATER BEST."

250. For this reason it often happens that if the water be shallow, and you are looking steeply down into it, the reflection of objects on the bank will consist simply of pieces of the bottom seen clearly through the water, and relieved by flashes of light, which are the reflection of the sky. Thus you may have to draw the reflected dark shape of a bush: but, inside of that shape, you must not draw the leaves of the bush, but the stones under the water; and, outside of this dark reflection, the blue or white of the sky, with no stones visible.

NOTE 5, p. 127.—"APPROACH STREAMS WITH REVERENCE."

251. I have hardly said anything about waves of torrents or waterfalls, as I do not consider them subjects for beginners to practise upon; but, as many of our younger artists are almost breaking their hearts over them, it may be well to state at once that it is physically impossible to draw a running torrent quite rightly, the lustre of its currents and whiteness of its foam being dependent on intensities of light which art has not at its ·command. This also is to be observed, that most young painters make their defeat certain by attempting to draw running water, which is a lustrous object in rapid motion, without ever trying their strength on a lustrous object standing still. Let them break a coarse green-glass bottle into a great many bits, and try to paint those, with all their undulations and edges of fracture, as they lie still on the table; if they cannot, of course they need not try the rushing crystal and foaming fracture of the stream. If they can manage the glass bottle, let them next buy a fragment or two of yellow fire-opal; it is quite a common and cheap mineral, and presents, as closely as anything can, the milky bloom

and colour of a torrent wave: and if they can conquer the opal, they may at last have some chance with the stream, as far as the stream is in any wise possible. But, as I have just said, the bright parts of it are *not* possible, and ought, as much as may be, to be avoided in choosing subjects. A great deal more may, however, be done than any artist has done yet, in painting the gradual disappearance and lovely colouring of stones seen through clear and calm water.

Students living in towns may make great progress in rock-drawing by frequently and faithfully drawing broken edges of common roofing-slates, of their real size.

NOTE 6, p. 153.—"NATURE'S ECONOMY OF COLOUR."

252. I heard it wisely objected to this statement, the other day, by a young lady, that it was not through economy that Nature did not colour deep down in the flower bells, but because "she had not light enough there to see to paint with." This may be true; but it is certainly not for want of light that, when she is laying the dark spots on a foxglove, she will not use any more purple than she has got already on the bell, but takes out the colour all round the spot, and concentrates it in the middle.

NOTE 7, p. 168.—"THE LAW OF REPETITION."

253. The reader may perhaps recollect a very beautiful picture of Vandyck's, in the Manchester Exhibition,[1] representing three children in court dresses of rich black and red. The law in question was amusingly illustrated, in the lower corner of that picture, by the introduction of two crows, in a similar colour of court dress, having jet black feathers and bright red beaks.

---

254. Since the first edition of this work was published, I have ascertained that there are two series of engravings from the Bible drawings mentioned in the list at p. 76. One of these is inferior to the other, and in many respects false to the drawings; the "Jericho," for instance, in the false series, has common bushes instead of palm trees in the middle distance. The original plates may be had at almost any respectable printseller's; and ordinary impressions, whether of these or any other plates mentioned in the list at p. 75, will be quite as useful as proofs; but, in buying Liber Studiorum, it is always well to get the best impressions that can be had, and if possible impressions of the original plates, published by Turner. In case these are not to be had, the copies which are in course of publication by Mr. Lupton[2] (4 Keppel Street, Russell Square) are good and serviceable; but no others are of any use.[3]

---

[1] [No. 660 in the catalogue: "'Three Children,' lent by Earl de Grey."]
[2] [For whom, see Vol. IX. p. 15 *n*. Lupton dedicated the copies to Ruskin.]
[3] [Note added in ed. 2, 1857.]

I have placed in the hands of Mr. Ward (Working Men's College) some photographs from the etchings made by Turner for the Liber; the original etchings being now unobtainable, except by fortunate accident. I have selected the subjects carefully from my own collection of the etchings; and though some of the more subtle qualities of line are lost in the photographs, the student will find these proofs the best lessons in pen-drawing accessible to him.[1]

---

[1] [The last seven lines of this note were added in ed. 3, 1859. Mr. William Ward, now of 2 Church Terrace, Richmond, Surrey, still supplies prints and photographs after Turner, etc., to illustrate Ruskin's works and teaching.]

II

THINGS TO BE STUDIED

255. THE worst danger by far, to which a solitary student is exposed,
is that of liking things that he should not. It is not so much his difficulties, as his tastes, which he must set himself to conquer: and although,
under the guidance of a master, many works of art may be made instructive, which are only of partial excellence (the good and bad of them
being duly distinguished), his safeguard, as long as he studies alone, will
be in allowing himself to possess only things, in their way, so free from
faults, that nothing he copies in them can seriously mislead him, and to
contemplate only those works of art which he knows to be either perfect
or noble in their errors. I will therefore set down, in clear order, the
names of the masters whom you may safely admire, and a few of the
books which you may safely possess. In these days of cheap illustration,
the danger is always rather of your possessing too much than too little.
It may admit of some question, how far the looking at bad art may set
off and illustrate the characters of the good; but, on the whole, I believe
it is best to live always on quite wholesome food, and that our enjoyment
of it will never be made more acute by feeding[1] on ashes; though it
may be well sometimes to taste the ashes, in order to know the bitterness
of them. Of course the works of the great masters can only be serviceable to the student after he has made considerable progress himself. It
only wastes the time and dulls the feelings of young persons, to drag
them through picture galleries; at least, unless they themselves wish to
look at particular pictures. Generally, young people only care to enter
a picture gallery when there is a chance of getting leave to run a race
to the other end of it; and they had better do that in the garden below.
If, however, they have any real enjoyment of pictures, and want to look
at this one or that, the principal point is never to disturb them in looking
at what interests them, and never to make them look at what does not.
Nothing is of the least use to young people (nor, by the way, of much
use to old ones), but what interests them; and therefore, though it is of
great importance to put nothing but good art into their possession, yet,
when they are passing through great houses or galleries, they should be
allowed to look precisely at what pleases them: if it is not useful to
them as art, it will be in some other way; and the healthiest way in

---

[1] [Ed. 1 reads:—
    ". . . by feeding, however temporarily, on ashes. Of course the
works . . ."]

which art can interest them is when they look at it, not as art, but because it represents something they like in Nature. If a boy has had his heart filled by the life of some great man, and goes up thirstily to a Vandyck portrait of him, to see what he was like, that is the wholesomest way in which he can begin the study of portraiture; if he loves mountains, and dwells on a Turner drawing because he sees in it a likeness to a Yorkshire scar or an Alpine pass, that is the wholesomest way in which he can begin the study of landscape; and if a girl's mind is filled with dreams of angels and saints, and she pauses before an Angelico because she thinks it must surely be like heaven, that is the right way for her to begin the study of religious art.

256. When, however, the student has made some definite progress, and every picture becomes really a guide to him, false or true, in his own work, it is of great importance that he should never look, with even partial admiration, at bad art; and then, if the reader is willing to trust me in the matter, the following advice will be useful to him. In which, with his permission, I will quit the indirect and return to the epistolary address, as being the more convenient.

First, in Galleries of Pictures :

1. You may look, with trust in their being always right, at Titian, Veronese, Tintoret,[1] Giorgione, John Bellini, and Velasquez; the authenticity of the picture being of course established for you by proper authority.

2. You may look with admiration, admitting, however, question of right and wrong,* at Van Eyck, Holbein, Perugino, Francia, Angelico, Leonardo da Vinci, Correggio, Vandyck, Rembrandt, Reynolds, Gainsborough, Turner, and the modern Pre-Raphaelites.† You had better look at no other painters than these, for you run a chance, otherwise, of being led far off the road, or into grievous faults, by some of the other great ones, as Michael Angelo, Raphael, and Rubens; and of being, besides, corrupted in taste by the base ones, as Murillo, Salvator, Claude, Gaspar Poussin, Teniers, and such others. You may look, however, for examples of evil, with safe universality of reprobation, being sure that everything you see is bad, at Domenichino, the Carracci, Bronzino, and the figure pieces of Salvator.[2]

Among those named for study under question, you cannot look too much at, nor grow too enthusiastically fond of, Angelico, Correggio, Reynolds, Turner, and the Pre-Raphaelites; but, if you find yourself getting especially fond of any of the others, leave off looking at them, for

* I do not mean necessarily to imply inferiority of rank in saying that this second class of painters have questionable qualities. The greatest men have often many faults, and sometimes their faults are a part of their greatness; but such men are not, of course, to be looked upon by the student with absolute implicitness of faith.

† Including, under this term, John Lewis, and William Hunt of the Old Watercolour, who, take him all in all, is the best painter of still life, I believe, that ever existed.

---

[1] [But see Two Paths, § 69, and Appendix i., where some qualification is made of the inclusion of Tintoret here.]

[2] [For Ruskin's other references to these painters, see General Index; while the list here may be compared with his classification given in Vol. IV. pp. xxxiv.–xxxv.]

you must be going wrong some way or other. If, for instance, you begin to like Rembrandt or Leonardo especially, you are losing your feeling for colour; if you like Van Eyck or Perugino especially, you must be getting too fond of rigid detail; and if you like Vandyck or Gainsborough especially, you must be too much attracted by gentlemanly flimsiness.

257. Secondly, of published, or otherwise multiplied, art, such as you may be able to get yourself, or to see at private houses or in shops, the works of the following masters are the most desirable, after the Turners, Rembrandts, and Dürers, which I have asked you to get first:

1. SAMUEL PROUT.*

All his published lithographic sketches are of the greatest value,[1] wholly unrivalled in power of composition, and in love and feeling of architectural subject. His somewhat mannered linear execution, though not to be imitated in your own sketches from Nature, may be occasionally copied, for discipline's sake, with great advantage: it will give you a peculiar steadiness of hand, not quickly attainable in any other way; and there is no fear of your getting into any faultful mannerism as long as you carry out the different modes of more delicate study above recommended.

If you are interested in architecture, and wish to make it your chief study, you should draw much from photographs of it; and then from the architecture itself, with the same completion of detail and gradation, only keeping the shadows of due paleness,—in photographs they are always about four times as dark as they ought to be,—and treat buildings with as much care and love as artists do their rock foregrounds, drawing all the moss, and weeds, and stains upon them. But if, without caring to understand architecture, you merely want the picturesque character of it, and to be able to sketch it fast, you cannot do better than take Prout for your exclusive master; only do not think that you are copying Prout by drawing straight lines with dots at the end of them. Get first his *Rhine*,[2] and draw the subjects that have most hills, and least architecture

* The order in which I place these masters does not in the least imply superiority or inferiority. I wrote their names down as they occurred to me; putting Rossetti's last because what I had to say of him was connected with other subjects; and one or another will appear to you great, or be found by you useful, according to the kind of subjects you are studying.

[1] [For a summary of Ruskin's references to Prout, see Introduction to the volume containing *Notes on Prout and Hunt* (Vol. XIV. pp. xxxiv.–xxxv.]
[2] [This was the first series of Prout's foreign drawings. It consisted of twenty-four (increased in a later edition to thirty) lithographs, published in oblong quarto in 1824 by Ackermann, with the title *Illustrations of the Rhine drawn from Nature and on Stone by S. Prout*. For the *Sketches in Flanders and Germany* (about 1833), see Vol. I. p. xxix.; Vol. III. p. 217; Vol. XIV. p. 433; and for the *Sketches in France, Switzerland, and Italy* (about 1839), Vol. III. p. 217 n. The full title of the other work referred to in the text is *Prout's Microcosm: The Artistic Sketch-book of Groups and Figures, Shipping and other Picturesque Objects. By Samuel Prout, F.S.A.* It contains twenty-four lithographs, and was published in 1841 (large quarto).]

in them, with chalk on smooth paper, till you can lay on his broad flat tints, and get his gradations of light, which are very wonderful; then take up the architectural subjects in the *Rhine*, and draw again and again the groups of figures, etc., in his *Microcosm*, and *Lessons on Light and Shadow*. After that, proceed to copy the grand subjects in the *Sketches in Flanders and Germany*; or in *Switzerland and Italy*, if you cannot get the Flanders; but the Switzerland is very far inferior. Then work from Nature, not trying to Proutise Nature, by breaking smooth buildings into rough ones, but only drawing *what you see*, with Prout's simple method and firm lines. Don't copy his coloured works. They are good, but not at all equal to his chalk and pencil drawings; and you will become a mere imitator, and a very feeble imitator, if you use colour at all in Prout's method. I have not space to explain why this is so, it would take a long piece of reasoning; trust me for the statement.

2. JOHN LEWIS.

His sketches in Spain, lithographed by himself, are very valuable. Get them, if you can, and also some engravings (about eight or ten, I think, altogether) of wild beasts, executed by his own hand a long time ago; they are very precious in every way. The series of the "Alhambra" is rather slight, and few of the subjects are lithographed by himself; still it is well worth having.[1]

But let *no* lithographic work come into the house, if you can help it, nor even look at any, except Prout's, and those sketches of Lewis's.

3. GEORGE CRUIKSHANK.

If you ever happen to meet with the two volumes of *Grimm's German Stories*, which were illustrated by him long ago,[2] pounce upon them instantly; the etchings in them are the finest things, next to Rembrandt's, that, as far as I know, have been done since etching was invented. You cannot look at them too much, nor copy them too often.

All his works are very valuable, though disagreeable when they touch on the worst vulgarities of modern life; and often much spoiled by a curiously mistaken type of face, divided so as to give too much to the mouth and eyes and leave too little for forehead, the eyes being set about two thirds up,

---

[1] [For another reference to Lewis's *Studies of Wild Animals*, see Vol. XII. p. 363. The other publications here referred to are: Lewis's *Sketches and Drawings of the Alhambra, made during a residence in Granada in 1833–1834*, drawn on stone by J. D. Harding . . . and J. F. L.: 1835, fol.; and Lewis's *Sketches of Spain and Spanish Character, made during his tour in that country in 1833–1834*, drawn on stone, *from his original sketches, by himself:* 1836. For Ruskin's other references to Lewis, see General Index.]

[2] [Published in 1826; for another reference to it, see Vol. V. p. xxiii., and for Cruikshank generally, see also Vol. II. p. xxxiii. and Vol. VI. p. 471. His *Cinderella, Jack and the Beanstalk*, and *Hop o' my Thumb* (for which Ruskin by a slip of the pen wrote "*Tom Thumb*") were published in separate parts of *George Cruikshank's Fairy Library* (about 1854).]

instead of at half the height of the head. But his manner of work is always right; and his tragic power, though rarely developed, and warped by habits of caricature, is, in reality, as great as his grotesque power.

There is no fear of his hurting your taste, as long as your principal work lies among art of so totally different a character as most of that which I have recommended to you; and you may, therefore, get great good by copying almost anything of his that may come in your way; except only his illustrations, lately published, to *Cinderella*, and *Jack and the Bean-stalk*, and *Hop o' my Thumb*, which are much over-laboured, and confused in line. You should get them, but do not copy them.

4. Alfred Rethel.[1]

I only know two publications by him; one, the "Dance of Death," with text by Reinick, published in Leipsic, but to be had now of any London bookseller for the sum, I believe, of eighteen pence, and containing six plates full of instructive character; the other, of two plates only, "Death the Avenger," and "Death the Friend." These two are far superior to the "Todtentanz," and, if you can get them, will be enough in themselves to show all that Rethel can teach you. If you dislike ghastly subjects, get "Death the Friend" only.

5. Bewick.

The execution of the plumage in Bewick's birds is the most masterly thing ever yet done in woodcutting; it is worked just as Paul Veronese would have worked in wood, had he taken to it. His vignettes, though too coarse in execution, and vulgar in types of form, to be good copies, show, nevertheless, intellectual power of the highest order; and there are pieces of sentiment in them, either pathetic or satirical,[2] which have never since been equalled in illustrations of this simple kind; the bitter intensity of the feeling being just like that which characterises some of the leading Pre-Raphaelites. Bewick is the Burns of painting.

6. Blake.[3]

The *Book of Job*, engraved by himself, is of the highest rank in certain characters of imagination and expression; in the mode of obtaining certain effects of light it will also be a very useful example to you. In expressing conditions of glaring and flickering light, Blake is greater than Rembrandt.

---

[1] [For a note on Rethel and his drawings for "The Dance of Death," see Vol. XII. p. 489; and for an account of the "two plates," *ibid.*, pp. 507, 508.]

[2] [As, for instance, in the case mentioned in Vol. XIII. p. 435, where, in the note, other references by Ruskin to Bewick are given.]

[3] [For Ruskin's other references to Blake, see Vol. V. p. 138; Vol. VIII. p. 256 *n.*; Vol. XIV. p. 354. *His Illustrations of the Book of Job* were engraved and published by him in 1825; a facsimile edition was published by J. M. Dent in 1902.]

7. RICHTER.

I have already told you what to guard against in looking at his works.[1] I am a little doubtful whether I have done well in including them in this catalogue at all; but the imaginations in them are so lovely and numberless, that I must risk, for their sake, the chance of hurting you a little in judgment of style. If you want to make presents of story-books to children, his are the best you can now get; but his most beautiful work, as far as I know, is his series of Illustrations to the Lord's Prayer.[2]

8. ROSSETTI.

An edition of Tennyson, lately published, contains woodcuts from drawings by Rossetti and other chief Pre-Raphaelite masters.[3] They are terribly spoiled in the cutting, and generally the best part, the expression of feature, *entirely* lost;* still they are full of instruction, and cannot be studied too closely. But observe, respecting these woodcuts, that if you have been in the habit of looking at much spurious work, in which sentiment, action, and style are borrowed or artificial, you will assuredly be offended at first by all genuine work, which is intense in feeling. Genuine art, which is merely art, such as Veronese's or Titian's, may not offend you, though the chances are that you will not care about it; but genuine works of feeling, such as *Maud* or *Aurora Leigh* in poetry,[4] or the grand Pre-Raphaelite designs in painting, are sure to offend you: and if you cease to work hard, and persist in looking at vicious and false art, they will continue to offend you. It will

---

* This is especially the case in the St. Cecily, Rossetti's first illustration to the *Palace of Art*, which would have been the best in the book had it been well engraved. The whole work should be taken up again, and done by line engraving, perfectly; and wholly from Pre-Raphaelite designs, with which no other modern work can bear the least comparison.

---

[1] [See above, p. 204. Adrian Ludwig Richter, painter and engraver (1803–1884), for many years Professor at the Dresden Academy. His illustrations to the Lord's Prayer were published in 1856 (" *Vater Unser*" in *Bildern von Ludwig Richter. In Holzschnitt ausgeführt von August Gaber: Dresden*), and in the same year, with English Text (" *The Lord's Prayer, with Illustrations by Ludwig Richter. Engraved on wood by A. Gaber, Dresden: Published by Gaber and Richter*"). Story-books illustrated by him are very numerous; for a complete bibliography see *Adrian Ludwig Richter: Maler und Radirer* (a Catalogue of his works by Johann Friedrich Hoff, Dresden: 1877).]

[2] [Ed. 1 reads: ". . . this catalogue at all; but the fancies in them are so pretty and numberless . . ."; and omits, at the end of the paragraph, the words "but his most beautiful work . . . Lord's Prayer."]

[3] [This was an edition of the *Poems* (the 1842 volume) with illustrations by Thomas Creswick, John Everett Millais, William Holman Hunt, William Mulready, John Callcott, Horsley, Dante Gabriel Rossetti, Clarkson Stanfield, and Daniel Maclise, published by Moxon in 1857. It was reprinted by Messrs. Macmillan in 1893, and by Freemantle & Co. in 1901 (with an introduction by Holman Hunt). The volume is the subject of a monograph by G. S. Layard, entitled *Tennyson and his Pre-Raphaelite Illustrators*: 1894.]

[4] [For Ruskin's appreciation of *Maud*, see Vol. V. p. 219 n. *Aurora Leigh* had just been published (1856) when this book appeared.]

be well, therefore, to have one type of entirely false art, in order to know what to guard against. Flaxman's outlines to Dante[1] contain, I think, examples of almost every kind of falsehood and feebleness which it is possible for a trained artist, not base in thought, to commit or admit, both in design and execution. Base or degraded choice of subject, such as you will constantly find in Teniers and others of the Dutch painters, I need not, I hope, warn you against; you will simply turn away from it in disgust; while mere bad or feeble drawing, which makes mistakes in every direction at once, cannot teach you the particular sort of educated fallacy in question. But, in these designs of Flaxman's, you have gentlemanly feeling, and fair knowledge of anatomy, and firm setting down of lines, all applied, in the foolishest and worst possible way; you cannot have a more finished example of learned error, amiable want of meaning, and bad drawing with a steady hand.* Retzsch's[2] outlines have more real material in them than Flaxman's, occasionally showing true fancy and power; in artistic principle they are nearly as bad, and in taste, worse. All outlines from statuary, as given in works on classical art, will be very hurtful to you if you in the least like them; and *nearly* all finished line engravings. Some particular prints I could name which possess instructive qualities, but it would take too long to distinguish them, and the best way is to avoid line engravings of figures altogether.†

---

* The praise I have given incidentally to Flaxman's sculpture in the *Seven Lamps*, and elsewhere,[3] refers wholly to his studies from Nature, and simple groups in marble, which were always good and interesting. Still, I have overrated him, even in this respect; and it is generally to be remembered that, in speaking of artists whose works I cannot be supposed to have specially studied, the errors I fall into will always be on the side of praise. For, of course, praise is most likely to be given when the thing praised is above one's knowledge; and, therefore, as our knowledge increases, such things may be found less praiseworthy than we thought. But blame can only be justly given when the thing blamed is below one's level of sight; and, practically, I never do blame anything until I have got well past it, and am certain that there is demonstrable falsehood in it. I believe, therefore, all my blame to be wholly trustworthy,[4] having never yet had occasion to repent of one depreciatory word that I have ever written, while I have often found that, with respect to things I had not time to study closely, I was led too far by sudden admiration, helped, perhaps, by peculiar associations, or other deceptive accidents; and this the more, because I never care to check an expression of delight, thinking the chances are, that, even if mistaken, it will do more good than harm; but I weigh every word of blame with scrupulous caution. I have sometimes erased a strong passage of blame from second editions of my books;[5] but this was only when I found it offended the reader without convincing him, never because I repented of it myself.

† Large line engravings, I mean, in which the lines, as such, are conspicuous. Small vignettes in line are often beautiful in figures no less than landscape; as, for instance, those from Stothard's drawings in Rogers's *Italy*;[6] and, therefore, I have just recommended the vignettes to Tennyson to be done by line engraving.

---

[1] [See the examples given in Vol. VI. pp. 371–373.]
[2] [For the works of Retzsch, see Vol. IV. pp. 259, 371, and Vol. XIII. p. 275.]
[3] [Vol. VIII. p. 44; and *Stones of Venice*, vol. i. (Vol. IX. p. 289 *n*.).]
[4] [Compare *The Two Paths*, Appendix i. (Vol. XVI.), and a passage in a letter on George Eliot given in a later volume: "I have always praised the living, and judged —the dead."]
[5] [See, for instance, Vol. III. pp. 529, 619.]
[6] [For other references to Stothard, see Vol. IV. p. 194 *n*.]

If you happen to be a rich person, possessing quantities of them, and if you are fond of the large finished prints from Raphael, Correggio, etc., it is wholly impossible that you can make any progress in knowledge of real art till you have sold them all,—or burnt them, which would be a greater benefit to the world. I hope that, some day, true and noble engravings will be made from the few pictures of the great schools, which the restorations undertaken by the modern managers of foreign galleries may leave us ; but the existing engravings have nothing whatever in common with the good in the works they profess to represent, and, if you like them, you like in the originals of them hardly anything but their errors.

258. Finally, your judgment will be, of course, much affected by your taste in literature. Indeed, I know many persons who have the purest taste in literature, and yet false taste in art, and it is a phenomenon which puzzles me not a little ; but I have never known any one with false taste in books, and true taste in pictures. It is also of the greatest importance to you, not only for art's sake, but for all kinds of sake, in these days of book deluge, to keep out of the salt swamps of literature, and live on a little rocky island of your own, with a spring and a lake in it, pure and good. I cannot, of course, suggest the choice of your library to you : every several mind needs different books ; but there are some books which we all need, and assuredly, if you read Homer,* Plato, Æschylus, Herodotus, Dante,† Shakspeare, and Spenser, as much as you ought, you will not require wide enlargement of shelves to right and left of them for purposes of perpetual study. Among modern books avoid generally magazine and review literature. Sometimes it may contain a useful abridgment or a wholesome piece of criticism ; but the chances are ten to one it will either waste your time or mislead you. If you want to understand any subject whatever, read the best book upon it you can hear of : not a review of the book. If you don't like the first book you try, seek for another ; but do not hope ever to understand the subject without pains, by a reviewer's help. Avoid especially that class of literature which has a knowing tone ; it is the most poisonous of all. Every good book, or piece of book, is full of admiration and awe ; it may contain firm assertion or stern satire, but it never sneers coldly, nor asserts haughtily, and it always leads you to reverence or love something with your whole heart. It is not always easy to distinguish the satire of the venomous race of books from the satire of the noble and pure ones ; but in general you may notice that the cold-blooded, Crustacean and Batrachian books will sneer at sentiment ; and the warm-blooded, human books, at sin. Then, in general, the more you can

---

* Chapman's, if not the original.[1]

† Cary's or Cayley's, if not the original. I do not know which are the best translations of Plato.[2] Herodotus and Æschylus can only be read in the original. It may seem strange that I name books like these for "beginners" : but all the greatest books contain food for all ages ; and an intelligent and rightly bred youth or girl ought to enjoy much, even in Plato, by the time they are fifteen or sixteen.

---

[1] [For Ruskin's appreciation of Chapman's Homer, see *Proserpina*, ch. v. (" Papaver Rhoeas "), and *Storm-Cloud of the Nineteenth Century*, Lecture ii.]

[2] [This was in 1857, and Jowett's translation of Plato, which Ruskin sometimes used (see *Fors Clavigera*, Letter 37), was not published till 1871. For his own exercises in translating Plato, see Vol. I. p. 494 *n*.]

restrain your serious reading to reflective or lyric poetry, history, and natural history, avoiding fiction and the drama, the healthier your mind will become. Of modern poetry, keep to Scott, Wordsworth, Keats, Crabbe, Tennyson, the two Brownings, Thomas Hood,[1] Lowell, Longfellow, and Coventry Patmore, whose *Angel in the House* is a most finished piece of writing, and the sweetest analysis we possess of quiet modern domestic feeling; while Mrs. Browning's *Aurora Leigh* is, as far as I know, the greatest poem which the century has produced in any language. Cast Coleridge at once aside, as sickly and useless; and Shelley, as shallow and verbose; Byron, until your taste is fully formed, and you are able to discern the magnificence in him from the wrong.[2] Never read bad or common poetry, nor write any poetry yourself; there is, perhaps, rather too much than too little in the world already.

259. Of reflective prose, read chiefly Bacon, Johnson, and Helps.[3] Carlyle is hardly to be named as a writer for "beginners," because his teaching, though to some of us vitally necessary, may to others be hurtful. If you understand and like him, read him; if he offends you, you are not yet ready for him, and perhaps may never be so; at all events, give him up, as you would sea-bathing if you found it hurt you, till you are stronger. Of fiction, read *Sir Charles Grandison*, Scott's novels, Miss Edgeworth's, and, if you are a young lady, Madame de Genlis', the French Miss Edgeworth;[4] making

---

[1] ["Thomas Hood" was first inserted here in ed. 3 (1859).]

[2] [In the General Index all Ruskin's references to, or citations from, the poets named above are given. A summary statement is here added. For Scott, Ruskin's admiration never wavered. His early admiration of Wordsworth is sufficiently shown by the numerous quotations in *Modern Painters*; the qualifications which he afterwards made were set out in the papers on *Fiction, Fair and Foul*. In the same papers he emphasised "the magnificence" in Byron, whom, it may be added, Ruskin himself had read from very early years (*Præterita*, i. ch. viii. § 163). Ruskin's admiration of Keats is indicated in many quotations in *Modern Painters*, and very strongly expressed in vol. v. pt. vi. ch. ix. § 9 n.; his changing attitude towards Shelley has already been noted (Vol. I. pp. 253–254 n.) For other references to Crabbe, see Vol. VI. p. 71, Vol. X. p. 231; to Tennyson, see (among many other passages) *Two Paths*, Appendix i. ; to Mrs. Browning, *Stones of Venice*, vol. i. (Vol. IX. p. 228 n.) ; to Robert Browning, Vol. VI. p. 449; to Thomas Hood, Vol. VI. p. 471 n. To Lowell, Ruskin refers as his "dear friend and teacher" in *Modern Painters*, vol. v. pt. ix. ch. xii. § 10 (see also *ibid.*, ch. viii. § 15 n.); for his admiration of Longfellow, see *Modern Painters*, vol. iii. (Vol. V. p. 229), vol. iv. (Vol. VI. p. 446), Vol. XII. p. 485. Ruskin's admiration of Coventry Patmore's work is fully shown in his letters to the poet, contained in a later volume of this edition ; see also *Sesame and Lilies*, § 65 and n. For a discussion of Coleridge, see Vol. IV. pp. 391, 392.]

[3] [Here, again, see the General Index for a list of Ruskin's references to the authors cited. His characterisation of Bacon is given in Vol. VI. p. 439; his debt to Johnson is explained in *Præterita*, i. ch. xii. §§ 251, 252; for the high place assigned to Helps, see Vol. V. p. 334, Vol. XI. p. 153 n. Among those to whom Carlyle was "vitally necessary" was Ruskin himself. For his admiration of Richardson, and especially of *Sir Charles Grandison*, see *Præterita*, ii. ch. iv. § 70. The same book contains repeated tributes of admiration to Miss Edgeworth; Ruskin was especially fond of her *Absentee* and *Helen*, which books he would often read aloud to his guests at Brantwood.]

[4] [For Madame de Genlis, see Vol. VI. p. 298. Ruskin was much interested in her books and in her life. In 1781 she had been appointed "gouverneur" in the household of the Duke of Orleans, and in 1793 she took refuge with her pupil,

these, I mean, your constant companions.   Of course you must, or will, read
other books for amusement once or twice ; but you will find that these have
an element of perpetuity in them, existing in nothing else of their kind ;
while their peculiar quietness and repose of manner will also be of the greatest
value in teaching you to feel the same characters in art.   Read little at a
time, trying to feel interest in little things, and reading not so much for the
sake of the story as to get acquainted with the pleasant people into whose
company these writers bring you.   A common book will often give you much
amusement, but it is only a noble book which will give you dear friends.[1]
Remember, also, that it is of less importance to you in your earlier years, that
the books you read should be clever than that they should be right.   I do
not mean oppressively or repulsively instructive ; but that the thoughts they
express should be just, and the feelings they excite generous.   It is not
necessary for you to read the wittiest or the most suggestive books : it is
better, in general, to hear what is already known, and may be simply said.
Much of the literature of the present day, though good to be read by persons
of ripe age, has a tendency to agitate rather than confirm, and leaves its
readers too frequently in a helpless or hopeless indignation, the worst possible
state into which the mind of youth can be thrown.   It may, indeed, become
necessary for you, as you advance in life, to set your hand to things that
need to be altered in the world, or apply your heart chiefly to what must
be pitied in it, or condemned ; but, for a young person, the safest temper is
one of reverence, and the safest place one of obscurity.   Certainly at present,
and perhaps through all your life, your teachers are wisest when they make
you content in quiet virtue, and that literature and art are best for you which
point out, in common life, and in familiar things, the objects for hopeful
labour, and for humble love.

Mademoiselle d'Orleans, in Switzerland.   At Bremgarten, in 1858, Ruskin came
across some memorials of her, as thus described in a letter to his father :—
    "30th May, Sunday [1858].— . . . Here it was that Madame de Genlis
lived with her pupil and her daughter in the Convent for two years before
their final separation.   The landlord of the inn, now deserted or nearly so,
is the son of one of their servants, and has still three drawings of flowers
which he showed me, signed in their pretty little courtly hands—now
almost invisible from the fading of the ink—'Louise Adèle,' 'Stephanie'
(Madame de Genlis), and 'Henriette' (Madame de Genlis' daughter).   They
were beautifully done in a quaint old way, founded on the Dutch flower
painting, but precise, complete, and delicate.   The Princess's, besides the
flowers, had four shells ranged symmetrically underneath, prettily rounded
and spotted ; Madame de Genlis' was of a white and purple tulip, with
guelder roses.   They were nearly all equally well done, the two girls
seeming to have entirely reached, without trying to improve upon it, the
manner of their mother and tutress."]
[1] [Compare *Sesame and Lilies*, § 6, and *Eagle's Nest*, § 206.]

A CATALOG OF SELECTED
DOVER BOOKS
IN ALL FIELDS OF INTEREST

A CATALOG OF SELECTED DOVER
BOOKS IN ALL FIELDS OF INTEREST

CONCERNING THE SPIRITUAL IN ART, Wassily Kandinsky. Pioneering work by father of abstract art. Thoughts on color theory, nature of art. Analysis of earlier masters. 12 illustrations. 80pp. of text. 5⅜ x 8½. 0-486-23411-8

CELTIC ART: The Methods of Construction, George Bain. Simple geometric techniques for making Celtic interlacements, spirals, Kells-type initials, animals, humans, etc. Over 500 illustrations. 160pp. 9 x 12. (Available in U.S. only.) 0-486-22923-8

AN ATLAS OF ANATOMY FOR ARTISTS, Fritz Schider. Most thorough reference work on art anatomy in the world. Hundreds of illustrations, including selections from works by Vesalius, Leonardo, Goya, Ingres, Michelangelo, others. 593 illustrations. 192pp. 7⅛ x 10¼. 0-486-20241-0

CELTIC HAND STROKE-BY-STROKE (Irish Half-Uncial from "The Book of Kells"): An Arthur Baker Calligraphy Manual, Arthur Baker. Complete guide to creating each letter of the alphabet in distinctive Celtic manner. Covers hand position, strokes, pens, inks, paper, more. Illustrated. 48pp. 8¼ x 11. 0-486-24336-2

EASY ORIGAMI, John Montroll. Charming collection of 32 projects (hat, cup, pelican, piano, swan, many more) specially designed for the novice origami hobbyist. Clearly illustrated easy-to-follow instructions insure that even beginning papercrafters will achieve successful results. 48pp. 8¼ x 11. 0-486-27298-2

BLOOMINGDALE'S ILLUSTRATED 1886 CATALOG: Fashions, Dry Goods and Housewares, Bloomingdale Brothers. Famed merchants' extremely rare catalog depicting about 1,700 products: clothing, housewares, firearms, dry goods, jewelry, more. Invaluable for dating, identifying vintage items. Also, copyright-free graphics for artists, designers. Co-published with Henry Ford Museum & Greenfield Village. 160pp. 8¼ x 11. 0-486-25780-0

THE ART OF WORLDLY WISDOM, Baltasar Gracian. "Think with the few and speak with the many," "Friends are a second existence," and "Be able to forget" are among this 1637 volume's 300 pithy maxims. A perfect source of mental and spiritual refreshment, it can be opened at random and appreciated either in brief or at length. 128pp. 5⅜ x 8½. 0-486-44034-6

JOHNSON'S DICTIONARY: A Modern Selection, Samuel Johnson (E. L. McAdam and George Milne, eds.). This modern version reduces the original 1755 edition's 2,300 pages of definitions and literary examples to a more manageable length, retaining the verbal pleasure and historical curiosity of the original. 480pp. 5³⁄₁₆ x 8¼. 0-486-44089-3

ADVENTURES OF HUCKLEBERRY FINN, Mark Twain, Illustrated by E. W. Kemble. A work of eternal richness and complexity, a source of ongoing critical debate, and a literary landmark, Twain's 1885 masterpiece about a barefoot boy's journey of self-discovery has enthralled readers around the world. This handsome clothbound reproduction of the first edition features all 174 of the original black-and-white illustrations. 368pp. 5⅜ x 8½. 0-486-44322-1

FRENCH STORIES/CONTES FRANÇAIS: A Dual-Language Book, Wallace Fowlie. Ten stories by French masters, Voltaire to Camus: "Micromegas" by Voltaire; "The Atheist's Mass" by Balzac; "Minuet" by de Maupassant; "The Guest" by Camus, six more. Excellent English translations on facing pages. Also French-English vocabulary list, exercises, more. 352pp. 5⅜ x 8½.   0-486-26443-2

CHICAGO AT THE TURN OF THE CENTURY IN PHOTOGRAPHS: 122 Historic Views from the Collections of the Chicago Historical Society, Larry A. Viskochil. Rare large-format prints offer detailed views of City Hall, State Street, the Loop, Hull House, Union Station, many other landmarks, circa 1904-1913. Introduction. Captions. Maps. 144pp. 9⅜ x 12¼.   0-486-24656-6

OLD BROOKLYN IN EARLY PHOTOGRAPHS, 1865-1929, William Lee Younger. Luna Park, Gravesend race track, construction of Grand Army Plaza, moving of Hotel Brighton, etc. 157 previously unpublished photographs. 165pp. 8⅞ x 11¾.
0-486-23587-4

THE MYTHS OF THE NORTH AMERICAN INDIANS, Lewis Spence. Rich anthology of the myths and legends of the Algonquins, Iroquois, Pawnees and Sioux, prefaced by an extensive historical and ethnological commentary. 36 illustrations. 480pp. 5⅜ x 8½.   0-486-25967-6

AN ENCYCLOPEDIA OF BATTLES: Accounts of Over 1,560 Battles from 1479 B.C. to the Present, David Eggenberger. Essential details of every major battle in recorded history from the first battle of Megiddo in 1479 B.C. to Grenada in 1984. List of Battle Maps. New Appendix covering the years 1967-1984. Index. 99 illustrations. 544pp. 6½ x 9¼.   0-486-24913-1

SAILING ALONE AROUND THE WORLD, Captain Joshua Slocum. First man to sail around the world, alone, in small boat. One of great feats of seamanship told in delightful manner. 67 illustrations. 294pp. 5⅜ x 8½.   0-486-20326-3

ANARCHISM AND OTHER ESSAYS, Emma Goldman. Powerful, penetrating, prophetic essays on direct action, role of minorities, prison reform, puritan hypocrisy, violence, etc. 271pp. 5⅜ x 8½.   0-486-22484-8

MYTHS OF THE HINDUS AND BUDDHISTS, Ananda K. Coomaraswamy and Sister Nivedita. Great stories of the epics; deeds of Krishna, Shiva, taken from puranas, Vedas, folk tales; etc. 32 illustrations. 400pp. 5⅜ x 8½.   0-486-21759-0

MY BONDAGE AND MY FREEDOM, Frederick Douglass. Born a slave, Douglass became outspoken force in antislavery movement. The best of Douglass' autobiographies. Graphic description of slave life. 464pp. 5⅜ x 8½.   0-486-22457-0

FOLLOWING THE EQUATOR: A Journey Around the World, Mark Twain. Fascinating humorous account of 1897 voyage to Hawaii, Australia, India, New Zealand, etc. Ironic, bemused reports on peoples, customs, climate, flora and fauna, politics, much more. 197 illustrations. 720pp. 5⅜ x 8½.   0-486-26113-1

THE PEOPLE CALLED SHAKERS, Edward D. Andrews. Definitive study of Shakers: origins, beliefs, practices, dances, social organization, furniture and crafts, etc. 33 illustrations. 351pp. 5⅜ x 8½.   0-486-21081-2

THE MYTHS OF GREECE AND ROME, H. A. Guerber. A classic of mythology, generously illustrated, long prized for its simple, graphic, accurate retelling of the principal myths of Greece and Rome, and for its commentary on their origins and significance. With 64 illustrations by Michelangelo, Raphael, Titian, Rubens, Canova, Bernini and others. 480pp. 5⅜ x 8½.   0-486-27584-1

HOW TO DO BEADWORK, Mary White. Fundamental book on craft from simple projects to five-bead chains and woven works. 106 illustrations. 142pp. 5⅜ x 8. 0-486-20697-1

THE 1912 AND 1915 GUSTAV STICKLEY FURNITURE CATALOGS, Gustav Stickley. With over 200 detailed illustrations and descriptions, these two catalogs are essential reading and reference materials and identification guides for Stickley furniture. Captions cite materials, dimensions and prices. 112pp. 6½ x 9¼. 0-486-26676-1

EARLY AMERICAN LOCOMOTIVES, John H. White, Jr. Finest locomotive engravings from early 19th century: historical (1804–74), main-line (after 1870), special, foreign, etc. 147 plates. 142pp. 11⅜ x 8¼. 0-486-22772-3

LITTLE BOOK OF EARLY AMERICAN CRAFTS AND TRADES, Peter Stockham (ed.). 1807 children's book explains crafts and trades: baker, hatter, cooper, potter, and many others. 23 copperplate illustrations. 140pp. 4⅝ x 6. 0-486-23336-7

VICTORIAN FASHIONS AND COSTUMES FROM HARPER'S BAZAR, 1867–1898, Stella Blum (ed.). Day costumes, evening wear, sports clothes, shoes, hats, other accessories in over 1,000 detailed engravings. 320pp. 9⅜ x 12¼. 0-486-22990-4

THE LONG ISLAND RAIL ROAD IN EARLY PHOTOGRAPHS, Ron Ziel. Over 220 rare photos, informative text document origin (1844) and development of rail service on Long Island. Vintage views of early trains, locomotives, stations, passengers, crews, much more. Captions. 8⅞ x 11¾. 0-486-26301-0

VOYAGE OF THE LIBERDADE, Joshua Slocum. Great 19th-century mariner's thrilling, first-hand account of the wreck of his ship off South America, the 35-foot boat he built from the wreckage, and its remarkable voyage home. 128pp. 5⅜ x 8½. 0-486-40022-0

TEN BOOKS ON ARCHITECTURE, Vitruvius. The most important book ever written on architecture. Early Roman aesthetics, technology, classical orders, site selection, all other aspects. Morgan translation. 331pp. 5⅜ x 8½. 0-486-20645-9

THE HUMAN FIGURE IN MOTION, Eadweard Muybridge. More than 4,500 stopped-action photos, in action series, showing undraped men, women, children jumping, lying down, throwing, sitting, wrestling, carrying, etc. 390pp. 7⅞ x 10⅝. 0-486-20204-6 Clothbd.

TREES OF THE EASTERN AND CENTRAL UNITED STATES AND CANADA, William M. Harlow. Best one-volume guide to 140 trees. Full descriptions, woodlore, range, etc. Over 600 illustrations. Handy size. 288pp. 4½ x 6⅜. 0-486-20395-6

GROWING AND USING HERBS AND SPICES, Milo Miloradovich. Versatile handbook provides all the information needed for cultivation and use of all the herbs and spices available in North America. 4 illustrations. Index. Glossary. 236pp. 5⅜ x 8½. 0-486-25058-X

BIG BOOK OF MAZES AND LABYRINTHS, Walter Shepherd. 50 mazes and labyrinths in all–classical, solid, ripple, and more–in one great volume. Perfect inexpensive puzzler for clever youngsters. Full solutions. 112pp. 8⅛ x 11. 0-486-22951-3

PIANO TUNING, J. Cree Fischer. Clearest, best book for beginner, amateur. Simple repairs, raising dropped notes, tuning by easy method of flattened fifths. No previous skills needed. 4 illustrations. 201pp. 5⅜ x 8½. 0-486-23267-0

HINTS TO SINGERS, Lillian Nordica. Selecting the right teacher, developing confidence, overcoming stage fright, and many other important skills receive thoughtful discussion in this indispensible guide, written by a world-famous diva of four decades' experience. 96pp. 5⅜ x 8½. 0-486-40094-8

THE COMPLETE NONSENSE OF EDWARD LEAR, Edward Lear. All nonsense limericks, zany alphabets, Owl and Pussycat, songs, nonsense botany, etc., illustrated by Lear. Total of 320pp. 5⅜ x 8½. (Available in U.S. only.) 0-486-20167-8

VICTORIAN PARLOUR POETRY: An Annotated Anthology, Michael R. Turner. 117 gems by Longfellow, Tennyson, Browning, many lesser-known poets. "The Village Blacksmith," "Curfew Must Not Ring Tonight," "Only a Baby Small," dozens more, often difficult to find elsewhere. Index of poets, titles, first lines. xxiii + 325pp. 5⅝ x 8¼. 0-486-27044-0

DUBLINERS, James Joyce. Fifteen stories offer vivid, tightly focused observations of the lives of Dublin's poorer classes. At least one, "The Dead," is considered a masterpiece. Reprinted complete and unabridged from standard edition. 160pp. $5\frac{3}{16}$ x 8¼. 0-486-26870-5

GREAT WEIRD TALES: 14 Stories by Lovecraft, Blackwood, Machen and Others, S. T. Joshi (ed.). 14 spellbinding tales, including "The Sin Eater," by Fiona McLeod, "The Eye Above the Mantel," by Frank Belknap Long, as well as renowned works by R. H. Barlow, Lord Dunsany, Arthur Machen, W. C. Morrow and eight other masters of the genre. 256pp. 5⅜ x 8½. (Available in U.S. only.) 0-486-40436-6

THE BOOK OF THE SACRED MAGIC OF ABRAMELIN THE MAGE, translated by S. MacGregor Mathers. Medieval manuscript of ceremonial magic. Basic document in Aleister Crowley, Golden Dawn groups. 268pp. 5⅜ x 8½. 0-486-23211-5

THE BATTLES THAT CHANGED HISTORY, Fletcher Pratt. Eminent historian profiles 16 crucial conflicts, ancient to modern, that changed the course of civilization. 352pp. 5⅜ x 8½. 0-486-41129-X

NEW RUSSIAN-ENGLISH AND ENGLISH-RUSSIAN DICTIONARY, M. A. O'Brien. This is a remarkably handy Russian dictionary, containing a surprising amount of information, including over 70,000 entries. 366pp. 4½ x 6⅛. 0-486-20208-9

NEW YORK IN THE FORTIES, Andreas Feininger. 162 brilliant photographs by the well-known photographer, formerly with *Life* magazine. Commuters, shoppers, Times Square at night, much else from city at its peak. Captions by John von Hartz. 181pp. 9¼ x 10¾. 0-486-23585-8

INDIAN SIGN LANGUAGE, William Tomkins. Over 525 signs developed by Sioux and other tribes. Written instructions and diagrams. Also 290 pictographs. 111pp. 6⅛ x 9¼. 0-486-22029-X

ANATOMY: A Complete Guide for Artists, Joseph Sheppard. A master of figure drawing shows artists how to render human anatomy convincingly. Over 460 illustrations. 224pp. 8⅜ x 11¼. 0-486-27279-6

MEDIEVAL CALLIGRAPHY: Its History and Technique, Marc Drogin. Spirited history, comprehensive instruction manual covers 13 styles (ca. 4th century through 15th). Excellent photographs; directions for duplicating medieval techniques with modern tools. 224pp. 8⅜ x 11¼. 0-486-26142-5

DRIED FLOWERS: How to Prepare Them, Sarah Whitlock and Martha Rankin. Complete instructions on how to use silica gel, meal and borax, perlite aggregate, sand and borax, glycerine and water to create attractive permanent flower arrangements. 12 illustrations. 32pp. 5⅜ x 8½. 0-486-21802-3

EASY-TO-MAKE BIRD FEEDERS FOR WOODWORKERS, Scott D. Campbell. Detailed, simple-to-use guide for designing, constructing, caring for and using feeders. Text, illustrations for 12 classic and contemporary designs. 96pp. 5⅜ x 8½. 0-486-25847-5

THE COMPLETE BOOK OF BIRDHOUSE CONSTRUCTION FOR WOODWORKERS, Scott D. Campbell. Detailed instructions, illustrations, tables. Also data on bird habitat and instinct patterns. Bibliography. 3 tables. 63 illustrations in 15 figures. 48pp. 5¼ x 8½. 0-486-24407-5

SCOTTISH WONDER TALES FROM MYTH AND LEGEND, Donald A. Mackenzie. 16 lively tales tell of giants rumbling down mountainsides, of a magic wand that turns stone pillars into warriors, of gods and goddesses, evil hags, powerful forces and more. 240pp. 5⅜ x 8½. 0-486-29677-6

THE HISTORY OF UNDERCLOTHES, C. Willett Cunnington and Phyllis Cunnington. Fascinating, well-documented survey covering six centuries of English undergarments, enhanced with over 100 illustrations: 12th-century laced-up bodice, footed long drawers (1795), 19th-century bustles, 19th-century corsets for men, Victorian "bust improvers," much more. 272pp. 5⅝ x 8¼. 0-486-27124-2

ARTS AND CRAFTS FURNITURE: The Complete Brooks Catalog of 1912, Brooks Manufacturing Co. Photos and detailed descriptions of more than 150 now very collectible furniture designs from the Arts and Crafts movement depict davenports, settees, buffets, desks, tables, chairs, bedsteads, dressers and more, all built of solid, quarter-sawed oak. Invaluable for students and enthusiasts of antiques, Americana and the decorative arts. 80pp. 6½ x 9¼. 0-486-27471-3

WILBUR AND ORVILLE: A Biography of the Wright Brothers, Fred Howard. Definitive, crisply written study tells the full story of the brothers' lives and work. A vividly written biography, unparalleled in scope and color, that also captures the spirit of an extraordinary era. 560pp. 6⅛ x 9¼. 0-486-40297-5

THE ARTS OF THE SAILOR: Knotting, Splicing and Ropework, Hervey Garrett Smith. Indispensable shipboard reference covers tools, basic knots and useful hitches; handsewing and canvas work, more. Over 100 illustrations. Delightful reading for sea lovers. 256pp. 5⅜ x 8½. 0-486-26440-8

FRANK LLOYD WRIGHT'S FALLINGWATER: The House and Its History, Second, Revised Edition, Donald Hoffmann. A total revision–both in text and illustrations–of the standard document on Fallingwater, the boldest, most personal architectural statement of Wright's mature years, updated with valuable new material from the recently opened Frank Lloyd Wright Archives. "Fascinating"–*The New York Times*. 116 illustrations. 128pp. 9¼ x 10¾. 0-486-27430-6

PHOTOGRAPHIC SKETCHBOOK OF THE CIVIL WAR, Alexander Gardner. 100 photos taken on field during the Civil War. Famous shots of Manassas Harper's Ferry, Lincoln, Richmond, slave pens, etc. 244pp. 10⅝ x 8¼. 0-486-22731-6

FIVE ACRES AND INDEPENDENCE, Maurice G. Kains. Great back-to-the-land classic explains basics of self-sufficient farming. The one book to get. 95 illustrations. 397pp. 5⅜ x 8½. 0-486-20974-1

A MODERN HERBAL, Margaret Grieve. Much the fullest, most exact, most useful compilation of herbal material. Gigantic alphabetical encyclopedia, from aconite to zedoary, gives botanical information, medical properties, folklore, economic uses, much else. Indispensable to serious reader. 161 illustrations. 888pp. 6½ x 9¼. 2-vol. set. (Available in U.S. only.)   Vol. I: 0-486-22798-7   Vol. II: 0-486-22799-5

HIDDEN TREASURE MAZE BOOK, Dave Phillips. Solve 34 challenging mazes accompanied by heroic tales of adventure. Evil dragons, people-eating plants, blood-thirsty giants, many more dangerous adversaries lurk at every twist and turn. 34 mazes, stories, solutions. 48pp. 8¼ x 11.   0-486-24566-7

LETTERS OF W. A. MOZART, Wolfgang A. Mozart. Remarkable letters show bawdy wit, humor, imagination, musical insights, contemporary musical world; includes some letters from Leopold Mozart. 276pp. 5⅜ x 8½.   0-486-22859-2

BASIC PRINCIPLES OF CLASSICAL BALLET, Agrippina Vaganova. Great Russian theoretician, teacher explains methods for teaching classical ballet. 118 illustrations. 175pp. 5⅜ x 8½.   0-486-22036-2

THE JUMPING FROG, Mark Twain. Revenge edition. The original story of The Celebrated Jumping Frog of Calaveras County, a hapless French translation, and Twain's hilarious "retranslation" from the French. 12 illustrations. 66pp. 5⅜ x 8½.
                    0-486-22686-7

BEST REMEMBERED POEMS, Martin Gardner (ed.). The 126 poems in this superb collection of 19th- and 20th-century British and American verse range from Shelley's "To a Skylark" to the impassioned "Renascence" of Edna St. Vincent Millay and to Edward Lear's whimsical "The Owl and the Pussycat." 224pp. 5⅜ x 8½.
                    0-486-27165-X

COMPLETE SONNETS, William Shakespeare. Over 150 exquisite poems deal with love, friendship, the tyranny of time, beauty's evanescence, death and other themes in language of remarkable power, precision and beauty. Glossary of archaic terms. 80pp. 5³⁄₁₆ x 8¼.   0-486-26686-9

HISTORIC HOMES OF THE AMERICAN PRESIDENTS, Second, Revised Edition, Irvin Haas. A traveler's guide to American Presidential homes, most open to the public, depicting and describing homes occupied by every American President from George Washington to George Bush. With visiting hours, admission charges, travel routes. 175 photographs. Index. 160pp. 8¼ x 11.   0-486-26751-2

THE WIT AND HUMOR OF OSCAR WILDE, Alvin Redman (ed.). More than 1,000 ripostes, paradoxes, wisecracks: Work is the curse of the drinking classes; I can resist everything except temptation; etc. 258pp. 5⅜ x 8½.   0-486-20602-5

SHAKESPEARE LEXICON AND QUOTATION DICTIONARY, Alexander Schmidt. Full definitions, locations, shades of meaning in every word in plays and poems. More than 50,000 exact quotations. 1,485pp. 6½ x 9¼. 2-vol. set.
                    Vol. 1: 0-486-22726-X   Vol. 2: 0-486-22727-8

SELECTED POEMS, Emily Dickinson. Over 100 best-known, best-loved poems by one of America's foremost poets, reprinted from authoritative early editions. No comparable edition at this price. Index of first lines. 64pp. 5³⁄₁₆ x 8¼. 0-486-26466-1

THE INSIDIOUS DR. FU-MANCHU, Sax Rohmer. The first of the popular mystery series introduces a pair of English detectives to their archnemesis, the diabolical Dr. Fu-Manchu. Flavorful atmosphere, fast-paced action, and colorful characters enliven this classic of the genre. 208pp. 5³⁄₁₆ x 8¼.   0-486-29898-1

THE MALLEUS MALEFICARUM OF KRAMER AND SPRENGER, translated by Montague Summers. Full text of most important witchhunter's "bible," used by both Catholics and Protestants. 278pp. 6⅝ x 10. 0-486-22802-9

SPANISH STORIES/CUENTOS ESPAÑOLES: A Dual-Language Book, Angel Flores (ed.). Unique format offers 13 great stories in Spanish by Cervantes, Borges, others. Faithful English translations on facing pages. 352pp. 5⅜ x 8½.
0-486-25399-6

GARDEN CITY, LONG ISLAND, IN EARLY PHOTOGRAPHS, 1869–1919, Mildred H. Smith. Handsome treasury of 118 vintage pictures, accompanied by carefully researched captions, document the Garden City Hotel fire (1899), the Vanderbilt Cup Race (1908), the first airmail flight departing from the Nassau Boulevard Aerodrome (1911), and much more. 96pp. 8⅞ x 11¾. 0-486-40669-5

OLD QUEENS, N.Y., IN EARLY PHOTOGRAPHS, Vincent F. Seyfried and William Asadorian. Over 160 rare photographs of Maspeth, Jamaica, Jackson Heights, and other areas. Vintage views of DeWitt Clinton mansion, 1939 World's Fair and more. Captions. 192pp. 8⅞ x 11. 0-486-26358-4

CAPTURED BY THE INDIANS: 15 Firsthand Accounts, 1750-1870, Frederick Drimmer. Astounding true historical accounts of grisly torture, bloody conflicts, relentless pursuits, miraculous escapes and more, by people who lived to tell the tale. 384pp. 5⅜ x 8½. 0-486-24901-8

THE WORLD'S GREAT SPEECHES (Fourth Enlarged Edition), Lewis Copeland, Lawrence W. Lamm, and Stephen J. McKenna. Nearly 300 speeches provide public speakers with a wealth of updated quotes and inspiration–from Pericles' funeral oration and William Jennings Bryan's "Cross of Gold Speech" to Malcolm X's powerful words on the Black Revolution and Earl of Spenser's tribute to his sister, Diana, Princess of Wales. 944pp. 5⅜ x 8⅜. 0-486-40903-1

THE BOOK OF THE SWORD, Sir Richard F. Burton. Great Victorian scholar/adventurer's eloquent, erudite history of the "queen of weapons"–from prehistory to early Roman Empire. Evolution and development of early swords, variations (sabre, broadsword, cutlass, scimitar, etc.), much more. 336pp. 6⅛ x 9¼.
0-486-25434-8

AUTOBIOGRAPHY: The Story of My Experiments with Truth, Mohandas K. Gandhi. Boyhood, legal studies, purification, the growth of the Satyagraha (nonviolent protest) movement. Critical, inspiring work of the man responsible for the freedom of India. 480pp. 5⅜ x 8½. (Available in U.S. only.) 0-486-24593-4

CELTIC MYTHS AND LEGENDS, T. W. Rolleston. Masterful retelling of Irish and Welsh stories and tales. Cuchulain, King Arthur, Deirdre, the Grail, many more. First paperback edition. 58 full-page illustrations. 512pp. 5⅜ x 8½. 0-486-26507-2

THE PRINCIPLES OF PSYCHOLOGY, William James. Famous long course complete, unabridged. Stream of thought, time perception, memory, experimental methods; great work decades ahead of its time. 94 figures. 1,391pp. 5⅜ x 8½. 2-vol. set.
Vol. I: 0-486-20381-6   Vol. II: 0-486-20382-4

THE WORLD AS WILL AND REPRESENTATION, Arthur Schopenhauer. Definitive English translation of Schopenhauer's life work, correcting more than 1,000 errors, omissions in earlier translations. Translated by E. F. J. Payne. Total of 1,269pp. 5⅜ x 8½. 2-vol. set.   Vol. 1: 0-486-21761-2   Vol. 2: 0-486-21762-0

MAGIC AND MYSTERY IN TIBET, Madame Alexandra David-Neel. Experiences among lamas, magicians, sages, sorcerers, Bonpa wizards. A true psychic discovery. 32 illustrations. 321pp. 5⅜ x 8½. (Available in U.S. only.)   0-486-22682-4

THE EGYPTIAN BOOK OF THE DEAD, E. A. Wallis Budge. Complete reproduction of Ani's papyrus, finest ever found. Full hieroglyphic text, interlinear transliteration, word-for-word translation, smooth translation. 533pp. 6½ x 9¼.
0-486-21866-X

HISTORIC COSTUME IN PICTURES, Braun & Schneider. Over 1,450 costumed figures in clearly detailed engravings–from dawn of civilization to end of 19th century. Captions. Many folk costumes. 256pp. 8⅜ x 11¼.   0-486-23150-X

MATHEMATICS FOR THE NONMATHEMATICIAN, Morris Kline. Detailed, college-level treatment of mathematics in cultural and historical context, with numerous exercises. Recommended Reading Lists. Tables. Numerous figures. 641pp. 5⅜ x 8½.
0-486-24823-2

PROBABILISTIC METHODS IN THE THEORY OF STRUCTURES, Isaac Elishakoff. Well-written introduction covers the elements of the theory of probability from two or more random variables, the reliability of such multivariable structures, the theory of random function, Monte Carlo methods of treating problems incapable of exact solution, and more. Examples. 502pp. 5⅜ x 8½.   0-486-40691-1

THE RIME OF THE ANCIENT MARINER, Gustave Doré, S. T. Coleridge. Doré's finest work; 34 plates capture moods, subtleties of poem. Flawless full-size reproductions printed on facing pages with authoritative text of poem. "Beautiful. Simply beautiful."–*Publisher's Weekly.* 77pp. 9¼ x 12.   0-486-22305-1

SCULPTURE: Principles and Practice, Louis Slobodkin. Step-by-step approach to clay, plaster, metals, stone; classical and modern. 253 drawings, photos. 255pp. 8⅜ x 11.
0-486-22960-2

THE INFLUENCE OF SEA POWER UPON HISTORY, 1660–1783, A. T. Mahan. Influential classic of naval history and tactics still used as text in war colleges. First paperback edition. 4 maps. 24 battle plans. 640pp. 5⅜ x 8½.   0-486-25509-3

THE STORY OF THE TITANIC AS TOLD BY ITS SURVIVORS, Jack Winocour (ed.). What it was really like. Panic, despair, shocking inefficiency, and a little heroism. More thrilling than any fictional account. 26 illustrations. 320pp. 5⅜ x 8½.
0-486-20610-6

ONE TWO THREE . . . INFINITY: Facts and Speculations of Science, George Gamow. Great physicist's fascinating, readable overview of contemporary science: number theory, relativity, fourth dimension, entropy, genes, atomic structure, much more. 128 illustrations. Index. 352pp. 5⅜ x 8½.   0-486-25664-2

DALÍ ON MODERN ART: The Cuckolds of Antiquated Modern Art, Salvador Dalí. Influential painter skewers modern art and its practitioners. Outrageous evaluations of Picasso, Cézanne, Turner, more. 15 renderings of paintings discussed. 44 calligraphic decorations by Dalí. 96pp. 5⅜ x 8½. (Available in U.S. only.)   0-486-29220-7

ANTIQUE PLAYING CARDS: A Pictorial History, Henry René D'Allemagne. Over 900 elaborate, decorative images from rare playing cards (14th–20th centuries): Bacchus, death, dancing dogs, hunting scenes, royal coats of arms, players cheating, much more. 96pp. 9¼ x 12¼.   0-486-29265-7

MAKING FURNITURE MASTERPIECES: 30 Projects with Measured Drawings, Franklin H. Gottshall. Step-by-step instructions, illustrations for constructing handsome, useful pieces, among them a Sheraton desk, Chippendale chair, Spanish desk, Queen Anne table and a William and Mary dressing mirror. 224pp. 8⅛ x 11¼.
0-486-29338-6

NORTH AMERICAN INDIAN DESIGNS FOR ARTISTS AND CRAFTSPEOPLE, Eva Wilson. Over 360 authentic copyright-free designs adapted from Navajo blankets, Hopi pottery, Sioux buffalo hides, more. Geometrics, symbolic figures, plant and animal motifs, etc. 128pp. 8⅜ x 11. (Not for sale in the United Kingdom.)   0-486-25341-4

THE FOSSIL BOOK: A Record of Prehistoric Life, Patricia V. Rich et al. Profusely illustrated definitive guide covers everything from single-celled organisms and dinosaurs to birds and mammals and the interplay between climate and man. Over 1,500 illustrations. 760pp. 7½ x 10⅛.   0-486-29371-8

VICTORIAN ARCHITECTURAL DETAILS: Designs for Over 700 Stairs, Mantels, Doors, Windows, Cornices, Porches, and Other Decorative Elements, A. J. Bicknell & Company. Everything from dormer windows and piazzas to balconies and gable ornaments. Also includes elevations and floor plans for handsome, private residences and commercial structures. 80pp. 9⅜ x 12¼.   0-486-44015-X

WESTERN ISLAMIC ARCHITECTURE: A Concise Introduction, John D. Hoag. Profusely illustrated critical appraisal compares and contrasts Islamic mosques and palaces—from Spain and Egypt to other areas in the Middle East. 139 illustrations. 128pp. 6 x 9.   0-486-43760-4

CHINESE ARCHITECTURE: A Pictorial History, Liang Ssu-ch'eng. More than 240 rare photographs and drawings depict temples, pagodas, tombs, bridges, and imperial palaces comprising much of China's architectural heritage. 152 halftones, 94 diagrams. 232pp. 10¾ x 9⅞.   0-486-43999-2

THE RENAISSANCE: Studies in Art and Poetry, Walter Pater. One of the most talked-about books of the 19th century, *The Renaissance* combines scholarship and philosophy in an innovative work of cultural criticism that examines the achievements of Botticelli, Leonardo, Michelangelo, and other artists. "The holy writ of beauty."—Oscar Wilde. 160pp. 5⅜ x 8½.   0-486-44025-7

A TREATISE ON PAINTING, Leonardo da Vinci. The great Renaissance artist's practical advice on drawing and painting techniques covers anatomy, perspective, composition, light and shadow, and color. A classic of art instruction, it features 48 drawings by Nicholas Poussin and Leon Battista Alberti. 192pp. 5⅜ x 8½.
0-486-44155-5

THE MIND OF LEONARDO DA VINCI, Edward McCurdy. More than just a biography, this classic study by a distinguished historian draws upon Leonardo's extensive writings to offer numerous demonstrations of the Renaissance master's achievements, not only in sculpture and painting, but also in music, engineering, and even experimental aviation. 384pp. 5⅜ x 8½.   0-486-44142-3

WASHINGTON IRVING'S RIP VAN WINKLE, Illustrated by Arthur Rackham. Lovely prints that established artist as a leading illustrator of the time and forever etched into the popular imagination a classic of Catskill lore. 51 full-color plates. 80pp. 8⅜ x 11.   0-486-44242-X

HENSCHE ON PAINTING, John W. Robichaux. Basic painting philosophy and methodology of a great teacher, as expounded in his famous classes and workshops on Cape Cod. 7 illustrations in color on covers. 80pp. 5⅜ x 8½.   0-486-43728-0

LIGHT AND SHADE: A Classic Approach to Three-Dimensional Drawing, Mrs. Mary P. Merrifield. Handy reference clearly demonstrates principles of light and shade by revealing effects of common daylight, sunshine, and candle or artificial light on geometrical solids. 13 plates. 64pp. 5⅜ x 8½. 0-486-44143-1

ASTROLOGY AND ASTRONOMY: A Pictorial Archive of Signs and Symbols, Ernst and Johanna Lehner. Treasure trove of stories, lore, and myth, accompanied by more than 300 rare illustrations of planets, the Milky Way, signs of the zodiac, comets, meteors, and other astronomical phenomena. 192pp. 8⅜ x 11. 0-486-43981-X

JEWELRY MAKING: Techniques for Metal, Tim McCreight. Easy-to-follow instructions and carefully executed illustrations describe tools and techniques, use of gems and enamels, wire inlay, casting, and other topics. 72 line illustrations and diagrams. 176pp. 8¼ x 10⅞. 0-486-44043-5

MAKING BIRDHOUSES: Easy and Advanced Projects, Gladstone Califf. Easy-to-follow instructions include diagrams for everything from a one-room house for bluebirds to a forty-two-room structure for purple martins. 56 plates; 4 figures. 80pp. 8¾ x 6⅜. 0-486-44183-0

LITTLE BOOK OF LOG CABINS: How to Build and Furnish Them, William S. Wicks. Handy how-to manual, with instructions and illustrations for building cabins in the Adirondack style, fireplaces, stairways, furniture, beamed ceilings, and more. 102 line drawings. 96pp. 8¾ x 6⅜. 0-486-44259-4

THE SEASONS OF AMERICA PAST, Eric Sloane. From "sugaring time" and strawberry picking to Indian summer and fall harvest, a whole year's activities described in charming prose and enhanced with 79 of the author's own illustrations. 160pp. 8¼ x 11. 0-486-44220-9

THE METROPOLIS OF TOMORROW, Hugh Ferriss. Generous, prophetic vision of the metropolis of the future, as perceived in 1929. Powerful illustrations of towering structures, wide avenues, and rooftop parks–all features in many of today's modern cities. 59 illustrations. 144pp. 8¼ x 11. 0-486-43727-2

THE PATH TO ROME, Hilaire Belloc. This 1902 memoir abounds in lively vignettes from a vanished time, recounting a pilgrimage on foot across the Alps and Apennines in order to "see all Europe which the Christian Faith has saved." 77 of the author's original line drawings complement his sparkling prose. 272pp. 5⅜ x 8½. 0-486-44001-X

THE HISTORY OF RASSELAS: Prince of Abissinia, Samuel Johnson. Distinguished English writer attacks eighteenth-century optimism and man's unrealistic estimates of what life has to offer. 112pp. 5⅜ x 8½. 0-486-44094-X

A VOYAGE TO ARCTURUS, David Lindsay. A brilliant flight of pure fancy, where wild creatures crowd the fantastic landscape and demented torturers dominate victims with their bizarre mental powers. 272pp. 5⅜ x 8½. 0-486-44198-9

Paperbound unless otherwise indicated. Available at your book dealer, online at **www.doverpublications.com**, or by writing to Dept. GI, Dover Publications, Inc., 31 East 2nd Street, Mineola, NY 11501. For current price information or for free catalogs (please indicate field of interest), write to Dover Publications or log on to **www.doverpublications.com** and see every Dover book in print. Dover publishes more than 500 books each year on science, elementary and advanced mathematics, biology, music, art, literary history, social sciences, and other areas.